The STEPS OF THE SAVIOR

365 DEVOTIONALS FROM THE GOSPEL OF LUKE

PHIL WARE

LEAFWOOD
P U B L I S H E R S

The Steps of the Savior
365 Devotionals from the Gospel of Luke

LEAFWOOD
PUBLISHERS

Copyright 2011 by Phil Ware

ISBN 978-0-89112-314-9

Printed in the United States of America

Cover design by Marc Whitaker

For information:
Leafwood Publishers, Abilene, Texas
1-877-816-4455 toll free
Visit our website: www.leafwoodpublishers.com

10 11 12 13 14 15 / 7 6 5 4 3 2 1

For Melody, Karen, Fitia, Tom, Anna, and Candy

Over the last several months, you have helped me remember that Luke's story of Jesus still reaches out to the hearts of sweet, genuine people when they read his story and experience his family. I love each you. I pray that you will come to fully understand the love Jesus has for you. I pray for the day that we can all sit at the table of the Lord as God's family and enjoy the fellowship of the Holy Spirit and the sweetness of each other's presence, knowing that distance, culture, and language are not barriers in the joyous family of our Resurrected Savior.

ACKNOWLEDGEMENTS

Luke wants us to know that Jesus brings salvation. This salvation is experienced in the joy we find in the Holy Spirit, in the genuine fellowship we share when eating together and recognizing Jesus is present at every meal, and in the moments of grace we experience with God in prayer.

Salvation is much more than a doctrine we hold. Salvation is an experience of the goodness and grace of God given us through Jesus and the power of his resurrection and the life the Holy Spirit brings to his followers. I got to experience this salvation in precious ways over the last several months with the kind of people Luke wrote his good news story of Jesus to reach.

I want to thank a special group that went to Thailand with me during a time of uncertainty—Samuel Cook, Larry and Kathy Musick, Kent Rideout. We never wavered in our commitment to do what God sent us to do. We never saw dangerous or threatening people. We were constantly surprised by God's grace and the Holy Spirit's leading. Jesus' fingerprints were all over our efforts. Robert and Jan Reagan, long time friends, were precious to us as we sought to serve the people they love and call their Thai family. Not only did God give us the opportunity to share the story of Jesus with the Thai people, but the Father also arranged it so that we could share this story with beautiful, attentive, and loving Chinese students. Many of these had never really heard of God, so the whole story of Jesus was new and fresh to them. Their hard, but honest questions and their genuine openness to find truth was refreshing and inspiring. We will never be the same because of this shared experience and our prayer is that they will never be the same either.

This cross-cultural evangelistic experience made Luke's story of Jesus more real to me than ever. Not only did we use the Gospel of Luke in our *Let's Start Talking* studies with the Thai and Chinese, we also experienced the joy of the Holy Spirit and the power of the resurrected Jesus as we worshiped and shared table fellowship with the brothers and sisters at the Christian Zone in Chiang Mai. Singing, playing games, telling the story of Jesus, sharing meals from a variety of cultures, praying together, experiencing the seven nations choir, the spiritual retreat at the shack on top of the mountain, and enjoying the heartfelt love of Christian family reminded us all that the family of Jesus is as real today as it was in those early days in the book of Acts.

I have also experienced these same things through the work of my own church family reaching out to students from Madagascar and to Bhutanese refugees from Nepal. The names may be hard for me to pronounce, but the faces of these new brothers and sisters in Christ are precious to my heart and joy to my bones! These are the constant reminders that the Gospel of Luke calls us to experience the life of salvation as we walk *In the Steps of the Savior!*

THE STEPS OF THE SAVIOR

Savior!

The word "Savior" means many things to many people, but to followers of Jesus, it means something quite special. Luke wrote his Gospel to tell the story of Jesus and help us understand what it means for us to follow in *The Steps of the Savior.*

Early in Luke's good news story of Jesus, we meet angels proclaiming Jesus as Savior to lowly shepherds on the hillside: *"Today your Savior was born in David's town. He is Christ, the Lord"* (Luke 2:11). Luke reminds us that Jesus brings *salvation* (word used ten times) and that Jesus *saves* us from all that is bad and *saves* (word used twenty-four times) us as community for a life in God. Jesus is concerned that the *lost* (word used eight times) be found. Salvation brings Jesus' followers *joy* (word used twenty-eight times) as they experience the presence of the Holy Spirit (title used fifty-five times). They share in this fellowship of joy as they *pray* (word used sixty times) and *eat* (concept found over sixty times) together in God's *Kingdom* (word used fifty-one times).

Far more than counting words, the joy of salvation is seen in the people Jesus touches and the stories that Jesus told. Luke is an outsider, a gentile, probably from the city of Antioch—the first place the early followers of Jesus really began to reach outside racial and social boundaries and share salvation with all people (Acts 11:19-21). So Luke is writing to help outsiders know the truth of the story of Jesus and let them know that Jesus came to include them in the good news of God's joyous Kingdom.

Luke reminds us that the despised shepherds are the first to know about the Savior's birth. He tells us that Jesus reaches out to all people, whether they are religious or despised sinners, respected men or sinful women from the city. Jesus notices bereaved widows, generous widows, a thankful Samaritan leper, hated tax collectors, forgotten fishermen, and Roman Centurions. Jesus makes a "good Samaritan" the hero of the story emphasizing righteousness. Jesus is a friend of women, some pay for his ministry, others he calls out of a life of sin and self-destruction, and others he praises for their devotion to him and for their faith in what God can do. Jesus tells stories about poor beggars being saved as well as stories about lost coins and lost sheep and lost sons being found and a persistent widow being heard. Jesus is the Savior of all people, and Luke reminds us that all different kinds of people find the joy of salvation in Jesus! We are not surprised that in Luke, Jesus describes his ministry with these words: *"The Son of Man came to find lost people and save them"* (Luke 19:10).

So as we begin our journey through Luke's good news story of Jesus, I want to encourage you to open your heart to this Savior who comes to bring you God's saving power and include you in his family of joy. As you read these daily devotionals, I hope you will also occasionally read through the whole Gospel of Luke at one sitting using different translations. Ask the Holy Spirit, a key interest of Luke, to open your heart to the joy salvation and the opportunity to share it with others.

Luke not only writes the good news story of Jesus we know as the Gospel of Luke, he also writes the Acts of the Apostles. Both are told as something we might call a travel biography or diary. Luke sees Jesus' earthly ministry as a journey to us and back to God (Gospel of Luke) and he describes the growth of the early church as the journeys of Jesus' followers to share the news of salvation with the world. So as you begin this yearlong devotional journey through the Gospel of Luke, you may find the following simple outline helpful as you read:

- The Journey of Jesus our Savior to Us—1:1-4:13
- The Journey of Jesus our Savior around Galilee—4:14-9:50
- The Journey of Jesus our Savior on the Way to Jerusalem—9:51-19:27
- The Journey of Jesus our Savior to through the Cross and Resurrection—19:28-24:53

Whether you use the outline or not, I hope you will listen to Luke's story of Jesus like you would a friend describing an exciting journey with twists and turns, joys and sorrows, memorable people and great stories, dangers and joys, heroes and villains, and listen to Jesus as he invites us all to journey with him in the joy of being found by our gracious Father! At every twist and turn of the journey, Luke invites us to join Jesus and follow in *The Steps of the Savior*.

Day 1

GOD'S PLAN COMPLETED!

Luke 1:1

Most Honorable Theophilus: Many others have tried to give a report
of the things that happened among us to complete God's plan.

KEY THOUGHT

Theophilus means friend of God. We can't be sure whether the name refers to an actual person or if it is symbolic to speak to each person who is seeking to live as a friend of God. Luke does want us to know that his Gospel is written after many other accounts of Jesus' life have been written. His story is about the work God had accomplished through the events of Jesus' life; Luke makes clear he believes that Jesus completes God's plan talked about in the Prophets, Moses, and the Jewish Scriptures (Luke 24:25-27). Luke's introduction is also his invitation to us.

TODAY'S PRAYER

Father, as I start this New Year reading through Luke, I want to know you
more fully through what Jesus did in his earthly ministry so that I can serve
you more fully in my daily life. Please reveal Jesus to me as I study his life
from the Gospel of Luke this coming year. In Jesus' name I pray. Amen.

CONTEXT: LUKE 1:1-4
Related Passages: Luke 11:9-13; Luke 7:16-17; John 1:17-18

Day 2

A CAREFUL COMPILATION

Luke 1:2-4

What they have written agrees with what we learned from the people who saw those events from the beginning. They also served God by telling people his message. I studied it all carefully from the beginning. Then I decided to write it down for you in an organized way. I did this so that you can be sure that what you have been taught is true.

KEY THOUGHT

Luke tells us he is organized in his work recording the story of Jesus for us. His Gospel is the longest and fullest account of Jesus' life we have in the New Testament. He carefully researched what he wrote. He wrote to give us assurance that we can know the story of Jesus' life accurately. As we journey through this Gospel, we will also see that Luke wants us to know that Jesus cares about all people—young and old, men and women, Jews and non-Jews, powerful and outcasts. Luke will tell us more about the Holy Spirit, Jesus' passion for prayer, and the importance of meals than the other Gospels. Most importantly, he wants us to know that Jesus came to bring salvation for all people, even us!

TODAY'S PRAYER

Father, I thank you for the gift of salvation that you have given to me through my faith in Jesus, your Son. I am touched to know that you love me and want me as your child. Thank you for preserving the story of Jesus in such detail so I can know about your Son and your love more fully. In Jesus' name I thank you. Amen.

CONTEXT: LUKE 1:1-4
Related Passages: Luke 19:1-10; 2 Timothy 3:14-15; Luke 2:29-32

Day 3

IT ALL BEGINS WITH FAITHFULNESS

Luke 1:5-7

During the time when Herod ruled Judea, there was a priest named Zechariah. He belonged to Abijah's group. His wife came from the family of Aaron. Her name was Elizabeth. Zechariah and Elizabeth were both good people who pleased God. They did everything the Lord commanded, always following his instructions completely. But they had no children. Elizabeth could not have a baby, and both of them were very old.

KEY THOUGHT

Sometimes, when things aren't going as well as we hope, we are tempted to give up on our righteous commitments to God. "What's the use?" we sometimes think. "It surely doesn't seem to be paying off for me!" God gives us Zechariah and Elizabeth to help us not give up in our discouragement, impatience, and frustration. Luke reminds us that the beginning of this chapter of Jesus' story is found in two old, faithful followers of God. They were righteous in God's eyes even though their most fervent desire to have a child had not been granted. They honored God because it was right. Their faithfulness opens the door for Jesus to come! So the next time you find yourself discouraged and ready to give up because your prayers seem unanswered, remember this old couple and their joyous surprise—seen in the following verses. It's worth the wait to share in God's glory!

TODAY'S PRAYER

Holy and righteous God, my Abba Father, forgive me for the times that I have let discouragement and impatience cause me to stumble and give up for a time. I do believe that you are at work in my life and want to use my life to help others find Jesus. Please give me strength to live before you righteously as Zechariah and Elizabeth did. In Jesus' name I pray. Amen.

CONTEXT: LUKE 1:5-25
Related Passages: Philippians 2:13; Matthew 6:31-33; Ephesians 2:1-10

Day 4

ONCE IN A LIFETIME

Luke 1:8-10
Zechariah was serving as a priest before God for his group. It was his group's time to serve. The priests always chose one priest to offer the incense, and Zechariah was the one chosen this time. So he went into the Temple of the Lord to offer the incense. There was a large crowd outside praying at the time the incense was offered.

KEY THOUGHT

In Zechariah's day, a priest often served God all of his life and never got to enter the sanctuary and burn incense before the Lord. But God chose this day to be Zechariah's day. So often, we "go to church" with little or no expectation of something great happening to us. Once again, Zechariah reminds us that God has a plan and purpose. He likes to surprise us with his faithfulness at just the right time. Don't give up on God's purpose for you! Keep on doing the next right thing and trust that God will not only see you through, but also that he just might surprise you with a once-in-a-lifetime experience right there "in church"!

TODAY'S PRAYER

Dear heavenly Father, fill me with expectation when I go to be with your people who are gathered to worship you. Great is your faithfulness, O Lord, so surprise me with your grace, mercy, and power when the time is right. Use me, dear Lord, to do your work in my world and to bring you glory. In Jesus' name I pray. Amen.

CONTEXT: LUKE 1:5-25
Related Passages: Romans 8:28-30; Psalm 122:1; Hebrews 10:19-25

Day 5
BEYOND FEAR

Luke 1:11-13

Then, on the right side of the incense table an angel of the Lord came and stood before Zechariah. When he saw the angel, Zechariah was upset and very afraid. But the angel said to him, "Zechariah, don't be afraid. Your prayer has been heard by God. Your wife Elizabeth will give birth to a baby boy, and you will name him John."

KEY THOUGHT

God has sent his presence, his messengers (angels), his love, and most of all his Son to us to cast out our fear. Zechariah is caught up in the whole exciting faithfulness of God that occurs with the coming of the Messiah. God has chosen Zechariah and his wife Elizabeth to play crucial roles in the fulfillment of God's greatest promises. This faithfulness was experienced as a very personal blessing as well. Zechariah experienced his once-in-a-lifetime opportunity to offer sacrifice at the great Temple. Zechariah received a visit from God's heavenly messenger, an angel. Zechariah was given a son in his old age. But he was also given a job: he was to name his son John. When we faithfully obey God, we are never completely sure what the result of that obedience will be. Often we feel that no one really knows whether we obey or not. Yet God is still at work through his people's obedience to bring about great things. Let's not take God's commands lightly. Who knows where that "simple" obedience may ultimately lead!

TODAY'S PRAYER

Father, please accept my obedience in the small, clear, and simple things I do. I want my obedience to be an offering of love to you. Take that obedience and bring glory to your name and a blessing to your people whether others know of my part in your plan or not. In Jesus' name, and to your glory, I offer you this prayer and my life. Amen.

CONTEXT: LUKE 1:5-25
Related Passages: Hebrews 1:14; 1 John 4:17-18; Hebrews 6:9-12

Day 6

A JOY TO MANY

Luke 1:14-16

*[The angel said] "You will be very happy, and many others will share your
joy over his birth. He will be a great man for the Lord. He will never drink
wine or beer. Even before he is born, he will be filled with the Holy Spirit.
John will help many people of Israel return to the Lord their God."*

KEY THOUGHT

Babies usually bring great joy with their arrival. Kinfolks and friends
are overjoyed for the family. This will be true of John, the son of Zechariah
and Elizabeth. They are blessed with joy in their old age. In addition, their
joy will be multiplied since John has a crucial role to play in the coming of
God's promised Messiah, Jesus. He will reach many hearts that the religion
of the day could not reach. John's life, even from the womb, is dedicated to
proclaiming God's Messiah. He will identify himself as a prophet through
his diet and wardrobe. His habits show that John is especially consecrated
to the work of God. But unlike the ascetics of the desert who withdrew from
sinful people, John spoke with the Spirit and fire of God to those people. They
flocked to hear his message and he prepared them to follow Jesus. With the
birth of any child, let's pray that he or she will bring glory to God and bring
many others to know his Son.

TODAY'S PRAYER

*Dear heavenly Father, Creator and Sovereign God of the entire universe,
please look down on the little babies I know [list several by name] in my
family and church family. Do mighty things through them. Guard their
parents. Nurture them in your truth. Bring experiences into their lives that
will make them most useful to you. In Jesus' name I pray. Amen.*

CONTEXT: LUKE 1:5-25
Related Passages: Judges 13:3-7; Luke 1:57-66; Galatians 4:19

Day 7

THE SPIRIT AND POWER OF ELIJAH

Luke 1:17

"John himself will go ahead of the Lord and make people ready for his coming. He will be powerful like Elijah and will have the same spirit. He will make peace between fathers and their children. He will cause people who are not obeying God to change and start thinking the way they should."

KEY THOUGHT

Israel looked forward to the return of Elijah, the prophet who was to precede the Messiah. Since he never died, but went straight to God, they believed he would return and continue his powerful ministry of proclaiming God's truth. John's message touched folks in a way that united them across generations and called people to life-changing repentance. Why? Why was his coming so important? His coming was necessary to prepare the people for Jesus. Isn't this the key reason God has put us where he has placed us? Doesn't the Father want our words and our actions to prepare those around us to know Jesus?

TODAY'S PRAYER

Holy and righteous God, my Abba Father, please use my life to prepare the way for Jesus in the lives of those I love and over whom I have influence. In Jesus' name I pray. Amen.

CONTEXT: LUKE 1:5-257
Related Passages: 1 Peter 3:13-17; Mark 13:11; Luke 9:23-26

Day 8

HOW CAN I KNOW?

Luke 1:18-20

*Zechariah said to the angel, "How can I know that what you say
is true? I am an old man, and my wife is also old."*

*The angel answered him, "I am Gabriel, the one who always stands ready before God.
He sent me to talk to you and to tell you this good news. Now, listen! You will not be
able to talk until the day when these things happen. You will lose your speech because
you did not believe what I told you. But everything I said will really happen."*

KEY THOUGHT

I'd like to think that I would not have doubted like Zechariah, but I am
not so sure. Even with his years of faithfulness, the experiences and goodness
that God poured out upon Zechariah this day were simply too much to
comprehend. Zechariah greeted God's promise with less than complete trust.
He wanted more proof. Our human doubt, even on our best days, helps us
understand this desire for proof. Yet God didn't take away his grace, his gifts,
or his promises simply because Zechariah couldn't quite trust the bewildering
promise he was given. He just lost his voice for a while so that when it
returned, folks would listen to God's amazing message! Let's use Zechariah's
doubt to remind us that God keeps his promises to us even when they are
more than we can comprehend.

TODAY'S PRAYER

*Father, I come before you with hushed silence in awe at your faithfulness. I bring
to you the best of my faith and ask you to help my belief grow. I thank you for your
many great promises—forgiveness, the Holy Spirit, the return of Jesus– and I commit
to live my life trusting in those promises. In Jesus' name I come to you. Amen.*

CONTEXT: LUKE 1:5-25
Related Passages: Acts 1:6-11; John 14:1-3; Acts 2:36-42

Day 9

HE RETURNED HOME

Luke 1:21-23

*Outside, the people were still waiting for Zechariah. They were surprised
that he was staying so long in the Temple. Then Zechariah came outside,
but he could not speak to them. So the people knew that he had seen a vision
inside the Temple. He was not able to speak, so he could only make signs
to the people. When his time of service was finished, he went home.*

KEY THOUGHT

In the first two chapters of Luke, God announces great news to people
through angels. God does great things that excite and thrill his faithful ones.
God's people are caught up in once-in-a-lifetime experiences. Yet at the end
of these experiences, they have to return home and live out their everyday
lives. "Mountain top experiences" are not the norm. They are the powerful
reminders of God's love and grace that move constantly behind the scenes of
our lives. When heaven's grace and glory break through in powerful ways, we
are blessed with an extraordinary gift. That gift is given so that we can return
to our regular lives with faith, power, and confidence to bless those around us.
Let's enjoy those mountain top experiences of faith, but let's also remember to
return home and share the blessings of our faith with those around us!

TODAY'S PRAYER

*Father in heaven, thank you for the mountain-top moments in my life when
you felt so close and my faith was so vibrant. Help me use the power of those
moments to come back home and live with passionate faith around the
people you have called me to serve. In Jesus' name I ask this. Amen.*

CONTEXT: LUKE 1:5-25
Related Passages: Mark 5:18-20; Luke 2:15-20; Luke 5:24-26

Day 10

TAKING AWAY DISGRACE

Luke 1:24-25

Later, Zechariah's wife Elizabeth became pregnant. So she did not go out of her house for five months. She said, "Look what the Lord has done for me! He decided to help me. Now people will stop thinking there is something wrong with me."

KEY THOUGHT

God's passion is to take away our disgrace—the disgrace of our failure, our misfortune, our sin, and yes, even the disgrace of circumstances. The old hymn says, "Bring Christ your broken life . . . . He will create anew, make whole again." What disgrace, disappointment, or disaster do you still have holding back your life? Why not openly confess it and the feelings that it fosters within you, and ask God to take it away?

TODAY'S PRAYER

Holy God, I thank you for the gift of memory and the ability to remember wonderful, joyous, and pleasant times in my life. However, dear Father, there are some memories in my life that I let Satan use to hold me back and keep me down. Please take away the disgrace of my past and heal those memories so that I can use those experiences and not be debilitated by them. In Jesus' name I pray. Amen.

CONTEXT: LUKE 1:5-25
Related Passages: Psalm 103:1-5; Psalm 51:7-13; Jeremiah 14:21

Day 11

A SIMPLE HUMILITY

Luke 1:26-29
During Elizabeth's sixth month of pregnancy, God sent the angel Gabriel to a virgin girl who lived in Nazareth, a town in Galilee. She was engaged to marry a man named Joseph from the family of David. Her name was Mary. The angel came to her and said, "Greetings! The Lord is with you; you are very special to him."

But Mary was very confused about what the angel said. She wondered, "What does this mean?"

KEY THOUGHT

When we were children, many of us imagined ourselves in special circumstances being chosen to do great things. As we mature, we hope and trust we can be useful to God, but genuine humility leads us to be surprised when we are chosen for a special task for God. Although undoubtedly young, Mary has this attitude of genuine humility. She is genuinely confused and somewhat unsettled by Gabriel's presence and announcement. A host of questions filled her heart: "How can I be highly favored by God? Why would I be visited by an angel from God?" It was Mary's faithful humility that made her the person God could trust as the mother of the Messiah. It is that same kind of genuine humility that makes us fit to do great things for our King as well!

TODAY'S PRAYER
Lord God Almighty, give me genuine humility—not a false humility that sees myself as deficient and unfit to do your work or answer your call, but genuine humility that recognizes your power and grace working in me and through my limitations. Please use me to bring you glory and to bless your people. In Jesus' name I ask this. Amen.

CONTEXT: LUKE 1:26-38
Related Passages: Romans 12:3-6a; Proverbs 15:33; 1 Peter 5:5-6

Day 12

DON'T BE AFRAID

Luke 1:30-33
*The angel said to her, "Don't be afraid, Mary, because God is very pleased
with you. Listen! You will become pregnant and have a baby boy. You will
name him Jesus. He will be great. People will call him the Son of the Most
High God, and the Lord God will make him king like his ancestor David. He
will rule over the people of Jacob forever; his kingdom will never end."*

KEY THOUGHT

Fear. It's overwhelming. It's paralyzing. So it should not surprise us that
one of the most often repeated commands in Scripture is, "Don't be afraid!"
In older translations, it is sometimes translated, "Fear not!" Fear of the
unknown, fear of complications, fear of death and dying, fear of a person,
fear of a circumstance, fear of the incomprehensible, and a host of other fears
can come crashing in on us. This is especially true in times of stress, danger,
and uncertainty. The great heroes of faith faced moments of fear, but God
guided them through it. Jesus' coming is about putting aside so many of our
fears. The announcement of Jesus' conception came with the command,
"Don't be afraid!" As you journey with Jesus each day, ask God to use Jesus in
your life to crowd out the influence of fear over your heart.

TODAY'S PRAYER
*Give me courage, O Almighty Father, so that fear will not cloud my thoughts or
weaken my faith. Fill me with your assurance and have Jesus chase the clouds of
fear away. In the name of Jesus your Son and my triumphant Lord, I pray. Amen.*

CONTEXT: LUKE 1:26-38
Related Passages: Matthew 1:18-21; John 6:16-21; Hebrews 2:14-18

Day 13

NO ORDINARY BABY!

Luke 1:34-35

Mary said to the angel, "How will this happen? I am still a virgin."

The angel said to Mary, "The Holy Spirit will come to you, and the power of the Most High God will cover you. The baby will be holy and will be called the Son of God."

KEY THOUGHT

Every baby is precious. God forms each child in the mother's womb (Ps. 139:13-16). In addition, Jesus is miraculously conceived by the Holy Spirit. Jesus is uniquely holy, the very Son of God, with no human father. This doesn't make sense to us any more than a person being raised from the dead makes sense. They are outside the natural order. They are outside our personal experience. Yet this is the miracle of baby Jesus. God comes to earth, walks among us, and personally shows us his love. If we will make room for him, this Jesus can bring us life and immortality. Do you believe? Maybe you are asking the same question that Mary did, "How will this happen?" But she did believe, and the world was forever changed. As we believe, our world is changed, too!

TODAY'S PRAYER

Lord God, my Abba Father, help my faith in Jesus be more real and vibrant. Make my relationship with him more real as I read his story and seek to follow his lead in my life. Change my world because of my faith in your Son, in whose name I pray. Amen.

CONTEXT: LUKE 1:26-38

Related Passages: John 1:9-14; Galatians 3:26-29; 4:3-7; Romans 1:2-4

Day 14

NOTHING IS IMPOSSIBLE

Luke 1:36-37

[The angel said] "And here's something else: Your relative Elizabeth is pregnant. She is very old, but she is going to have a son. Everyone thought she could not have a baby, but she has been pregnant now for six months. God can do anything!"

KEY THOUGHT

It's almost as if the angel is saying, "How about a little help with that impossible thing to believe, Mary? Go check with your old cousin Elizabeth. The impossible has really happened to her! She's pregnant!" God's great promises to his people often happened with miraculous conceptions that were beyond experience and that stretched their faith. Mary is given assurance that God not only can do, but he actually does do the impossible in the lives of everyday folks. What does God want to do in you? How does he want to use you for his glory? Don't think it's possible? Go ask Mary who first asked Elizabeth! NOTHING is impossible for God!

TODAY'S PRAYER

Father, shake loose my "too little" dreams. Please give me a heart of faith to believe in your ability to do great things through everyday folks like me. Give me the gift of faith to believe that you are doing great things through your people. Take me, mold me, and use me to your glory. In Jesus' name I pray. Amen.

CONTEXT: LUKE 1:26-38
Related Passages: Ephesians 3:14-21; Matthew 14:14-21; Matthew 19:23-26

Day 15

I AM THE LORD'S SERVANT

Luke 1:38
*Mary said, "I am the servant of the Lord God. Let this thing you
have said happen to me!" Then the angel went away.*

KEY THOUGHT

The greatest in the Kingdom of God is a servant. So we should not be
surprised when God's Son and our Savior explained his role as a servant,
should we? Jesus conviction about the greatest being a servant wasn't theory:
his mother was a great example of this truth when she offered herself to
God by saying, "I am the Lord's servant." Have you said it? Have you offered
yourself as a servant to God Almighty? Mary did! Her son, who was also God's
Son, did!

TODAY'S PRAYER

*O Lord God, Creator of the universe and the Father who created me in the womb
of my mother, I offer myself to you as your servant. I am not sure if you will fill
my earthly life with wonder like Mary's or if it will be filled with sorrow, also like
Mary's. But I do, dear Lord, want to serve you in this world, knowing that I will sit
at your side as your dear child in the world to come. In Jesus' name I pray. Amen.*

CONTEXT: LUKE 1:26-38
Related Passages: 2 Corinthians 4:5-7; Matthew 18:1-5; Mark 10:42-45

Day 16

CONNECTED GRACE!

Luke 1:39-45

Mary got up and went quickly to a town in the hill country of Judea. She went into Zechariah's house and greeted Elizabeth. When Elizabeth heard Mary's greeting, the unborn baby inside her jumped, and she was filled with the Holy Spirit.

In a loud voice she said to Mary, "God has blessed you more than any other woman. And God has blessed the baby you will have. You are the mother of my Lord, and you have come to me! Why has something so good happened to me? When I heard your voice, the baby inside me jumped with joy. Great blessings are yours because you believed what the Lord said to you! You believed this would happen."

KEY THOUGHT

What a glorious way God connected two different promises delivered by the angel to two precious women! He promised Elizabeth that her son would be filled by the Spirit from the womb, and sure enough, her son stirs at the voice of Mary and the presence of the newly conceived Messiah. He also promised Mary that Elizabeth was pregnant and that this pregnancy was the confirmation of God's miracle in her. Mary's faith was strengthened and both women were blessed. While we may never have experienced an encounter with the angel Gabriel, we have received a host of promises from God that can be accepted only by faith. However, our faith remains small and often unblessed until we begin to act on that faith. That active faith then opens the door for God's blessing and confirmation. So what promise from Scripture has God laid on your heart recently that you have not acted on because of your doubt? Why not prayerfully re-examine that promise and then act obediently in response to God's Word?

TODAY'S PRAYER

O glorious God and Father, "I believe, but help my unbelief!" Forgive me for letting my doubt and my circumstances interfere with my obedience. Give me courage to obey your commands and to respond to your promises in faith. In Jesus' name I pray. Amen.

CONTEXT: LUKE 1:39-568
Related Passages: Mark 9:20-29; Matthew 7:21; Ephesians 2:8-10

$$Day\ 17$$

A BURST OF PRAISE

Luke 1:46-56

Then Mary said, "I praise the Lord with all my heart. I am very happy because God is my Savior. I am not important, but he has shown his care for me, his lowly servant. From now until the end of time, people will remember how much God blessed me. Yes, the Powerful One has done great things for me. His name is very holy. He always gives mercy to those who worship him. He reached out his arm and showed his power. He scattered those who are proud and think great things about themselves. He brought down rulers from their thrones and raised up the humble people. He filled the hungry with good things, but he sent the rich away with nothing. God has helped Israel—the people he chose to serve him. He did not forget his promise to give us his mercy. He has done what he promised to our ancestors, to Abraham and his children forever." Mary stayed with Elizabeth for about three months and then went home.

KEY THOUGHT

Two thoughts immediately strike me about Mary's song—known as the Magnificat. First, notice how easily she slips into praise passages from the Old Testament to speak her praise to God. Imagine being that familiar with the language of praise. What a wonderful thing for us to do—to let the language and idiom of praise from the Bible become our own! Second, Mary was probably very young when this happened. We often shoot way too low in our expectations of our children's knowledge of Scripture. So let's be touched by Mary's praise and then let's take these two principles and turn them loose in our lives and our families.

TODAY'S PRAYER

O righteous God, my Heavenly Father, forgive me for my inadequate words of praise. Give me a heart that desires to honor you with my life and my words. Through your Spirit, give my mind extraordinary ability to to recall the praise I read in Scripture so that my limited language to express my love to you will be enriched. In Jesus' name I ask this. Amen.

CONTEXT: LUKE 1:39-56
Related Passages: Psalm 147:1-7; Romans 11:33-35; Ephesians 3:20-21

Day 18

REJOICE!

Luke 1:57-58

When it was time for Elizabeth to give birth, she had a boy. Her neighbors and relatives heard that the Lord was very good to her, and they were happy for her.

KEY THOUGHT

So often today it seems that those who are not blessed with unexpected joys are jealous, even critical, of those who do receive them. Isn't it wonderful that Elizabeth's neighbors weren't that way? We can follow their lead and rejoice with those who rejoice. Find things in your friends' lives for which you can honestly rejoice. That makes their blessings a source of blessing for you, too!

TODAY'S PRAYER

Seems as if, dear God and Almighty Lord, that there is so much bad news these days. I don't seem to find the good in the things around me. Give me a heart that rejoices with the blessings of others. Make that joy contagious. I ask for this grace in Jesus' name. Amen.

CONTEXT: LUKE 1:57-66
Related Passages: Romans 12:15; Philippians 4:4-8; Psalm 22:26

Day 19

OBEDIENCE PURE AND SIMPLE!

Luke 1:59-64

When the baby was eight days old, they came to circumcise him.
They wanted to name him Zechariah because this was his father's
name. But his mother said, "No, he will be named John."

The people said to Elizabeth, "But no one in your family has that name."
Then they made signs to his father, "What would you like to name him?"

Zechariah asked for something to write on. Then he wrote, "His name is John." Everyone
was surprised. Then Zechariah could talk again, and he began praising God.

KEY THOUGHT

What is the big deal about the name they give this miracle baby born to
Elizabeth? It's all about obedience, pure and simple. There was no reason to
name him John—no relatives or heroes in the family of that name. But the
angel had said, "You will name him John." So they did! God's approval was
shown in the removal of Zechariah's inability to speak. This conception, this
birth, this child is no accident of late-life passion. This is the work of God!
Obedience—pure and simple obedience—opens up a pathway for the work of
God, and no one's life illustrates that more than John ben Zechariah, the one
we know as John the Baptizer.

TODAY'S PRAYER

Holy and righteous God, full of compassion and mercy, please forgive me
for sometimes treating my responsibility to obey your will as optional.
Give me a holy passion to honor you in word and in deed with a heart
of pure and simple obedience. In Jesus' name I pray. Amen.

CONTEXT: LUKE 1:57-66
Related Passages: 1 Samuel 15:17-23; James 1:21-25; Colossians 1:19-23

Day 20

WHAT ABOUT THIS CHILD?

Luke 1:65-66

And all their neighbors were afraid. In all the hill country of Judea people continued talking about these things. Everyone who heard about these things wondered about them. They thought, "What will this child be?" They could see that the Lord was with him.

KEY THOUGHT

Speculation about a newborn is nothing new. Parents, family, and friends have looked down on a sleeping newborn and wondered, "What will this child turn out to be?" It was natural that people did this with John. However, they went beyond the normal speculation because they had reason to believe he was special. And he was! He was conceived in Elizabeth's old age after his dad was on service in the Temple and lost his ability to speak. Add in his surprising name and the return of his father's speech and you have an unforgettable birth. So their wonder and amazement led them to believe that the Lord was with him. And God was at work in John to do something spectacular. At the same time, we need to remember that God is at work in each child, from the moment of conception, to do something spectacular. Let's make a commitment to bless each child that God puts into our circle of influence and help that child know he or she is special to God.

TODAY'S PRAYER

O glorious God, you alone are Creator of the universe and giver of life! Please use me to bless your precious children. Work in the hearts of our people so that we can value each child as you do. In Jesus' name I ask for this grace. Amen.

CONTEXT: LUKE 1:57-66
Related Passages: Psalm 139:13-16; Philippians 2:13; Genesis 1:26-27

Day 21

THE VOICE OF THE REDEEMED

Luke 1:67-75

Then Zechariah, John's father, was filled with the Holy Spirit and told the people a message from God: "Praise to the Lord God of Israel. He has come to help his people and has given them freedom. He has given us a powerful Savior from the family of his servant David. This is what he promised through his holy prophets long ago. He will save us from our enemies and from the power of all those who hate us. God said he would show mercy to our fathers, and he remembered his holy agreement. This was the promise he made to our father Abraham, a promise to free us from the power of our enemies, so that we could serve him without fear in a way that is holy and right for as long as we live."

KEY THOUGHT

Mary praised God in her youth, from the bottom of her heart, in words steeped in Scripture. Now, Zechariah praises God in his old age, from the bottom of his heart, in words steeped in Scripture. Redemption knows no boundaries of gender or age. Praise can't be confined to an age group. Passion doesn't belong to just the young and scriptural knowledge to just the old. God's grace is a river that exceeds its banks and brings its joy to young and old alike. So let's open our hearts to God's grace. Let's open our minds to his Word. Let's praise him for his work of redemption and his love that brought him to visit his people.

TODAY'S PRAYER

I praise you, O God, the incomparable Almighty. I praise you for your power exhibited in your creation. I praise you for your patience and faithfulness to your promises. I praise you for your love and sacrifice. I praise you for your power over sin and death. I praise you for being who you are and doing what you do. In Jesus' name I praise you. Amen.

CONTEXT: LUKE 1:75-80
Related Passages: Galatians 3:26-29; 1 John 2:12-14; Psalm 148:7-13

Day 22

GREAT EXPECTATIONS!

Luke 1:76-79

"Now you, little boy, will be called a prophet of the Most High God. You will go first before the Lord to prepare the way for him. You will make his people understand that they will be saved by having their sins forgiven.

"With the loving mercy of our God, a new day from heaven will shine on us. It will bring light to those who live in darkness, in the fear of death. It will guide us into the way that brings peace."

KEY THOUGHT

At first glance, this is a passage about great expectations that parents have for their child. On closer inspection, it is really about the great expectations that people have for God. The birth of John is the dawn of God's great time of fulfillment. Many of the promises to the people of God, spoken over many centuries in the Old Testament, are now coming true. John will be a tool in God's hand. John will be a sign that the time of fulfillment has come. John will be a servant to the Almighty. However, the work is God's work. The deliverance is God's salvation. The triumph is God's victory. The fulfillment is God's faithfulness. The dawn has come and darkness is being driven away by a holy light.

TODAY'S PRAYER

Father, I praise you for being completely faithful to your promises. I thank you for using everyday human beings to be your vessels through whom your work is done. I appreciate you for choosing Zechariah and Elizabeth to receive your miraculous blessing of John. I honor you for loving your people and bringing them hope in their night of despair. I am in awe that the gospel begins with John the Baptizer. Thank you for your plan to bring us salvation. In Jesus' name I pray. Amen.

CONTEXT: LUKE 1:67-80
Related Passages: 2 Corinthians 4:5-7; Deuteronomy 7:6-9; Psalm 136:2

Day 23

SPIRIT MADE

Luke 1:80
And so the little boy John grew up and became stronger in spirit.
Then he lived in areas away from other people until the time when
he came out to tell God's message to the people of Israel.

KEY THOUGHT

John was filled with the Holy Spirit from his mother's womb according to the promise of the angel. We should not be surprised that he grows strong in the Spirit. While we can debate whether the "s" in spirit should be lower case or upper case, the truth is, the Holy Spirit filled John's spirit and empowered his life. John was not shaped by the culture of the city or by the ways of the Temple. God shaped John in the same way God shaped Israel before they reached the Promised Land—the desert. John's role was unique; his ways seem strange and bizarre to us. The point Luke wants us to know, however, is that John was Spirit-led. His work sets the stage for the dawning of the age of the Spirit and the New Covenant. That Spirit is ours when we become Christians. He leads, guides, transforms, equips, and informs us as the children of God. We, too, can become strong in the Spirit!

TODAY'S PRAYER

Father, I know that your Son poured out the Holy Spirit upon me when I
became a Christian. I know your Spirit lives in me and makes my body
a holy temple where you live. So I ask that you make me strong in the
Spirit. May your will and your character take shape in my life as the Holy
Spirit has more control of my will. In Jesus' name I pray. Amen.

CONTEXT: LUKE 1:67-80
Related Passages: Acts 2:36-39; Titus 3:3-7; Ephesians 3:14-21

Day 24

HISTORICAL REALITY!

Luke 2:1-3

It was about that time that Augustus Caesar sent out an order to all people in the countries that were under Roman rule. The order said that everyone's name must be put on a list. This was the first counting of all the people while Quirinius was governor of Syria. Everyone traveled to their own hometowns to have their name put on the list.

KEY THOUGHT

The Good News of God does not occur in a vacuum. Luke wants us to know that Jesus' life was lived out in the real world, at a real time, with real people, who dealt with real problems. God does not want us to live our lives isolated and separated from his presence. He does not want us to have to reach beyond our grasp to find him. He wants us to know that he understands the limits of our mortal world. In Jesus, God has entered our real world to draw us near! The real question is this: Will we let him into our lives and then live out his will in our everyday world?

TODAY'S PRAYER

Loving Father, Almighty God, I open my life to you. You are welcome here. Come and draw near. Change me at your will. I long to be your child—not just in name, but also in closeness and in character. In Jesus' name I offer my heart to you. Amen.

CONTEXT: LUKE 2:1-7
Related Passages: Acts 17:24-28; John 1:14-18; Matthew 7:7-8

DAVID'S TOWN

Luke 2:4-5

So Joseph left Nazareth, a town in Galilee, and went to the town of Bethlehem in Judea. It was known as the town of David. Joseph went there because he was from the family of David. Joseph registered with Mary because she was engaged to marry him. (She was now pregnant.)

KEY THOUGHT

Bethlehem may not have been much of a town in Jesus' day, but it was King David's town. More importantly, Luke helps us establish a link in Jesus' heritage to King David. Jesus, however, is not just any descendant of David; he is THE successor. Jesus is the one who will reign on David's throne forever. Before Jesus arrives on the scene, we know a little something of his identity and his role, yet he will be King. The issue for you and me is whether we allow him to be King, Lord, and Master of our lives.

TODAY'S PRAYER

Almighty God and loving Father, I want Jesus to rule over my heart. I want him to be Lord of my passions. I want him to redeem the weak, broken, and unholy parts of my character. I want him to be Master of my future. Father, I don't want this because I am worthless and have no value, but because I know that my true value as a person will never be unlocked until I truly let Jesus rule my life. Please shape me and mold me, Lord Jesus, so that just as you obeyed your Father's will, I can learn to do the same. Amen.

CONTEXT: LUKE 2:1-7
Related Passages: 2 Samuel 7:8-13; 1 Kings 9:5; 2 Chronicles 13:5

Day 26

THE TIME CAME

Luke 2:6-7

While Joseph and Mary were in Bethlehem, the time came for her to have the baby. She gave birth to her first son. She wrapped him up well and laid him in a box where cattle are fed. She put him there because the guest room was full.

KEY THOUGHT

We all wait on tiptoe for the birth of a child in our families. No one can be sure of the exact arrival time. Doctors and nurses will talk about subtle body signals, dilation, and effacement, but they can't be sure. Young children awaiting a new sibling will drive everyone crazy by asking every day for months if this is the day. So imagine the excitement among the angels of heaven at Jesus' birth! It wasn't just Joseph and Mary, but the hosts of heaven that awaited his arrival. So at "just the right time," the "time came for her baby to be born." Like any good mother, Mary welcomed her child and God began his gracious and sacrificial journey through humanity, swaddled at his birth like every other baby, but with his bed made in a manger—a feeding box for animals. The question you and I face is whether or not we will give God a room in the most important place of our hearts.

TODAY'S PRAYER

How do I comprehend your gracious and sacrificial love, dear Father? Coming in human flesh as a baby! Swaddled in strips of cloth like the babies of that day! Making your bed in a manger! Holy God, my Abba Father, please know that I want you to make your home in my heart. You are welcome here. Thank you for the grace of coming in Jesus. Thank you for your grace of also coming to live in me through your Spirit. In Jesus' name I thank you. Amen.

CONTEXT: LUKE 2:1-7
Related Passages: Galatians 4:4; John 1:14-18; 1 Peter 1:8-12

Day 27

THE KING'S ADDRESS

Luke 2:8-12

That night, some shepherds were out in the fields near Bethlehem watching their sheep. An angel of the Lord appeared to them, and the glory of the Lord was shining around them. The shepherds were very afraid. The angel said to them, "Don't be afraid. I have some very good news for you—news that will make everyone happy. Today your Savior was born in David's town. He is Christ, the Lord. This is how you will know him: You will find a baby wrapped in pieces of cloth and lying in a feeding box."

KEY THOUGHT

Incredibly, when the angels of God announced the birth of God's Son, the King, they give his address as "lying in a feeding box"—or manger as we traditionally say. Luke wants us to grasp three powerful truths in this simple description. First, God is tapping into the long line of imagery that ties him and his work to shepherds. Second, even though shepherds were not respected in Jesus' day, God announces the birth of his Son to them first—it is part of Luke's emphasis on God's desire to reach all kinds of people across every strata of life. Third, the Savior enters the world in humble circumstances, born to an ordinary and otherwise unnoticeable family. The grand and the forgotten, the glorious and the abandoned, the promised ones and the hopeful are all combined into God's story of love, grace, and salvation. The needle that sews this tapestry of grace is God's love. His thread is the Holy Spirit. His good news is that Jesus, his Son and our Savior, has arrived at an address we can all find, knocking on the door of our hearts.

TODAY'S PRAYER

Holy and magnificent God, thank you for making yourself accessible and reachable in your Son. Most of all, thank you for taking away my greatest reason to be afraid by coming with your salvation for me in Jesus, in whose name I give you thanks. Amen.

CONTEXT: LUKE 2:8-20
Related Passages: Isaiah 53:1-2; Isaiah 40:9-11; 1 Peter 2:25

Day 28

LET'S GO SEE!

Luke 2:13-15

Then a huge army of angels from heaven joined the first angel, and they were all praising God, saying, "Praise God in heaven, and on earth let there be peace to the people who please him."

The angels left the shepherds and went back to heaven. The shepherds said to each other, "Let's go to Bethlehem and see this great event the Lord has told us about."

KEY THOUGHT

Here's our invitation. We're invited to join the shepherds to go see the wonderful thing that God has done by sending Jesus. Yes, God has told us about this great event—through his Old Testament prophets, through the yearning of our hearts for a Savior, and through our need for answers to life's greatest dilemmas. So let's join the shepherds at the manger. But, let's not just stop at the manger; God invites us to journey all the way through the story. After all, Luke isn't writing a biography about Jesus, but is instead telling the story of our salvation through God's promised Savior. So let's strengthen our resolve to pursue Jesus all this year through Luke's story of God's saving love. Let's go "see this great event the Lord has told us about" and find God's grace, love, and salvation in Jesus.

TODAY'S PRAYER

Father, make my heart yearn to know you, your love, and your story of grace more. Teach me as I seek you in Luke's story of Jesus. I pray this in his name. Amen.

CONTEXT: LUKE 2:8-20
Related Passages: Hebrews 1:1-3; Acts 4:8-12; John 1:35-39

Day 29

ASTONISHMENT, TREASURE, AND PRAISE

Luke 2:16-20

So they went running and found Mary and Joseph. And there was the baby, lying in the feeding box. When they saw the baby, they told what the angels said about this child. Everyone was surprised when they heard what the shepherds told them. Mary continued to think about these things, trying to understand them. The shepherds went back to their sheep, praising God and thanking him for everything they had seen and heard. It was just as the angel had told them.

KEY THOUGHT

If we will allow it to touch us, the birth of Jesus can produce the same reactions in us as it did in those three groups touched by it. The villagers were astonished at the story—and so are we, because God would love us this much. Mary stored up the words and events in her heart like treasure—and so do we, when we read the story of Jesus with love, joy, and anticipation. The shepherds returned to their work, but they do so with joy and praise knowing that their world would never be the same. God has come and visited us. He has shown us his love. He has reminded us that life doesn't have to have its normal boundaries. So we greet this story and this child with astonishment, taking in each story and every word as a treasure, while offering our heartfelt praise to God for his gracious love.

TODAY'S PRAYER

O Almighty God, so majestic and yet so accessible, thank you for drawing near us when we could not draw near you. In Jesus' name I pray. Amen.

CONTEXT: LUKE 2:8-20
Related Passages: Mark 6:45-51; Matthew 13:44; Mark 11:8-10

Day 30

HIS PLACE IN HIS WORLD

Luke 2:21-24

When the baby was eight days old, he was circumcised, and he was named Jesus. This name was given by the angel before the baby began to grow inside Mary.

The time came for Mary and Joseph to do the things the Law of Moses taught about being made pure. They brought Jesus to Jerusalem so that they could present him to the Lord. It is written in the law of the Lord: "When a mother's first baby is a boy, he shall be called 'special for the Lord.'" The law of the Lord also says that people must give a sacrifice: "You must sacrifice two doves or two young pigeons." So Joseph and Mary went to Jerusalem to do this.

KEY THOUGHT

Jesus' parents followed the requirements of the Old Testament Law and had him circumcised. After Mary's forty-day period of purification, she and Joseph took Jesus to the Temple where they went through the ceremony of dedication and redemption of the firstborn. Their offering of two young pigeons rather than a lamb indicates their status as common poor folks. Luke makes perfectly clear that the people out of whom the hope of all people came were poor, devout, obedient, simple, and faithful. Even today, when people recognize they are not above God's call to obedience, and when they are faithful, God works to bring salvation. This is not a story about the power of the high and mighty of Jesus day, but of poor devout folks who were faithful to the Almighty!

TODAY'S PRAYER

O God, Master of the universe and ruler of my heart, give me a heart of faithful obedience like I see in Zechariah, Elizabeth, Joseph, and Mary. Help me raise up my children with examples of faithfulness and obedience. Banish arrogance and self-seeking, not only from my heart, but from all in my influence for generations to come. Use us as a place to give birth to hope through your Son, in whose name I pray. Amen.

CONTEXT: LUKE 2:21-40
Related Passages: Galatians 4:4-5; Matthew 5:17; Philippians 2:5-8

Day 31

LED BY THE SPIRIT

Luke 2:25-27

A man named Simeon lived in Jerusalem. He was a good man who was devoted to God. He was waiting for the time when God would come to help Israel. The Holy Spirit was with him. The Holy Spirit told him that he would not die before he saw the Christ from the Lord. The Spirit led Simeon to the Temple. So he was there when Mary and Joseph brought the baby Jesus to do what the Jewish law said they must do.

KEY THOUGHT

Simeon is a great figure, an example of Old Testament devotion—he was righteous and devout. He is also a great figure of what will be New Testament devotion—filled with the Holy Spirit, enlightened by the Holy Spirit, and led by the Holy Spirit. In this blending of old and new, we find something fresh, vital, and life-changing: people whose hearts are fully committed to honor God, but acknowledge that their power to be holy comes from the Holy Spirit. Like Simeon, let's make sure we take up the new and not neglect the old. God wants us to be filled with a holy passion for him, his Kingdom, and his hope!

TODAY'S PRAYER

Father, thank you for giving me the Holy Spirit when I became a Christian. I pray that my heart will seek after you and your ways passionately. However, dear Father, I know that my best efforts are not enough. I need the power and leading of your Spirit to be all that I want to be as I seek to live for Jesus, in whose name I pray. Amen.

CONTEXT: LUKE 2:21-40
Related Passages: Titus 3:3-8; Romans 8:5-11; Galatians 5:22-25

Day 32

OLD EYES, NEW LIGHT

Luke 2:27-32

The Spirit led Simeon to the Temple. So he was there when Mary and Joseph brought the baby Jesus to do what the Jewish law said they must do. Simeon took the baby in his arms and thanked God: "Now, Lord, you can let me, your servant, die in peace as you said. I have seen with my own eyes how you will save your people. Now all people can see your plan. He is a light to show your way to the other nations. And he will bring honor to your people Israel."

KEY THOUGHT

"You can't teach an old dog new tricks!" It's one of those "truisms" that we all accept as an excuse for becoming staid and cynical as we age. I don't know about you, but I'm no dog! I believe I can change—or better yet, I believe that God's Spirit can transform me . . . at any age. Here is old Simeon, old eyes and all, and he is the one who gets to see God's new light. Why? Because Simeon believed God would do something great in his day, and he kept on believing even when he was old. God still longs to do glorious things in our day, even if we are old! Keep believing, listening, trusting, and following, and most of all, keep expecting! God is faithful and he will surprise you with glorious things.

TODAY'S PRAYER

O Father, my tender Shepherd, please do not let my passion dim or my faith grow tired as I grow older. I want to live a vibrant life of faith, expecting and experiencing your great acts of mercy and power all the way to my dying day. In Jesus' name I pray this. Amen.

CONTEXT: LUKE 2:21-40
Related Passages: Psalm 92:12-14; Isaiah 46:3-4; Joshua 14:10-13

Day 33

A CHILD OF DECISION

Luke 2:33-35

Jesus' father and mother were amazed at what Simeon said about him. Then Simeon blessed them and said to Mary, "Many Jews will fall and many will rise because of this boy. He will be a sign from God that some will not accept. So the secret thoughts of many will be made known. And the things that happen will be painful for you—like a sword cutting through your heart."

KEY THOUGHT

While Jesus came to bring "goodness and light," he came to a world infected by sin and enslaved to the principles of darkness, decay, and death. His life would not be about ease and escape, but about decision, confrontation, and truth. Darkness had to be driven away. Decay had to be destroyed. Death had to be defeated. To do that meant taking on everything the powers of this world had used to maintain their hold on the hearts of people. Yes, liberation would bring joy to the rescued, but it would mean a high cost for those who wanted to preserve the status quo and did not accept the liberation. Jesus' coming forces us to decide which side we are on. He came as Lord, not as a sweet, do-gooder pal. Only when we surrender our hearts to him as Lord does he become our friend and brother. But there is no middle ground. He is not just a good guy, come to do good things, and to make good people happy. He is Savior, Lord, and King. So our joy is Mary's pain. Our victory is Jesus' agony. Our hope is God's sacrifice. Simeon's words remind us that we must make a decision about this Jesus. There is no middle ground or middle emotion.

TODAY'S PRAYER

Give me the courage, O Lord God, to choose Jesus completely. I want him to be my Lord as well as my Savior, my King as well as my friend, my Master as well as my brother. Thank you for paying such a huge price to make him Savior, friend, and brother. I offer my heart to him as Lord and King . In the name of my Lord, Jesus Christ, I pray. Amen.

CONTEXT: LUKE 2:21-40
Related Passages: Matthew 10:32-39; Joshua 24:14-15; 2 Corinthians 5:9-10

Day 34

AN OLD HOPE AND A LONG DELIGHT

Luke 2:36-38

Anna, a prophetess, was there at the Temple. She was from the family of Phanuel in the tribe of Asher. She was now very old. She had lived with her husband seven years before he died and left her alone. She was now 84 years old. Anna was always at the Temple; she never left. She worshiped God by fasting and praying day and night.

Anna was there when Joseph and Mary came to the Temple. She praised God and talked about Jesus to all those who were waiting for God to free Jerusalem.

KEY THOUGHT

Anna had lost her husband, but not her hope. She had lost the life of her dreams, but not the ability to dream. Life can be hard for all of us. Some get hit with crushing wounds early in their journey. These wounds don't have to destroy their lives. While they may carry the memory and the scars through all of their years, God can be their sufficiency and strength. This was true with Anna. Her walk with God stands up there with Elijah and Enoch. She found him sufficient for her needs and worthy of her praise. God gave her the delight of her life and an opportunity to do what the prophets had foretold: "Both your sons and daughters will prophesy!" She was privileged to declare the arrival of the Messiah to everyone in the Temple. What a long wait! What a glorious conclusion! What an awesome privilege! Come to think of it, we have the privilege of declaring Jesus, too!

TODAY'S PRAYER

Father, I do not know what life will bring me, but please give me the faith to trust that you will be there to help me find my way through it until I find the joy that awaits me in you. In Jesus' name I pray. Amen.

CONTEXT: LUKE 2:21-40
Related Passages: Psalm 46:1-3, 7; Acts 2:16-18; Luke 10:38-42

Day 35

HE GREW UP!

Luke 2:39-40

Joseph and Mary finished doing all the things that the law of the Lord commanded.
Then they went home to Nazareth, their own town in Galilee. The little boy Jesus
was developing into a mature young man, full of wisdom. God was blessing him.

KEY THOUGHT

Think how amazing these statements are. God came to visit our world in
Jesus! Yet before he could minister to us and teach us, he had to be born and
grow up like us. It boggles the mind. The amazing part of this passage is not
that God placed his favor on Jesus, but that he favored us by choosing to share
our human experiences. Amazing! And why did he do it? So we could know
that he has been where we are and that we would call out to him to help us in
our times of struggle, weakness, vulnerability, and temptation.

TODAY'S PRAYER

I praise you, Lord God Almighty, for choosing to come live among
us as one of us. Thank you for being so gracious and glorious to us,
your human children. In Jesus' name I praise you. Amen.

CONTEXT: LUKE 2:21-40
Related Passages: Hebrews 2:14-16; Hebrews 4:14-16; Luke 18:15-17

Day 36

ESTABLISHING FAITH AT AN EARLY AGE

Luke 2:41-47

Every year Jesus' parents went to Jerusalem for the Passover festival. When Jesus was twelve years old, they went to the festival as usual. When the festival was over, they went home, but Jesus stayed in Jerusalem. His parents did not know about it. They traveled for a whole day thinking that Jesus was with them in the group. They began looking for him among their family and close friends, but they did not find him. So they went back to Jerusalem to look for him there.

After three days they found him. Jesus was sitting in the Temple area with the religious teachers, listening and asking them questions. Everyone who heard him was amazed at his understanding and wise answers.

KEY THOUGHT

So often parents wait until their children are older or in trouble to begin trying to get them involved in spiritual matters. By then, it can be too late to make a big difference. God wants us to start early in our children's lives! That way it is a lifelong foundation that goes with them every step of their way. Don't waste a moment; don't neglect an opportunity to read Bible stories, discuss life, and pray lovingly with your children or grandchildren!

TODAY'S PRAYER

Father in heaven, please bless my efforts to pass on a vibrant faith to my children and grandchildren. Help me keep my priorities and my schedule in order so I can fulfill this awesome responsibility and this glorious opportunity with the children that I love. In Jesus' name I pray. Amen.

CONTEXT: LUKE 2:41-52
Related Passages: 2 Timothy 3:14-17; Deuteronomy 6:4-9; Ephesians 6:1-4

Day 37

MY FATHER'S HOUSE

Luke 2:48-50

When his parents saw him, they wondered how this was possible. And his mother said, "Son, why did you do this to us? Your father and I were very worried about you. We have been looking for you."

Jesus said to them, "Why did you have to look for me? You should have known that I must be where my Father's work is." But they did not understand the meaning of what he said to them.

KEY THOUGHT

Jesus had a growing sense of purpose as he grew older. While he would apprentice in Joseph's carpenter shop, Jesus felt the pull to be about his Heavenly Father's work. An Old Testament passage that was associated with Jesus' cleansing of the Temple later in his ministry reads, "Passion for God's house burns within me" (John 2:17). That passion was with him even at twelve years old. No matter the age of your child or grandchild (or nephew or niece), don't hesitate to teach them how important it is that God's reign in their hearts and his holy influence on their choices should begin today.

TODAY'S PRAYER

Father, I pray for those children over whom I have influence. Please use me to encourage them and to show them how precious they are. Please use me to show them how important it is that they live for you. In Jesus' name I pray. Amen.

CONTEXT: LUKE 2:41-52
Related Passages: John 2:13-17; Matthew 18:7-10; Ecclesiastes 12:1-7

Day 38

HE GREW UP A GOOD KID

Luke 2:51-52

Jesus went with them to Nazareth and obeyed them. His mother was still thinking about all these things. As Jesus grew taller, he continued to grow in wisdom. God was pleased with him and so were the people who knew him.

KEY THOUGHT

Luke lets us know that Jesus was a "good kid." As Jesus grew up, he was obedient, he grew smarter, he made God proud, and he was liked by others. Like any loving parent, Mary stored up the memories of his childhood in her heart. There were no shortcuts for the Messiah. God's Son had to grow up and live a life of character in a family just like any other child. His wisdom came as he grew. Yet all the while, God's mission for him lay ahead. Think of it: If we cannot fathom God fully in human flesh, what must it have been like for Mary and Joseph? Yet in this divine mystery lie our healing, God's grace, and the Savior's glory. Now God calls us to grow, in all ways, to be like his Son.

TODAY'S PRAYER

Father, you know that I sometimes get tired and distracted in my spiritual development. Forgive my past times of spiritual laziness and stir in me a holy passion to be conformed and grow ever more fully into the person you want me to be. In the name of Jesus and by the power of his transforming Spirit may this be so. Amen.

CONTEXT: LUKE 2:41-52
Related Passages: Philippians 2:5-11; 2 Corinthians 3:17-18; Galatians 4:19

Day 39

GOD'S MESSAGE COMES TO JOHN

Luke 3:1-2

It was the 15th year of the rule of Tiberius Caesar. These men were under Caesar: Pontius Pilate, the ruler of Judea; Herod, the ruler of Galilee; Philip, Herod's brother, the ruler of Iturea and Trachonitis; Lysanias, the ruler of Abilene.

Annas and Caiaphas were the high priests. During this time, John, the son of Zechariah, was living in the desert, and he received a message from God.

KEY THOUGHT

We often think that it is our setting or our location or the time in our life that determines when God's influence is most felt by us. The beginning of the Jesus story reminds us that God is greater than any setting, location, or time in history. God's message came to John when Israel was occupied by Roman power, influence, and politics. Yet this was the time that God chose to speak and to act to fulfill his promises and to redeem all peoples. No matter where you are in the circumstances of your life, don't think that God can't act and bring change, deliverance, and salvation. God is greater than any circumstance. The real issue is whether or not our hearts are yearning for his mighty works and his powerful words to change us regardless of our setting, location, or time in history.

TODAY'S PRAYER

Abba Father, may your name be revered with holy passion and your words and works be honored today as they are by the hosts of heaven. Break through in this time and show your glory and splendor, holiness and honor, righteousness and justice, before all people. Keep my heart's fervor vibrantly passionate for you and your will. In Jesus' name. Amen.

CONTEXT: LUKE 3:1-9
Related Passages: Matthew 6:9-10; Jeremiah 32:17-20; Deuteronomy 30:16

A CALL TO TURN

Luke 3:2-3

Annas and Caiaphas were the high priests. During this time, John, the son of Zechariah, was living in the desert, and he received a message from God. So he went through the whole area around the Jordan River and told the people God's message. He told them to be baptized to show that they wanted to change their lives, and then their sins would be forgiven.

KEY THOUGHT

John came to prepare the way for Jesus. For that to happen in most people's lives, they have to re-orient their priorities and values, no longer living by their own instincts and values, but according to God's will. One of the biggest problems with postmodern secular culture is that many have an arrogant heart that chooses its own path based upon what seems right to itself. For true conversion to take place, one has to surrender this arrogance and genuinely turn to God. Are you committed to obeying God's will? Or, are you still trying to live based on what seems right to you? You see, repentance isn't just about being sorry for our mistakes, wrongs, transgressions, sins, or hurtful things we've done; it's about turning from them to God and living by God's holy standards. Our own ways are flawed and destructive. Without doing the things of God, we will invariably find ourselves hurting others and ourselves. Let's turn our hearts and lives fully in the direction of God!

TODAY'S PRAYER

Forgive me, dear Heavenly Father, for so often seeking things based upon my own will and wisdom. Humble me gently and turn me to your ways. I know your will for me is life and blessing, so I renounce my own ways as destructive and selfish and seek to turn my will fully over to you, seeking to serve, honor, and obey you each day. In Jesus' name I pray. Amen.

CONTEXT: LUKE 3:1-9
Related Passages: Proverbs 16:25; 2 Corinthians 7:10; 1 Thessalonians 1:2-10

Day 41

A BULLDOZER FROM HEAVEN

Luke 3:4-6
This is like the words written in the book of Isaiah the prophet: "There is someone shouting in the desert: 'Prepare the way for the Lord. Make the road straight for him. Every valley will be filled, and every mountain and hill will be made flat. Crooked roads will be made straight, and rough roads will be made smooth. Then everyone will see how God will save his people!'"

KEY THOUGHT

Isaiah had foretold of a "bulldozer from heaven" that would make straight roads, leveling the hills and filling in the valleys, so that people could find the Savior. Does your life do that for others? Does it help them see Jesus more clearly? Does it show the transforming power of God at work? All of us are called to be like John in the road-smoothing work of making it easier for others to come to know Jesus.

TODAY'S PRAYER

O Lord God, please use my life to influence others to come to know your salvation. May my life never be a stumbling block, but instead, may it be a help to others looking for your hope and healing. I ask this in Jesus' name. Amen.

CONTEXT: LUKE 3:1-9
Related Passages: 1 Peter 3:13-16; Matthew 5:13-16; Colossians 4:5-6

Day 42

NO FALSE PRIDE IN OUR HERITAGE

Luke 3:7-9

Crowds of people came to be baptized by John. But he said to them, "You are all snakes! Who warned you to run from God's judgment that is coming? Change your hearts! And show by your lives that you have changed. I know what you are about to say—'but Abraham is our father!' That means nothing. I tell you that God can make children for Abraham from these rocks! The ax is now ready to cut down the trees. Every tree that does not produce good fruit will be cut down and thrown into the fire."

KEY THOUGHT

Often we want to take the efforts of those around us, and those who have gone before us, and claim them as our own. Faith is aided by a long heritage, but all genuine faith is always first generation faith—no one can believe for us. Many in Jesus' day wanted to claim lineage, race, and heritage as their spiritual guarantee. John reminds all people of all races of any time that heritage and pedigree don't mean a thing unless our faith is genuine. Let's show the genuineness of our faith in what we do, not in who we claim as our parents or what religious group we claim as our home.

TODAY'S PRAYER

Father, may my faith be my own and may it be as real in my daily behavior as it is in my heart and my heritage. Empower me to live out the faith I profess. In Jesus' name I pray. Amen.

CONTEXT: LUKE 3:1-9
Related Passages: James 2:14, 17-20; Matthew 7:15-23; 1 Peter 3:8-12

Day 43

WHAT SHOULD WE DO?

Luke 3:10-14

The people asked John, "What should we do?"

*He answered, "If you have two shirts, share with someone who
does not have one. If you have food, share that too."*

*Even the tax collectors came to John. They wanted to be baptized.
They said to him, "Teacher, what should we do?"*

He told them, "Don't take more taxes from people than you have been ordered to collect."

The soldiers asked him, "What about us? What should we do?"

*He said to them, "Don't use force or lies to make people give
you money. Be happy with the pay you get."*

KEY THOUGHT

As Luke tells the story of Jesus' earthly ministry (the Gospel of Luke) and
the story of Jesus' heavenly ministry (the Acts of the Apostles), he comes back
to this question again and again: "What must we [I] do?" This is THE question
Luke wants all of us to ask. Luke is looking for more than just, "What must I
believe?" God uses Luke to speak to our times when goodness and godliness
are associated only with what we feel or what we think. Yes, God wants our
hearts, minds, and souls to be thoroughly convicted and passionate. Yes,
without faith and love, all action is hollow and vain. But the Bible makes clear
that real faith leads us to action. When Jesus enters our world, he changes it.
When Jesus enters our lives, he changes them. So the ultimate question of
faith is this: "What, Lord, should I do?" So why not begin each day by asking
Jesus that question?

TODAY'S PRAYER

*O God, guide my steps and lead my heart and form my character. I want
my faith to be more than mental. I want my love for you to be displayed
in what I do and how I do it. In Jesus' name I pray. Amen.*

CONTEXT: LUKE 3:10-20
Related Passages: Acts 2:36-40; Acts 16:25-34; Luke 10:25

Day 44

GREATER THAN I

Luke 3:15-17

Everyone was hoping for the Christ to come, and they wondered about John. They thought, "Maybe he is the Christ."

John's answer to this was, "I baptize you in water, but there is someone coming later who is able to do more than I can. I am not good enough to be the slave who unties his sandals. He will baptize you with the Holy Spirit and with fire. He will come ready to clean the grain. He will separate the good grain from the straw, and he will put the good part into his barn. Then he will burn the useless part with a fire that cannot be stopped."

KEY THOUGHT

The Super Bowl has come and gone for another year. If you're interested in football, you might remember several key plays about this year's game. What I find interesting, however, is that invariably the outcome of the Super Bowl, along with other key games, often depends upon the guys who are frequently overlooked—the men in the trenches, the offensive and defensive linemen. Most coaches say that turnovers and skill position people are crucial to a victory. That may be true, but the outcome of the game is usually determined by the players whose work is seldom discussed unless they mess up. John was one of those men in the trenches. He could have kept a huge following for himself. He was immensely popular. Instead, John kept his integrity and didn't change his message for anyone, including an adulterous king. John stuck to his purpose: pointing others to Jesus and away from himself. Jesus emphasized that this sort of servant is the greatest in his Kingdom. Jesus said this kind of servant is also the greatest kind of person we can be!

TODAY'S PRAYER

Father, make me a servant. I want to live knowing that I am pleasing you and honoring Jesus. If folks can't remember me, but they know Jesus because I've touched their lives, then make their praise of your Son satisfaction enough for me. In Jesus' name I pray. Amen.

CONTEXT: LUKE 3:10-20
Related Passages: Philippians 2:3-4, 19-21; Luke 7:24-28; John 3:26-30

Day 45

WARNINGS AND GOOD NEWS?

Luke 3:18
John said many other things like this to encourage the people
to change, and he told them the Good News.

KEY THOUGHT

The warning in the previous verses and the Good News in this verse
don't seem to go together, do they? Hmm, how do they fit together? When
everlasting life and eternal destruction are the options, rejecting the Good
News about Jesus means choosing destruction. Each of the gospels (Matthew,
Mark, Luke, and John) emphasizes the radical nature of the choice we must
make about the Kingdom of God and the coming of Jesus. Jesus is Good
News. Jesus brings Good News. However, if we reject Jesus and the call of the
Kingdom of God, we must hear the warnings of that choice. In a world like
ours, where few want ultimate choices and the vast majority resents having
to deal with lasting consequences for moral and spiritual choices, John the
Baptizer's preaching still has a penetrating, invigorating, and for some,
irritating echo. Like it or not, Jesus confronts us with a decision about who will
rule our lives. The choice we make means everything!

TODAY'S PRAYER

Father, help me to hear the radical call of your Kingdom on my heart. I know that the
message of Jesus is Good News! At the same time, I don't want to take lightly your call
for me to live my life with holiness, integrity, honor, righteousness, compassion, goodness,
and godly character. May your will reign in my heart and may my life reflect the Good
News of the Kingdom to which you have called me. I ask this in Jesus' name. Amen.

CONTEXT: LUKE 3:10-20
Related Passages: Acts 4:8-12; John 14:6-7; I John 5:9-13

Day 46

THE TRUTH

Luke 3:19-20

John criticized Herod the ruler for what he had done with Herodias, the wife of Herod's brother, as well as for all the other bad things he had done. So Herod added another bad thing to all his other wrongs: He put John in jail.

KEY THOUGHT

I've heard it said that our true character is revealed in what we do and who we are when no one is looking. For most of us that is probably true. However, there is another test of character and truth-telling. Will we tell the truth to everyone, even those who have power over us and who don't want us to tell it? One of the stark reminders of Satan's reality in the world is the long line of martyrs for the cause of Jesus and the Kingdom. That line begins with John (Luke 9:9), who tells the truth to Herod just as he did to commoners. John teaches us integrity. Many others have followed his example. May God give us the grace to do the same if confronted with such a choice.

TODAY'S PRAYER

Holy and righteous God, please give me the courage and strength to speak truth regardless of the situation that confronts me. Help me speak the truth in love, but to speak the truth with conviction and clarity. In Jesus' name. Amen.

CONTEXT: LUKE 3:10-20
Related Passages: Luke 12:8-12; Acts 4:8-20; 1 Peter 3:13-17

Day 47

THE HEAVENS OPENED

Luke 3:21-22
When all the people were being baptized, Jesus came and was baptized too.
And while he was praying, the sky opened, and the Holy Spirit came down
on him. The Spirit looked like a real dove. Then a voice came from heaven
and said, "You are my Son, the one I love. I am very pleased with you."

KEY THOUGHT

Jesus comes as part of the genuine movement of God among common
people and is baptized. That event happens not only at a human level, but
also at a heavenly level. Part of what is happening at the heavenly level is
prayer, which is such a powerful dynamic in the work of the Holy Spirit. God's
approval of Jesus and affection for him as his child are articulated. When we
are baptized, we follow the example of Jesus and need to realize that God's
approval and affection rest upon us as well—"You are my beloved child,"
our Father tells us, "and I am fully pleased with you!" Isn't it incredible that
God gave us the invitation to follow his Son and receive his blessing? Isn't it
amazing that we get to do something that was important to our Savior? Isn't
it truly a blessing to know how God feels about us when we turn our hearts
toward him? Amazing!

TODAY'S PRAYER

Holy and righteous God, thank you for the gift of baptism. What a blessing it is
to have the opportunity to share in this same experience that your Son and my
Savior did so many years ago. Thank you that it is more than a mere human
event, but one in which your Spirit moves and also one in which I can find my
assurance of your approval and affection. Thank you in Jesus' name. Amen.

CONTEXT: LUKE 3:21-38
Related Passages: Acts 2:36-41; Titus 3:3-7; Acts 22:16

Day 48

BEGINNINGS

Luke 3:23
When Jesus began to teach, he was about 30 years old. People thought that Jesus was Joseph's son. Joseph was the son of Eli.

KEY THOUGHT

Jesus has accepted baptism, been anointed with the Spirit, and received affirmation from God. Now he begins his public ministry. If he was simply Joseph's son from Nazareth, there would have been little reason to describe any part of his life as public. From a small, nondescript little town, no one of importance would have known or cared about Jesus. Now he begins his public ministry that will touch billions of people over the course of time. Just as Jesus' beginnings were small, so also was his family small and insignificant. But, they are connected to a long line of folks—some of whom are important, many of whom are not—that extends back to Abraham and ultimately back to Adam and indeed all the way back to God. So in three ways, Jesus begins his ministry as God's Son: First, he is God's Son by conception of the Spirit; second, he is God's Son through the anointing of the Holy Spirit at his baptism; and finally, he is God's son as all of us are, a child of humanity that traces its beginnings back to the creative work of God. We all have to begin some place. The key is to start. Have you started? What are you waiting for?

TODAY'S PRAYER

O glorious God and Father of the Lord Jesus Christ, thank you for having your Messiah, my Savior, begin his ministry in a way that makes sense to us mortals. Thank you for his connections to us through human frailty and flesh. Thank you that he shared an experience that I too can share, the grace of baptism. Thank you for the Holy Spirit who makes me your child, similar in some ways to the way Jesus was your child. Thank you for a beginning point. Now I ask, dear Lord, to help me as I seek to move beyond the beginning point to what you would have me do. In Jesus' name I pray. Amen.

CONTEXT: LUKE 3:21-38
Related Passages: Galatians 3:26-29; Philippians 1:3-6; 2:13; 2 Corinthians 5:14-17

Day 49

MORE THAN NAMES

Luke 3:24-38

Eli was the son of Matthat. Matthat was the son of Levi. Levi was the son of Melchi. Melchi was the son of Jannai. Jannai was the son of Joseph. Joseph was the son of Mattathias. Mattathias was the son of Amos. Amos was the son of Nahum. Nahum was the son of Esli. Esli was the son of Naggai. Naggai was the son of Maath. Maath was the son of Mattathias. Mattathias was the son of Semein. Semein was the son of Josech. Josech was the son of Joda. Joda was the son of Joanan. Joanan was the son of Rhesa. Rhesa was the son of Zerubbabel. Zerubbabel was the son of Shealtiel. Shealtiel was the son of Neri. Neri was the son of Melchi. Melchi was the son of Addi. Addi was the son of Cosam. Cosam was the son of Elmadam. Elmadam was the son of Er. Er was the son of Joshua. Joshua was the son of Eliezer. Eliezer was the son of Jorim. Jorim was the son of Matthat. Matthat was the son of Levi. Levi was the son of Simeon. Simeon was the son of Judah. Judah was the son of Joseph. Joseph was the son of Jonam. Jonam was the son of Eliakim. Eliakim was the son of Melea. Melea was the son of Menna. Menna was the son of Mattatha. Mattatha was the son of Nathan. Nathan was the son of David. David was the son of Jesse. Jesse was the son of Obed. Obed was the son of Boaz. Boaz was the son of Salmon. Salmon was the son of Nahshon. Nahshon was the son of Amminadab. Amminadab was the son of Admin. Admin was the son of Arni. Arni was the son of Hezron. Hezron was the son of Perez. Perez was the son of Judah. Judah was the son of Jacob. Jacob was the son of Isaac. Isaac was the son of Abraham. Abraham was the son of Terah. Terah was the son of Nahor. Nahor was the son of Serug. Serug was the son of Reu. Reu was the son of Peleg. Peleg was the son of Eber. Eber was the son of Shelah. Shelah was the son of Cainan. Cainan was the son of Arphaxad. Arphaxad was the son of Shem. Shem was the son of Noah. Noah was the son of Lamech. Lamech was the son of Methuselah. Methuselah was the son of Enoch. Enoch was the son of Jared. Jared was the son of Mahalaleel. Mahalaleel was the son of Cainan. Cainan was the son of Enos. Enos was the son of Seth. Seth was the son of Adam. Adam was the son of God.

KEY THOUGHT

These are more than names. When nights seem dark and hopes distant, they are our reminder that God keeps his promises. He has for generations and he will for us.

TODAY'S PRAYER

Father, give me a heart of faith as deep and as long as the line of faith that has been passed down to me through the ages. In Jesus' name I pray. Amen.

Day 50

SPIRIT LED

Luke 4:1-2

Now filled with the Holy Spirit Jesus returned from the Jordan River. And then the Spirit led him into the desert. There the devil tempted Jesus for 40 days. Jesus ate nothing during this time, and when it was finished, he was very hungry.

KEY THOUGHT

"The devil is in the details." While the old saying is true, it is even truer that the devil tries to compromise anyone led by the Spirit. That is especially true early in a person's commitment. If the evil one can derail the early passion of a Christian when the presence of the Spirit is new and fresh, then he doesn't have to keep coming back to try to derail that believer. Just as Jesus will overcome temptation and Satan by his commitment to honor God and by his knowledge of Scripture—as we will see in the following verses—we also must hear Luke's key point: The Holy Spirit empowered and led Jesus through these trials. In the book of Acts, the strength of the early Christians was found in the power of the Holy Spirit who lived in them and worked through them. As Jesus' followers, Luke wants us to be like our great Teacher and follow his path to victory over Satan—through the power of Holy Spirit, our commitment to honor God, and the truth of the Scriptures alive in our hearts.

TODAY'S PRAYER

O Lord God, as your child, I know your Spirit lives in me. Please empower me by your Spirit and help me resist the temptations of the devil and to triumph over his attempts to dilute and to divert my loyalty and whole-hearted devotion to you. In Jesus' name I pray. Amen.

CONTEXT: LUKE 4:1-13
Related Passages: Romans 8:5-14; Galatians 5:19-25; Ephesians 5:15-21

Day 51

MORE THAN BREAD

Luke 4:3-4

The devil said to him, "If you are the Son of God, tell this rock to become bread."

Jesus answered, "The Scriptures say, 'It is not just bread that keeps people alive.'"

KEY THOUGHT

"If you are the Son of God . . . ." God had affirmed his relationship with his Son at his baptism: "You are my Son, the one I love. I am very pleased with you." Jesus had no reason to doubt his relationship with his Father. With his knowledge of Scripture, he could easily answer Satan's well-timed temptation. But what are we to learn from this battle? First, Satan knows when, where, and how to attack our vulnerabilities. Second, his enticements are often targeted as a shortcut to a real need. However, our relationship with God, the power of the Holy Spirit in us, and our internalization of biblical truth all can help us win our battles, just as they helped Jesus. The real challenge is for us to keep each of these three areas of our faith strong. So which one most needs your attention?

TODAY'S PRAYER

Father in heaven, the glorious and Almighty, please deepen my relationship with you as I seek to draw closer to you. Have your Spirit take a greater influence in my life as I intentionally seek to yield to your will and your influence in my life. As I read the Bible, press your truth into the fiber of my soul. In Jesus' name I pray. Amen.

CONTEXT: LUKE 4:1-13
Related Passages: Ephesians 6:10-13; 2 Corinthians 11:14-15; 1 Peter 5:8

Day 52

SHORTCUT OR SUFFERING

Luke 4:5-8

Then the devil took Jesus and in a moment of time showed him all the kingdoms of the world. The devil said to him, "I will make you king over all these places. You will have power over them, and you will get all the glory. It has all been given to me. I can give it to anyone I want. I will give it all to you, if you will only worship me."

Jesus answered, "The Scriptures say, 'You must worship the Lord your God. Serve only him.'"

KEY THOUGHT

This is a great demonstration of Jesus' love for us. His crucifixion would not have happened if he had not resisted the devil here. He is offered a shortcut to world dominion, one that would not require his suffering and death. Yet he chooses the long hard road that leads to Golgotha because of his love for us. Jesus will not compromise on this one truth of truths: only God is to be worshiped and honored as God! No matter the risks, costs, or consequences, Jesus reminds us that we are to serve God alone!

TODAY'S PRAYER

Father in heaven, only you are the one, true, living God whose love endures from one generation to another. Give me an undivided heart to serve you whole-heartedly and without rival. In Jesus' name I pray. Amen.

CONTEXT: LUKE 4:1-13
Related Passages: Deuteronomy 13:4; Luke 10:25-28; 1 John 5:21

Day 53

SHOW HE'S WITH YOU!

Luke 4:9-12

Then the devil led Jesus to Jerusalem and put him on a high place at the edge of the Temple area. He said to him, "If you are the Son of God, jump off! The Scriptures say, 'God will command his angels to take care of you.' It is also written, 'Their hands will catch you so that you will not hit your foot on a rock.'"

Jesus answered, "But the Scriptures also say, 'You must not test the Lord your God.'"

KEY THOUGHT

The devil is baiting Jesus to try to get him to show that God is really with him. It is as if the devil is telling Jesus, "Before it comes to the crucial showdown between you and me at Calvary, show that God is behind you. It will give you more courage and strength if it is really true and if you can really trust him!" Jesus saw through the whole charade. He would not test God, because to put God to the test is to distrust God's faithfulness. Yes, we will all pass through the fires of trial and temptation. Yes, we want to be confident in God's presence. But, we never want to doubt his faithfulness to his keep his promises to us. We don't need to test his faithfulness; it's been proven over the course of centuries. We are the ones who will be tested! Our job is to be faithful to our Father as our Father is faithful to us.

TODAY'S PRAYER

O God, the Heavenly Father who has proven himself faithful for generations, forgive me for those times I have been presumptuous, pompous, or cynical. I confess my all-too-human desire for assurance and security. Give me courage to be faithful in the face of ridicule and scorn from others, and in the face of doubt within myself. I do believe that you have been, are, and will be faithful. May I be found faithful, too. In Jesus' name I ask this. Amen.

CONTEXT: LUKE 4:1-13
Related Passages: 2 Timothy 2:8-13; James 1:12-15; Psalm 107:1-2

Day 54

UNTIL ANOTHER TIME

Luke 4:13

The devil finished tempting Jesus in every way and went away to wait until a better time.

KEY THOUGHT

There is a haunting and ominous tone to Luke's summary of the devil's departure. While Jesus may have won this encounter, Luke wants us to know that the evil one will be lurking nearby for another opportune moment. Defeated this time, the awful deceiver will choose his time and his methods carefully. We know that ultimately the greatest test will occur in the Garden of Gethsemane and on a hill we call Calvary. Of course, there will be skirmishes in between. Jesus will win them all. No demon, no evil, no power can stand against him. However, the evil schemer will not sit idly by while Jesus' ministry soars. He will use Jesus' own follower, Judas, for his plan of betrayal, mockery, and death. He will crush Jesus' strongest and most vocal supporter, Peter. He will bewilder all of Jesus followers and they will forsake their Rabbi and abandon him in his moment of need. Yes, the devil is a dirty street fighter who plays by his own rules, with only one goal—to destroy all that is good and godly. Never doubt the reality, the deviousness, or the ferocity of our opportunistic adversary. But also realize that the Jesus you worship has triumphed over the devil and sent us his Spirit to help us win our victories, too.

TODAY'S PRAYER

Glorious God, the great Almighty, give me confidence and courage because of Jesus' victory over the devil in every battle, big and small. Please help me share in the ultimate victory when the Lord Jesus returns in his glory. In Jesus' name I pray. Amen.

CONTEXT: LUKE 4:1-13
Related Passages: 2 Corinthians 4:3-4; 2 Corinthians 10:3-5; James 4:4-8

Day 55

FILLED WITH THE HOLY SPIRIT'S FIRE!

Luke 4:14-15

Jesus went back to Galilee with the power of the Spirit. Stories about him spread all over the area around Galilee. He began to teach in the synagogues, and everyone praised him.

KEY THOUGHT

Jesus' example reminds us that when we face down the devil's attacks, schemes, and temptations (see the verses preceding this passage), we can emerge from our battles stronger, with the Spirit's power more at work within us. While we don't like periods of trial, God can use them for our benefit, his glory, and the devil's defeat. So don't give up in difficult times. Stand firm and hold onto faith. Know that God will provide you a way of escape and the power of his Spirit to overcome the challenges you face!

TODAY'S PRAYER

Give me the faith and courage, O Lord, to trust that your Spirit will help me through my times of temptation, testing, and trial. Keep me from giving up. Instead, help me emerge from these tough times with deeper faith and with the Spirit's taking a more influential role in my life. In Jesus' name I pray. Amen.

CONTEXT: LUKE 4:14-30
Related Passages: Hebrews 10:35-39; Ephesians 3:14-21; Ephesians 5:15-21

Day 56

WHEN IT WAS FULFILLED!

Luke 4:16-21

Jesus traveled to Nazareth, the town where he grew up. On the Sabbath day he went to the synagogue as he always did. He stood up to read. The book of Isaiah the prophet was given to him. He opened the book and found the place where this is written: "The Spirit of the Lord is on me. He has chosen me to tell good news to the poor. He sent me to tell prisoners that they are free and to tell the blind that they can see again. He sent me to free those who have been treated badly and to announce that the time has come for the Lord to show his kindness."

Jesus closed the book, gave it back to the helper, and sat down. As everyone in the synagogue watched him closely, he began to speak to them. He said, "While you heard me reading these words just now, they were coming true!"

KEY THOUGHT

I can't think of a more powerful moment for a synagogue worshiper. The scroll is unrolled. The Scripture is read. Then, with breathless wonder, the words are heard: "Today this Scripture is fulfilled!" Luke wants us to know that Jesus' ministry is Spirit anointed, Spirit led, Spirit empowered, and Spirit fulfilled. Jesus connects his actions to God and to the Old Testament promises inspired by the Holy Spirit. Deliverance will come at the hands of this Jesus who ministers to outcasts because of the work of the Spirit. His ministry is no accident; it was Spirit prophesied. So what's there to learn for us in this? Ministry must be Spirit led and must be consistent with the promises of Scripture and the example of the Savior. Clearly in this case, that means it is about deliverance, grace, and reaching outcasts. How does our ministry compare?

TODAY'S PRAYER

Father, I know that you have placed your Holy Spirit within me and within your church. Yet, Father, we so often block the Spirit's leadership and ignore the Spirit's opportunities. Not only forgive us, dear Father, but please ignite in us a holy passion to be your servants to the lost, defeated, broken, and forgotten as your Spirit equips, empowers, and guides us. Please fulfill this old Scripture again, today, in us. In Jesus' name I humbly ask this. Amen.

CONTEXT: LUKE 4:14-30
Related Passages: 1 Corinthians 3:16-17; 1 Corinthians 12:4-7; John 20:19-23

Day 57

HOME COURT DISADVANTAGE

Luke 4:22-24

Everyone there said good things about Jesus. They were amazed to hear him speak such wonderful words. They said, "How is this possible? Isn't he Joseph's son?"

Jesus said to them, "I know you will tell me the old saying: 'Doctor, heal yourself.' You want to say, 'We heard about the things you did in Capernaum. Do those same things here in your own hometown!'" Then he said, "The truth is, a prophet is not accepted in his own hometown."

KEY THOUGHT

In sports, teams play all season to have the home-court advantage in the playoffs. Yet the ancient proverb is true in matters religious: "The truth is, a prophet is not accepted in his own hometown." While we can think of lots of reasons why this might be true, the bottom line is that we expect our experts to be from out of town, with credentials that include places we haven't been, and with degrees we haven't earned. To have someone from among us be used by God in special ways can provoke jealousy and stir cynicism. That's why it was so important that Jesus was one of us—specifically showing us that the way we are to honor God is possible. That there were no great expectations of Jesus by those among whom he was raised should not surprise us. That he grew up like all of us did (with family and friends in a real-life historical setting) should motivate us to reach for more than our shallow dreams often allow. While we may be saddened by Jesus' rejection by his hometown folks, let's not let the same thing happen with those whom God would use mightily among us. Let's encourage them to Kingdom greatness and believe that God can make any among us—young or old, big or small, including you and me—into something great for his use.

TODAY'S PRAYER

Father, use me to encourage your people to find their gifts to serve you. Use my faith and conviction to help them dream bigger dreams for your Kingdom. Raise up from our congregation great leaders for the future of your Kingdom and for the cause of Christ. In Jesus' name I pray. Amen.

CONTEXT: LUKE 4:14-30
Related Passages: Ephesians 4:4-7, 11-16; 1 Timothy 4:11-16; John 1:10-12

Day 58

GOD CARES FOR MORE THAN JUST US!

Luke 4:25-27

During the time of Elijah it did not rain in Israel for three and a half years. There was no food anywhere in the whole country. There were many widows in Israel during that time. But the fact is, Elijah was sent to none of those widows in Israel. He was sent only to a widow in Zarephath, a town in Sidon.

"And there were many people with leprosy living in Israel during the time of the prophet Elisha. But none of them were healed; the only one was Naaman. And he was from the country of Syria, not Israel."

KEY THOUGHT

God didn't love Israel just to love Israel. God chose Abraham and his descendants through Isaac to bring his gracious blessings to all people. God loves all people—people of all races, all cultures, and all languages. So not only does he want us to minister to the broken and the outcast, but he also wants us to minister to the broken and outcast of those who consider us their "enemies" and to those who do not share our faith. Jesus reminds us of this through two startling examples—the widow of Zarephath and Naaman. Both were non-Israelites. One was hopeless and forgotten. The other was the leader of an enemy—a stark reminder that loving our enemies and caring for those we may not perceive as redeemable is not a theory, but a passion for the God of all redemption.

TODAY'S PRAYER

Open my eyes, Lord, and open the eyes of your people. While our world struggles with conflict and hatred, please use us to be your ambassadors of reconciliation and redemption. Give us courage to share your grace in places and with people who need it regardless of their race, culture, or language. Use us to touch the nations with your grace. In Jesus' name I pray that use us to your glory. Amen.

CONTEXT: LUKE 4:14-30
Related Passages: Luke 24:44-49; Acts 1:3-8; Acts 28:28

Day 59

A STRONG RESPONSE TO THE SERMON

Luke 4:28-30

When the people in the synagogue heard this, they were very angry. They got up and forced Jesus to go out of town. Their town was built on a hill. They took Jesus to the edge of the hill to throw him off. But he walked through the middle of the crowd and went away.

KEY THOUGHT

In many church cultures, after a message is given, an invitation is offered for people to respond. Well, Jesus got a response to his message in the synagogue, that's for sure. They were furious. This reminds us that not all truth will be well received. Sometimes the truth of God provokes deep anger, especially among those whose faith is couched in prejudice and a false sense of ethnic or religious superiority. When those claiming to be God's people display prejudice, the presence of Jesus leaves them and moves to people who will share his grace. Let's eradicate all racial and cultural hatred and any sense of ethnic or religious superiority from our midst. It is by grace that we are saved. That grace should move us to share God's love with others with gentleness and respect, regardless of how alike or different from us they may appear to be.

TODAY'S PRAYER

Open our eyes, dear God, so that we may see that the fields are white to harvest, even in this time of rancor and hatred in our world. Use me, use us your people, to be your tools of grace to break down barriers that divide races, cultures, peoples, and nations so that when we worship you together in heaven, it will not be the first time we have worshiped in joyous diversity and multi-cultural praise. In Jesus' name I pray. Amen.

CONTEXT: LUKE 4:14-30
Related Passages: Revelation 7:9-12; Acts 15:6-9; Galatians 3:26-29

Day 60

WITH AUTHORITY!

Luke 4:31-32

Jesus went to Capernaum, a city in Galilee. On the Sabbath day he taught the people. They were amazed at his teaching because he spoke with authority.

KEY THOUGHT

Some people have positional authority—they've been appointed to a position. Some use that position wisely, while some misuse it to boss others around. Some folks have personal authority because of who they are and how they conduct themselves. Some folks speak with an authenticity and clarity that give them authority. Jesus had all three—God sent him, he lived with integrity, and he taught God's truth. That's why he stood out. That's also why his opponents viewed him as dangerous. The point for us, however, is that we need to listen to what Jesus says! Jesus comes and gives us God's truth for our lives. Will we listen and follow him?

TODAY'S PRAYER

Holy and righteous God, thank you for speaking to me so clearly through Jesus. His life and his words are powerful. Open my mind and heart as I seek to understand and apply his words and his example to my life. In Jesus' name I pray. Amen.

CONTEXT: LUKE 4:31-44
Related Passages: Luke 6:40; Matthew 28:18-20; Hebrews 1:1-3

Day 61

AUTHORITY OVER DEMONS

Luke 4:33-37

In the synagogue there was a man who had an evil spirit from the devil inside him. The man shouted loudly, "Jesus of Nazareth! What do you want with us? Did you come here to destroy us? I know who you are—God's Holy One!" But Jesus warned the evil spirit to stop. He said, "Be quiet! Come out of the man!" The evil spirit threw the man down on the ground in front of everyone. Then the evil spirit left the man and did not hurt him.

The people were amazed. They said to each other, "What does this mean? With authority and power he commands evil spirits and they come out." And so the news about Jesus spread to every place in the whole area.

KEY THOUGHT

Jesus' authority extended over Satan and the demonic world. His command cast them out. So many of us today struggle with Satan because we've given him a foothold in our lives through deception, bitterness, lust, or some other "secret" sin. Jesus still has power over Satan and the demonic world. As we confront those strongholds we've let Satan build in our lives because of our sinfulness, we must bring Jesus' authority to bear. That means, first, confessing our sin openly to God in Jesus' name and, second, asking for our sin to be forgiven. Third, we need not to keep that sin secret, but confess our struggle to a strong believer—this often needs to be someone of our same gender. Fourth, we need to ask that person to hold us accountable and encourage us. Fifth, we need to pray in the name of Jesus for deliverance from that sin and for the power to resist its temptation, asking for the power of the Holy Spirit to transform us. Finally, we need to keep our hearts exposed to what is pure rather than flirting with the evil that has captured us. Does this work? Well, it's not a recipe or a simple formula. But for most believers over the centuries, this is the path to victory—a path can be ours as well!

TODAY'S PRAYER

Father, remove the devil's power of deception in my life and help me confront the areas of my weakness, stubbornness, rebellion, and sin so that I can be completely yielded to your direction. In Jesus' name I ask you for this transformation. Amen.

CONTEXT: LUKE 4:31-44
Related Passages: Acts 26:9-18; Colossians 1:9-14; Colossians 2:12-15, 20

Day 62

HEALING WITH A WORD

Luke 4:38-39

Jesus left the synagogue and went to Simon's house. Simon's mother-in-law was very sick. She had a high fever. They asked Jesus to do something to help her. He stood very close to her and ordered the sickness to go away. The sickness left her, and she got up and began serving them.

KEY THOUGHT

Jesus shows the authority of his words over illness. Here, Jesus rebukes the fever and it leaves. His words are powerful and healing. This woman was not only instantly made well, but she was restored to health, vitality, and usefulness. Jesus' words still have power to do that for us today if we will obey them. When we believe and obey his message, Jesus' words restore our spiritual health, vitality, and usefulness. His words have the power of an expert surgeon to cut through the diseased tissue, to excise what is decaying and false, and to restore spiritual life. So as we journey through Luke, let's do more than read the words of Jesus: let's ask God to use them to make us whole.

TODAY'S PRAYER

God Almighty, my heavenly Father, as I spend this year listening to the words of your Son and observing his life, please use Jesus' words to convict me, instruct me, rehabilitate me, liberate me, restore me, and make of me what you would have me be. In Jesus' name I ask for this grace. Amen.

CONTEXT: LUKE 4:31-44
Related Passages: Hebrews 4:12-13; John 6:61-69; Luke 6:46-49

Day 63

THE POWER TO MAKE BETTER!

Luke 4:40-41
When the sun went down, the people brought their sick friends to Jesus. They had many different kinds of sicknesses. Jesus laid his hands on each sick person and healed them all. Demons came out of many people. The demons shouted, "You are the Son of God." But Jesus gave a strong command for the demons not to speak, because they knew he was the Christ.

KEY THOUGHT

If you've ever had a loved one who hurt, you know what a precious gift it is to be able to make things better and what a maddening frustration it is when you can't help at all. Jesus could make things better—not just a few things, but all things. Disease, demons, and even death were impotent to stop his power of making things better. His words, the touch of his hand, and power of his presence brought healing, deliverance, and comfort. Even now, he longs for us to invite him into our lives, into our problems, so he can make things better for us. While all our short-term, physical problems won't necessarily go away, they will dim in the light of his presence and his promise to bring us through them and bring us his ultimate blessing.

TODAY'S PRAYER

Dear Jesus, you are welcome in my life. I need your presence as I seek to deal with the hurt, anger, frustration, fears, difficulties, and troubles that I face. I want you to be at work in my life doing your will and leading me in the direction you want me to go. Amen.

CONTEXT: LUKE 4:31-44
Related Passages: Romans 8:18; Romans 8:28-30; Romans 8:31-39

Day 64

STICKING WITH THE MISSION

Luke 4:42-44

The next day Jesus went to a place to be alone. The people looked for him. When they found him, they tried to stop him from leaving. But he said to them, "I must tell the Good News about God's kingdom to other towns too. This is why I was sent." Then Jesus told the Good News in the synagogues in Judea.

KEY THOUGHT

The wilderness was the quiet place Jesus went to be alone with God; it was a place of renewal and relationship for Jesus. It was a place of renewal because this was where he reconnected with his Father and his Father's will. It was a place of relationship because Jesus would speak directly and privately with his Father. After being wildly successful blessing people and making things better, Jesus is now fully committed to going to other villages and sharing the gospel because that was his mission. If Jesus took time to be alone with God in a special place, then we must follow his example and do the same. If we don't, we will continue to be distracted by urgent things and lose our focus on the things most essential to our mission.

TODAY'S PRAYER

Father, forgive me for trying to do too much of my ministry on my own. I recognize that my wisdom is shallow and lacking, especially when there are so many urgent demands. Please show me your will and help me to stay focused on your mission for my life. In Jesus' name I pray. Amen.

CONTEXT: LUKE 4:31-44
Related Passages: Luke 5:16; Luke 11:1-4; James 1:5-8

Day 65

HUNGER FOR THE WORD OF GOD

Luke 5:1

As Jesus stood beside Lake Galilee, a crowd of people pushed to get closer to him and to hear the teachings of God. Jesus saw two boats at the shore of the lake.

KEY THOUGHT

Even though we are living in a skeptical age with a cultural environment in which people reject standards of any kind, many people still hunger for an authentic message from God. Jesus spoke that authentic message and people came to hear it. The authority of his words was unparalleled. The power in his words caught their attention and captured their hearts. Many people still yearn for that message and look for people who can speak it with conviction, character, and compassion. Let's be people who know the message of Jesus, who live the lifestyle of that message with passion, and who share that message with others. They will still draw near to listen if what we speak is the Word of God.

TODAY'S PRAYER

Righteous Father, the one true and holy God, please teach me your will as I seek for your guidance in Scripture and from the leading of your Spirit. Then, dear Father, use me to share that message to bless others and lead them to you! In Jesus' name I pray. Amen.

CONTEXT: LUKE 5:1-11
Related Passages: Acts 1:8; Acts 28:28-31; Amos 8:11

Day 66

IF YOU SAY SO!

Luke 5:2-7

Jesus saw two boats at the shore of the lake. The fishermen were washing their nets. Jesus got into the boat that belonged to Simon. He asked Simon to push off a little from the shore. Then he sat down in the boat and taught the people on the shore.

When Jesus finished speaking, he said to Simon, "Take the boat into the deep water. If all of you will put your nets into the water, you will catch some fish."

Simon answered, "Master, we worked hard all night trying to catch fish and caught nothing. But you say I should put the nets into the water, so I will." The fishermen put their nets into the water. Their nets were filled with so many fish that they began to break. They called to their friends in the other boat to come and help them. The friends came, and both boats were filled so full of fish that they were almost sinking.

KEY THOUGHT

Simon (Peter) was a fisherman. Being a fisherman was his life. Being a fisherman was his trade. So when Jesus came up and told him to fish in a certain place and at a certain time that Peter "knew" was wrong from all of his experience, he must have had to swallow hard to follow this carpenter's instructions. But he did! He fully obeyed what seemed to be questionable. He basically told Jesus, "If YOU say to do it, then I'll do it!" Let's be honest. There are times when what Jesus tells us to do seems at best counter-intuitive and sometimes a bit dangerous or crazy. Just a cursory reading of the Sermon on the Mount (Matthew 5-7) gives us more than enough to chew on for a lifetime. That's when our love for Jesus and our submission to his lordship really are tested. Are we willing to be like Peter and say, "Master, because you said to do it, I will"?

TODAY'S PRAYER

Compassionate Father, please give me a pliable heart and a willing spirit. I want to obey what your Son has taught and do what his lordship calls me to do. I ask for this help in Jesus' name. Amen.

CONTEXT: LUKE 5:1-11
Related Passages: John 6:60-69; 1 Peter 1:21-23; 1 Peter 1:24-25

Day 67

USEFUL TO THE MASTER!

Luke 5:8-11

The fishermen were all amazed at the many fish they caught. When Simon Peter saw this, he bowed down before Jesus and said, "Go away from me, Lord. I am a sinful man!" James and John, the sons of Zebedee, were amazed too. (James and John worked together with Simon.)

Jesus said to Simon, "Don't be afraid. From now on your work will be to bring in people, not fish!"

The men brought their boats to the shore. They left everything and followed Jesus.

KEY THOUGHT

Nothing prepares the way for the Messiah's work better than humility. We saw that principle clearly demonstrated in the life of John the Baptizer. In this encounter, we see humility demonstrated from an unlikely source, Simon Peter. Peter recognized he was in the presence of greatness when he was in the presence of Jesus. Compared to Jesus, Peter knew he didn't come close to measuring up even on his best day. He was a sinner. He was limited. He experienced failures. He kept having his closed mind blown open by someone far greater. To his credit, Peter was honest with himself when comparing himself to Jesus. Throughout his long ministry, Peter would have to learn the lesson time and time again: he was most valuable to the Master when he served out of a genuine humility.

TODAY'S PRAYER

Father, humble me gently and help me correctly evaluate myself in light of Jesus' glory, grace, and character. I am a sinner. I am thankful, dear Father, that you have saved me by your grace and have equipped me to serve you. Please forgive, repair, and equip me for your service. In Jesus' name I pray. Amen.

CONTEXT: LUKE 5:1-11
Related Passages: 1 Timothy 1:15-17; Romans 5:6-11; 1 Peter 5:5-7

Day 68

TWO PERSPECTIVES OF GRACE

Luke 5:12-13

One time Jesus was in a town where a very sick man lived. This man was covered with leprosy. When the man saw Jesus, he bowed before Jesus and begged him, "Lord, you have the power to heal me if you want."

Jesus said, "I want to heal you. Be healed!" Then he touched the man, and immediately the leprosy disappeared.

KEY THOUGHT

We see two powerful perspectives on grace in this simple, yet astounding, story. First, we see an awesome faith in Jesus. The man believed Jesus could cure the incurable and give him back his life. That awesome faith brought him to Jesus, face down in the dust, to honor Jesus and to ask for help. Second, we see the tenderness of Jesus. While the man is cured at the spoken word of Jesus (remember, one of the key themes that runs through several of the recent stories about Jesus is the power and authority of his words), here the focus is on the touch of Jesus. This touch is not about healing; healing occurs through Jesus' spoken word. In this instance, grace comes through the touch of Jesus! Jesus touches a man who was ritually unclean and lets that man know that he is loved even in his diseased and unclean condition. The message for us is clear: we come to Jesus claiming nothing and knowing he is everything. As we offer ourselves to him, we find that he not only gives us what we want, but he also blesses us with what we most need—the personal love and acceptance from our Creator and Lord!

TODAY'S PRAYER

O wonderfully gracious God Almighty, how can I fully fathom your love? You are majestic and limitless and I am finite and fallen. Thank you for reaching out to me with your hand of grace in Jesus and choosing to include me in your grace. In Jesus' name I praise you and thank you. Amen.

CONTEXT: LUKE 5:12-16
Related Passages: 1 John 4:9-10; Romans 5:6-8; Colossians 1:18-22

Day 69

WHO SETS THE AGENDA?

Luke 5:14-16

Then Jesus said, "Don't tell anyone about what happened. But go and let the priest look at you. And offer a gift to God for your healing as Moses commanded. This will show people that you are healed."

But the news about Jesus spread more and more. Many people came to hear him and to be healed of their sicknesses. Jesus often went away to other places to be alone so that he could pray.

KEY THOUGHT

Jesus did not want to become a miracle sideshow. His purpose in healing the leper was to love and bless the leper and re-integrate him back into community. Jesus wasn't trying to attract more folks looking to see something amazing. So as the crowds grew because they heard of his great and powerful deeds, Jesus withdrew. His withdrawal wasn't to hide from people. It was a time to be alone with God and renew his sense of mission and purpose. Jesus knew it was crucial not to let the crowd determine the direction of his ministry. He was on earth to do God's work. That work was centered in making hope, freedom, healing, life, and salvation possible for all of us. That was going to be done in a lasting way only if his Father set the agenda. Jesus withdrew to be alone with God and to have God, not the crowds and not his own ego, remain in control of his ministry! This is a powerful example for all of us—especially those who lead God's people.

TODAY'S PRAYER

Forgive me, dear Father, for I have often sought my own way based upon my "wisdom" and my own desires before I have sought your guidance. I am not sure if that is the sin of arrogance or if it is just willful stupidity, but I want to confess to you that I know I make a mess of things when I go my own way. Draw my heart to you, O God, and not only cleanse me, but also give me a holy hunger for your holy presence. In Jesus' name I ask this. Amen.

CONTEXT: LUKE 5:12-16
Related Passages: John 2:23-25; Proverbs 14:12; John 6:14-15

Day 70

THE HELP OF FRIENDS

Luke 5:17-20

One day Jesus was teaching the people. The Pharisees and teachers of the law were sitting there too. They had come from every town in Galilee and Judea and from Jerusalem. The Lord was giving Jesus the power to heal people. There was a man who was paralyzed, and some other men were carrying him on a mat. They tried to bring him and put him down before Jesus. But there were so many people that they could not find a way to Jesus. So they went up on the roof and lowered the crippled man down through a hole in the ceiling. They lowered the mat into the room so that the crippled man was lying before Jesus. Jesus saw how much faith they had and said to the sick man, "Friend, your sins are forgiven."

KEY THOUGHT

Sometimes Jesus sees the faith of people who need healing and blesses them based upon their faith. Sometimes faith is not mentioned and doesn't appear to be an issue in his healing ministry. This time, however, Jesus sees the faith of the four friends lowering their paralyzed friend. Their love, concern, effort, and faith all cry out to Jesus for help, so Jesus helps the man. This is a "get your hands dirty digging through the roof" kind of faith. It is a faith that takes great risks because of love. I wonder how many of our friends need us to get our hands dirty taking risks to help them meet Jesus? To whom do we need to be a "willing to get our hands dirty" friend?

TODAY'S PRAYER

Father, I'm thinking about several friends who need to let go of their calloused indifference and to find answers to their questions and concerns so that they can come to you. Please empower me to help them find their way home to you. In Jesus' name I pray. Amen.

CONTEXT: LUKE 5:17-26
Related Passages: Luke 24:45; 1 Peter 3:15-16; John 3:16-17

Day 71

THE GREATER NEED

Luke 5:21-26

The Jewish teachers of the law and the Pharisees thought to themselves, "Who is this man who dares to say such things? What an insult to God! No one but God can forgive sins."

But Jesus knew what they were thinking and said, "Why do you have these questions in your minds? The Son of Man has power on earth to forgive sins. But how can I prove this to you? Maybe you are thinking it was easy for me to say, 'Your sins are forgiven.' There's no proof that it really happened. But what if I say to the man, 'Stand up and walk'? Then you will be able to see that I really have this power." So Jesus said to the paralyzed man, "I tell you, stand up! Take your mat and go home!"

The man immediately stood up in front of everyone. He picked up his mat and walked home, praising God. Everyone was completely amazed and began to praise God. They were filled with great respect for God's power. They said, "Today we saw amazing things!"

KEY THOUGHT

Having just received a call about a friend who is terminally ill, this passage is a powerful reminder. So often my perspective focuses me on the physical needs. That is not bad. It moves me to act with compassion. It brings me to my knees in prayer. However, Jesus reminds me in this passage that forgiveness of sin is the greatest need we all have as humans. Spiritual healing that brings deliverance from sin and its guilt is what we most need and the greatest gift Jesus can give. As we look at the people around us, let's not forget what the greatest need in their lives truly is!

TODAY'S PRAYER

Eternal and gracious God, my Abba Father, forgive me when I get so distracted by lesser things. Stir me to act with compassion and genuine care toward those with physical needs. Help me also to act with compassion and genuine care toward those around me with the greatest need—the need for your grace and forgiveness. Please give me spiritual vision to see what needs to be done in the lives of those around me. In Jesus' name I pray. Amen.

CONTEXT: LUKE 5:17-26
Related Passages: Psalm 32:1-4; 1 Timothy 1:15-17; Romans 4:24-25

Day 72

JESUS' SENSE OF MISSION

Luke 5:27-32

After this Jesus went out and saw a tax collector sitting at his place
for collecting taxes. His name was Levi. Jesus said to him, "Follow
me!" Levi got up, left everything, and followed Jesus.

Then Levi gave a big dinner at his house for Jesus. At the table there were
many tax collectors and some other people too. But the Pharisees and those
who taught the law for the Pharisees began to complain to the followers of
Jesus, "Why do you eat and drink with tax collectors and other sinners?"

Jesus answered them, "It is the sick people who need a doctor, not
those who are healthy. I have not come to ask good people to change.
I have come to ask sinners to change the way they live."

KEY THOUGHT

Jesus came for a number of reasons, but reaching out to sinners was clearly
one of the central ones. Jesus' harshest words are reserved for those who
"think they are good people." Religious people are often critical when their
"itch isn't scratched" by their church or church leaders. However, any church
that seeks to minister as the presence of Christ in the world (i.e., to genuinely
be the Body of Christ) will have to live with the same values Jesus lived. Clearly
one of those values is a passion to reach those outside of grace rather than
catering to those who have already received it. Imagine if all of Jesus' followers
today could capture that passion!

TODAY'S PRAYER

O Lord, I confess that the church today is all too often worried about placating those who
are already saved and are fussy about how they want things in their church. Pour out your
Holy Spirit in a special way among your people, gripping us with a deep concern about
those who do not know Jesus and have no hope in his grace. In Jesus' name I pray. Amen.

CONTEXT: LUKE 5:27-39
Related Passages: Luke 15:25-32; Luke 19:5-10; Romans 15:5-7

Day 73

SOMETHING NEW, SOMETHING FRESH, SOMEONE AMAZING

Luke 5:33-35

They said to Jesus, "John's followers often fast and pray, the same as the followers of the Pharisees. But your followers eat and drink all the time."

Jesus said to them, "At a wedding you can't ask the friends of the bridegroom to be sad and fast while he is still with them. But the time will come when the groom will be taken away from them. Then his friends will fast."

KEY THOUGHT

Jesus is basically telling folks that his presence means that it won't be "business as usual." Jesus' presence changes everything! This reality and the people's decision about that reality become the basis for everything else that follows. Jesus is something new, something fresh, and most importantly, he is someone amazing. God has come to visit his people in Jesus. Things are not the same. A new era has dawned—an era of joy, salvation, and celebration. Yes, when he goes away, there will be moments of sorrow, of repentance, and of prayer that call for fasting. But while he is present, there is no time for business as usual! The same will be true when he comes again! The challenge for us is to maintain the joy of his first coming and anticipation of his second coming as we live in the time in between.

TODAY'S PRAYER

Thank you, dear Heavenly Father, for changing everything by sending Jesus. I know that there are times of sorrow and of hardship in this world. Yet, dear Father, I also know they are not permanent. By sending Jesus, you showed me your heart's desire for me. So, help me live with the joy and the courage that faith inspires until the day my faith becomes sight. In Jesus' name I pray this. Amen.

CONTEXT: LUKE 5:27-39
Related Passages: Luke 2:30-31; Luke 7:11-17; Revelation 21:1-5

Day 74

DON'T TRY TO LIMIT GOD'S NEWNESS

Luke 5:36-38

Jesus told them this story: "No one takes cloth off a new coat to cover a hole in an old coat. That would ruin the new coat, and the cloth from the new coat would not be the same as the old cloth. Also, no one ever pours new wine into old wineskins. The new wine would break them. The wine would spill out, and the wineskins would be ruined. You always put new wine into new wineskins."

KEY THOUGHT

Jesus' point is clear: Don't try to limit God's new life in Christ. Don't try to contain it with your old religious categories. Don't try to dilute it with your old religious practices. Jesus brings something new. Celebrate it. Enjoy its blessings. Be challenged by its demands and rejoice in its promises. But don't try to simply attach it to what you had before. The call of Christ is new, fresh, and all encompassing. Begin each day with the expectation that the Lord will do something you have never seen or expected. You won't feel safe. It won't be predictable. But it will be marvelous!

TODAY'S PRAYER

Forgive me, dear Father, for limiting the awesome power you have brought me in Jesus. Open my mind and my heart and my eyes and my ears so that I can imagine more fantastically, believe more completely, see more fully, and hear more richly all that you have done, are doing, and will do in my life in Jesus. It is in his name I pray. Amen.

CONTEXT: LUKE 5:27-39
Related Passages: 2 Corinthians 5:16-18; Ephesians 3:20-21; Philippians 2:13

Day 75

THE LURE OF THE FAMILIAR

Luke 5:39
[Jesus said] "No one who drinks old wine wants new wine." They say, 'The old wine is just fine.'"

KEY THOUGHT

The Israelites in the wilderness may be the best example of it, but we all have a tendency to do it. We look back on the past, what we once had or did, with nostalgia and imagine it better than it was. The Israelites were slaves, but wanted to go back to Egypt because they imagined it as better than what they were facing in the wilderness. We tend to do the same thing in our walk of faith. The old life and its temptations lure us back. So often we succumb. The old religious way of thinking, one based on works righteousness and earning our own salvation, easily seeps back into our Christian way of thinking, robbing us of vitality. The lure of the familiar is powerful. It is also a deadly thief, robbing our new life in Christ of its grace, joy, and victory. Let's not go back and mix some other form of religion from our past and dilute the radical and liberating call of Jesus!

TODAY'S PRAYER

Dear Father in heaven, please give me the courage and spiritual insight to resist anything that would take me back from the marvelous way of life you have given me in your Son, Jesus, in whose name I pray. Amen.

CONTEXT: LUKE 5:27-39
Related Passages: 2 Peter 2:20-22; Hebrews 3:12-14; Galatians 1:6-9

Day 76

BEATING THEM AT THEIR OWN GAME

Luke 6:1-4

One time on a Sabbath day, Jesus was walking through some grain fields. His followers picked the grain, rubbed it in their hands, and ate it. Some Pharisees said, "Why are you doing that? It is against the Law of Moses to do that on the Sabbath day."

Jesus answered, "You have read about what David did when he and the people with him were hungry. David went into God's house. He took the bread that was offered to God and ate it. And he gave some of the bread to the people with him. This was against the Law of Moses, which says that only the priests can eat that bread."

KEY THOUGHT

Legalism is a curse. It's so much a curse that the book of Galatians was written specifically to combat it. Jesus had to battle those who used their knowledge of the Scriptures to challenge him to justify what his followers did. So Jesus, on several occasions, beat them at their own game. If they are going to make what his followers are doing into a sin by "straining gnats" of the Law and their tradition, then Jesus will answer them doing the same. Jesus had already made his point repeatedly in the preceding story: with Jesus, God is doing something new and there will be no business as usual. "If David could do it," Jesus said to them in his use of argument, "then surely my followers can do it since the 'one greater than David' is here." The point? Don't mess with Jesus using legalism; you'll always lose! But then, why should you try to use legalistic arguments, now that grace has come and Jesus is here?

TODAY'S PRAYER

Father, please help me never abuse your Scriptures to try to justify what I do or don't do to make myself look better than other folks seeking to honor you. Forgive me for the times when I have done this. I am genuinely sorry. In the name of Jesus I ask. Amen.

CONTEXT: LUKE 6:1-11
Related Passages: Luke 11:46-52; Luke 16:15; Luke 10:25-29

Day 77

GREATER

Luke 6:5
Then Jesus said to the Pharisees, "The Son of Man is Lord over the Sabbath day."

KEY THOUGHT

There were three great attributes of the Jewish faith in Jesus' day: the Temple in Jerusalem, circumcision of all Jewish males, and keeping the Sabbath. There is no way to emphasize how radical Jesus' statement would have sounded in the ears of those who heard it and hated him. He was declaring himself more important than the Sabbath. If they had missed any of Jesus' other statements, they surely couldn't miss this one. He is confronting them with a choice—believe me and follow me totally, or reject me and go back to your old dying religion. That message is equally as powerful for us today. So much of what passes as Christianity is just modern culture with a religious good-luck charm attached. Christianity, by its very definition, is counter-culture living that reflects the character of Jesus. Jesus calls us beyond mere church going and church stuff to a lifestyle that shows he is our Lord.

TODAY'S PRAYER

*Righteous Father, make me passionately Christian—a true follower
of Jesus—your child whose life reflects the character, compassion,
and mission of your Son, in whose name I pray. Amen.*

CONTEXT: LUKE 6:1-11
Related Passages: Luke 11:29-32; Hebrews 8:7-13; John 14:6

Day 78

WHAT A WASTE!

Luke 6:6-7

On another Sabbath day Jesus went into the synagogue and taught the people. A man with a crippled right hand was there. The teachers of the law and the Pharisees were watching Jesus closely. They were waiting to see if he would heal on the Sabbath day. They wanted to see him do something wrong so that they could accuse him.

KEY THOUGHT

What a sad story and what a waste of a wonderful opportunity for genuine worship. Here are religious folks that have presumably gone to honor God but with totally false agendas: they've gone to be critical of someone else. What a shame! What a sham! What a waste of a great worship opportunity. Surely nobody would do that today, would they? Hmm!

TODAY'S PRAYER

Father, forgive me for being critical of your children and wasting my worship time with your people by thinking harshly of others for whom Christ has died. Give me a deeper love for my brothers and sisters in Christ and a holy passion for genuine worship. In Jesus' name I pray. Amen.

CONTEXT: LUKE 6:1-11
Related Passages: Luke 6:27-42; James 4:11-12; Romans 14:1

Day 79

SAVED FROM DESTRUCTION

Luke 6:8-9

But Jesus knew what they were thinking. He said to the man with the crippled hand, "Get up and stand here where everyone can see." The man got up and stood there. Then Jesus said to them, "I ask you, which is the right thing to do on the Sabbath day: to do good or to do evil? Is it right to save a life or to destroy one?"

KEY THOUGHT

The way the religious folks in Jesus' day had figured it out in their tradition, if an infirmity wasn't life threatening and it was the Sabbath, then healing could wait until tomorrow. Jesus saw it differently. To not do what you can do to bless someone in need is "to do evil" and to choose to "destroy" a life. We are not sure if we will get tomorrow, so we'd better do that thing needed to bless others while we have the opportunity. It may not come again. Jesus' example reminds us that to do good for someone trumps legalistic, religious rules, permissions, and procedures every time!

TODAY'S PRAYER

Give me eyes to see the opportunities to bless others today and each day, O Lord, and help that spiritual vision to live in me until you bring me home. In Jesus' name I pray. Amen.

CONTEXT: LUKE 6:1-11
Related Passages: James 4:13-17; Galatians 6:7-10; Luke 6:31

Day 80

NOT SWAYED BY THE CRITICS

Luke 6:10

*Jesus looked around at all of them, then said to the man, "Hold out
your hand." The man held out his hand, and it was healed.*

KEY THOUGHT

Jesus refused to let his critics determine his course of action. His ministry
would be determined by the will of God and the mission God had given him.
Part of that mission was to bless those who needed God's blessing and to
liberate those who needed God's freedom. Nothing and no one would stop
him from this opportunity to do what is good, even if doing it cost him dearly.
How passionate are we to bless those around us? How about those who are not
popular? How about those who go unnoticed? How about those who might
cause us to fall out of favor with the "in group" or the "in crowd"? Let's be like
Jesus and "do good" to everyone.

TODAY'S PRAYER

*Father, give me more courage so that I can stand up for folks who are forgotten or rejected.
Use me to minister to those whom others neglect. Help me not be so self-conscious of
how others view my involvement with people who may not be popular or powerful. Make
me more like Jesus in the way I interact with others. In Jesus' name I pray. Amen.*

CONTEXT: LUKE 6:1-11
Related Passages: Luke 4:18-21; James 1:27; Romans 5:6-8

Day 81

CONDEMNED FOR RIGHTEOUSNESS

Luke 6:11

The Pharisees and the teachers of the law got so mad they couldn't think straight. They talked to each other about what they could do to Jesus.

KEY THOUGHT

One of the things we must understand from the life of Jesus is this: doing the right things doesn't mean we will be treated in the right way. There are people who get angry and hostile when people do what is righteous. John the Baptizer paid with his life because of this. Jesus will, too. Some of us may have to do the same. Does that mean God has abandoned us or not heard our prayers? Absolutely not! Remember the passage that says God works all things together for our good (Rom. 8:28)? Did you ever notice how it ends? We're going to be conformed to Christ (Rom. 8:29)! If our hero was crucified for doing the right things, don't you think some of us will be mistreated as well? But in the end, in the longest stretch of life, we'll experience the joy of a proud and loving Father who will say, "Well done! You lived just like my Son!"

TODAY'S PRAYER

Father, give courage to all of your servants worldwide who are facing hardship, difficulty, and possibly even death for their faith and their deeds of kindness. In Jesus' name I pray. Amen.

CONTEXT: LUKE 6:1-11
Related Passages: Romans 8:28-30; 2 Timothy 3:10-14; Romans 8:17-18

Day 82

THE IMPORTANCE OF PRAYER

Luke 6:12-13

A few days later, Jesus went out to a mountain to pray. He stayed there all night praying to God. The next morning he called his followers. He chose twelve of them and called them apostles. These are the ones he chose . . .

KEY THOUGHT

Few events were more important in Jesus' ministry than his selection of apostles. How would Jesus select twelve from the mob that followed him? These men would be asked to change the world. Could he actually find twelve who could do that? Jesus knew what was in the hearts of people. Would anyone be able to stand up to the challenges that he would have to face as one of Jesus' chosen twelve? Jesus withdrew to the mountains to be alone with God and pray as he faced this momentous decision. He didn't choose twelve and then ask God to bless his choice. No, he spent the night in prayer before he chose them. When faced with decisions, whether they appear important or not, let's follow the example of our Lord!

TODAY'S PRAYER

Holy and loving Father, stir my heart with a deeper yearning for prayer. I need your guidance every day, so please bless me with the discipline of daily, fervent prayer. Particularly in those times when I face hard decisions, let your Holy Spirit stir my spirit with a longing to come into your presence and find my guidance and peace in you. In Jesus' name, and because of Jesus' example, I pray. Amen.

CONTEXT: LUKE 6:12-19
Related Passages: Luke 5:16; Mark 1:35-39; James 1:5-8

Day 83

REAL PEOPLE

Luke 6:14-16

Simon (Jesus named him Peter), Andrew, brother of Peter, James, John, Philip, Bartholomew, Matthew, Thomas, James, the son of Alphaeus, Simon, called the Zealot, Judas, the son of James, Judas Iscariot (the one who turned against Jesus).

KEY THOUGHT

We easily forget that our Bible heroes were real people. They had names, but like many of us, their friends gave them nicknames. They had personal histories; like many of us, their names are associated with those histories. They came from families; some of them were known by their relationship with a parent or sibling. Unfortunately, one of them lived in such a way to forever stain his name. Who we are is based upon our idiosyncrasies, our heritage, and choices. The wonderful thing about Jesus, however, is that who we become does not have to be forever tied to our past. Jesus can take the good in our past and make us far better (2 Cor. 5:17). Jesus can take the bad in our past and make us new and use those failures to be the beginning point of ministry. So before we place the apostles on a pedestal, let's remember that they were ordinary guys whose lives were changed by Jesus. If he can do that with them, he can surely do that with us!

TODAY'S PRAYER

Heavenly Father, the God who created me in my mother's womb, please continue your work of creation in me as I yield my heart to the leading of your Spirit. Don't leave me where I am, but make me into a vessel fit for service in your Kingdom. In the name of Jesus, your royal Son and my King, I pray. Amen.

CONTEXT: LUKE 6:12-19
Related Passages: 2 Corinthians 5:16-21; Philippians 1:3-6; Philippians 3:7-9

Day 84

THE OVERWHELMING OPPORTUNITY

Luke 6:17

Jesus and the apostles came down from the mountain. Jesus stood on a flat place. A large crowd of his followers was there. Also, there were many people from all around Judea, Jerusalem, and the seacoast cities of Tyre and Sidon.

KEY THOUGHT

The twelve followers Jesus chose to be his apostles didn't have to wait long to be overwhelmed with opportunity. After being called by the Master, they were immediately surrounded by the masses yearning to find the grace that God offered through Jesus. Who is sufficient for such a challenge? None of them! None of us! Yet the issue isn't our sufficiency, but the one on whom we rely. Jesus equips and prepares us for service in his Kingdom. He is the one who makes us perfect in our weakness to be a blessing to those searching for grace. Let's not be discouraged by our insufficiencies, but draw near to the Lord and depend upon his grace to be sufficient for us and through us.

TODAY'S PRAYER

Father, I confess that I have sometimes limited your work in my life by trying to do that work by my own power. I truly believe, dear Lord, that you long to do greater things in me than I can imagine. However, I know that my limited faith often keeps me from being useful to you. This is not because you cannot be sufficient in my weakness, but because I do not look to you to make my weakness a perfect place for your strength to be displayed. Please change my heart, so that I can be fully useful to you. In Jesus' name I pray. Amen.

CONTEXT: LUKE 6:12-19
Related Passages: 1 Corinthians 1:23-31; Hebrews 11:32-34; 2 Corinthians 12:10

Day 85

THE SOURCE OF HEALING AND CURE

Luke 6:18-19

They all came to hear Jesus teach and to be healed of their sicknesses. He healed the people who were troubled by evil spirits. Everyone was trying to touch him, because power was coming out from him. Jesus healed them all.

KEY THOUGHT

So often in ministry we get to thinking that we have the power to make people better. Not only is this arrogant, but it is dangerously wrong. The best we can hope to be is a conduit of Jesus' grace. Jesus is the one who brings healing, not us. So as we seek to bless others, let's remember where we are trying to point them: not to something in us or about us, but to Jesus.

TODAY'S PRAYER

Almighty God, use me to help others find their way to Jesus. Please don't let my ego or my weaknesses interfere with others finding Jesus as their source of healing and cure. In Jesus' name I pray. Amen.

CONTEXT: LUKE 6:17-26
Related Passages: 2 Corinthians 4:5-7; Ephesians 4:11-13; 1 Timothy 1:15-17

Day 86

THE BLESSINGS OF DISCIPLESHIP

Luke 6:20

Jesus looked at his followers and said, "Great blessings belong
to you who are poor. God's kingdom belongs to you."

KEY THOUGHT

Even though the crowds had mobbed Jesus for healing, Jesus uses this
moment to teach his followers. The words given here are not general promises
to all people, but blessings given to those who surrendered to the call of
Jesus and followed him with all their hearts. The Kingdom, Jesus reminds
his followers, is for those who are poor—for Luke, "the poor" are folks who
depend upon God and who know that they do not have the power or wealth
to cause change or to provide for life on their own. Those who are poor in this
way trust in the power of the Lord and seek his power in their lives. Without
the Lord, they know they have no hope and no power in this world. In such a
heart, the Kingdom comes with power and hope.

TODAY'S PRAYER

Father of all wealth and power, teach me that I am poor. I know that my best is nothing.
I know that my greatest claim to fame is valueless. Without you, without your Kingdom,
my dreams are all earthbound and my strength is a shadow. In Jesus' name I confess
my weakness and pray to be strengthened by your grace through the Holy Spirit. Amen.

CONTEXT: LUKE 6:17-26
Related Passages: 2 Corinthians 8:1-5; 1 Timothy 6:6-10; James 2:5

Day 87

FOOD FOR THE BODY AND THE SOUL

Luke 6:21a

[Jesus said] "Great blessings belong to you who are hungry now. You will be filled."

KEY THOUGHT

We all have hunger. Yes, we do have the daily physical hunger, but that physical hunger should point us to a deeper hunger: we are hungry for God. Sometimes we try to find comfort in physical food to compensate for the hunger we feel in our souls. But, there is a place in each of us that longs for God, that hungers for his presence, and that yearns for his fullness. If we will acknowledge our hunger for God, then we can be satisfied—he will come to us and make his home in us (John 14:18-23).

TODAY'S PRAYER

O Father, give me this day the daily bread I need for my body. In addition, give me the living bread of your presence in Jesus that feeds my soul and sustains my life. Help me recognize, dear Father, that I am hungry for you. Please, come fill my emptiness, heal my brokenness, and feed my soul. In Jesus' name I pray. Amen.

CONTEXT: LUKE 6:17-26
Related Passages: Matthew 6:11; Acts 17:22-28; John 6:32-35

Day 88

A TIME OF WEEPING

Luke 6:21b
[Jesus said] "Great blessings belong to you who are crying
now. You will be happy and laughing."

KEY THOUGHT

Sorrow is inescapable. Sooner or later, sorrow will touch each heart. Sorrow at the loss of a loved one, sorrow over the world's evil, sorrow at the gross inhumanity of people, sorrow at the world's rejection of God's grace, or sorrow because of persecution for righteousness' sake will not be forgotten. God will not allow a single teardrop to be forgotten. He will wipe away every tear and have our sorrow swallowed up in the joy of his presence and in our victory over sin and death at Jesus' coming. God's blessing awaits all who bear the pain of righteous sorrow.

TODAY'S PRAYER

Holy God, sorrow touches many a heart today. Please be near and make your presence known in the life of each of your children who sorrows. I know that sorrow is part of our earthly travels, but please encourage us, your children, with the presence of your Spirit and the promises of the great joy that awaits us. In Jesus' name I pray. Amen.

CONTEXT: LUKE 6:17-26
Related Passages: Revelation 7:13-17; Matthew 5:4; Ecclesiastes 3:1, 4

Day 89

BLESSINGS FOR THOSE ABUSED FOR JESUS

Luke 6:22-23

[Jesus said] "People will hate you because you belong to the Son of Man. They will make you leave their group. They will insult you. They will think it is wrong even to say your name. When these things happen, know that great blessings belong to you. You can be happy then and jump for joy, because you have a great reward in heaven. The ancestors of those people did the same things to the prophets."

KEY THOUGHT

The New Testament writers operated under the assumption that Christianity would always be a rejected counter-culture. The values of the Kingdom are not the values of the majority of people. The demands of the King are thought to be silly, harsh, or judgmental by those outside the Kingdom of God. Because many of us live in a watered down, pseudo-Christian culture, we are sometimes surprised when Christians are ridiculed, ostracized, and persecuted. Yet a night or two of television, a day or two watching hearings on possible judge appointees, and even a casual conversation overheard at the office water cooler reveals that Christians who seek to truly follow Jesus are the objects of disdain. Let's make sure that if we suffer for the name of Christ, it is because we have been people of character and respect, not because we have been obnoxious or self-righteous. At the same time, let's also remember that suffering for the name of Jesus is part of being Christian. Rather than being surprised, let's view these troubles as opportunities to show the character and grace of our Lord! When we do, we can be sure of God's blessing!

TODAY'S PRAYER

O Lord, God Almighty, help me to bring your blessings to others. May that be true in my casual encounters with others during the day. May it be true in those I am seeking to bring to Jesus. May it be true of those with whom I share faith. May it also be true when I find myself under attack for my faith. May my life always reflect the generous grace and the committed character of my Savior, Jesus, in whose name I pray. Amen.

CONTEXT: LUKE 6:17-26
Related Passages: 2 Timothy 3:10-14; 1 Peter 2:11-12; 1 Peter 3:13-17

Day 90

STUCK IN THE HERE AND NOW

Luke 6:24

[Jesus said] "But how bad it will be for you rich people, because you had your easy life."

KEY THOUGHT

So often we let our treasures become the things that are stuck "in the here and now." They do not have the lasting power to sustain us in this life, much less in the life to come. There is a very real sense that Christians should live "in the here and now" with a sense of urgency and awareness, but not focused on the material things of the "here and now." We should be fully alive every moment, because we know that what we do in this life matters for all of eternity. However, we must learn to build our hopes on what is lasting and eternal, not what is fleeting and subject to decay. Sorrows do await those who trust in their riches because those riches will not keep them from death and those riches will not go with them in death. All the happiness that they will ever receive is what they experience on earth. They lose out on the glory of the Kingdom. Let's invest in treasures that last—love for God, love for his children, and love for his praise. These are things that we know last forever!

TODAY'S PRAYER

O glorious God, give me eyes to see so that I can focus on what is truly important and not get distracted by the glitter of the things that are fleeting. In Jesus' name I pray. Amen.

CONTEXT: LUKE 6:17-26
Related Passages: Matthew 6:19-21; Luke 12:13-21; Luke 18:24-27

Day 91

CARELESS AND CARE-LESS JOY

Luke 6:25

*[Jesus said] "How bad it will be for you people who are full now,
because you will be hungry. How bad it will be for you people who
are laughing now, because you will be sad and cry."*

KEY THOUGHT

Jesus enjoyed the fellowship of sinners to redeem them and welcome them into God's family. Jesus knew how to enjoy a party! Remember the party that Matthew threw to introduce his sinful friends to Jesus (Luke 5:27-32)? Jesus talked about God's joyous party for returning sinners (Luke 15). However, Jesus had no part of "care less joy." "Care less joy" is that self-satisfied, look what I've done, arrogant joy that could care less if anyone else is unhappy or mistreated. This shallow joy cannot survive the hardships of life and the permanence of death. It is a vain attempt to escape from the hollowness of life without the Savior. Sorrow, awful hunger, and mourning await those who live such a life.

TODAY'S PRAYER

God of mercy and justice, I am concerned about the many people who fill their days with "care less joy" who are trying to drive out the emptiness in their hearts. Use me to help them find the wellspring of eternal joy found in your grace and the presence of your Holy Spirit. In Jesus' name I pray. Amen.

CONTEXT: LUKE 6:17-26
Related Passages: Luke 12:13-21; Luke 18:18-23; 2 Thessalonians 1:5-10

Day 92

THE CROWD'S HERO

Luke 6:26

[Jesus said] "How bad it is when everyone says nothing but good about you. Just look at the false prophets. Their ancestors always said good things about them."

KEY THOUGHT

For whom and for what do you live? Jesus warned us to avoid living for the approval of the crowd. He demonstrated the importance of this principle in his own life. Sometimes the crowd wildly accepted him. At other times, the crowd wanted to make him king, yet in just a matter of hours, they completely turned away from following him. The crowd cried out, "Hosanna! Hail, King of the Jews!" to praise him. Then a week later, the fickle crowd screamed, "Crucify him!" Jesus didn't trust the will of the crowd. He doesn't want us to either. When we live for the approval of the crowd, we give away the rule of our hearts to the will of the masses. We lose the direction in our lives in the process. We replace the approval of God with the call of the crowd, like the false prophets who led God's people and themselves into destruction.

TODAY'S PRAYER

Give me the courage, dear God, to live for you regardless of what those around me think of me. Make me a person of integrity, holy character, and graciousness. In Jesus' name I pray. Amen.

CONTEXT: LUKE 6:17-26
Related Passages: Acts 12:20-23; John 12:37-43; Galatians 1:10

Day 93

WHAT TO DO WITH ENEMIES?

Luke 6:27

*[Jesus said] "But I say to you people who are listening to me,
love your enemies. Do good to those who hate you."*

KEY THOUGHT

Can you think of anything more convicting than these words of Jesus? The
goal of a Christian is to be like the Master. That means we are redemptive in
all that we do. With Jesus as our example, there is no question about what our
attitude should be toward our enemies. Our only question is whether or not
we have the courage and the commitment to be willing to listen to Jesus and to
do what he asks us to do?

TODAY'S PRAYER

*Father, I confess that doing good to and loving my enemy is not something I enjoy
doing or find easy. Please use your Holy Spirit to transform me and empower me
to be more like your Son as I deal with my enemies. Give me wisdom to know how
to stand for righteousness and truth, to oppose evil and those who promote it, and
not to become corrupted by the power of hate. In Jesus' name I pray. Amen.*

CONTEXT: LUKE 6:27-36
Related Passages: Luke 23:32-38; Acts 7:54-60; 1 Peter 1:21-25

Day 94

THE POWER OF PRAYER TO CHANGE
AND REDEEM

Luke 6:28
*[Jesus said] "Ask God to bless the people who ask for bad things to
happen to you. Pray for the people who are mean to you."*

KEY THOUGHT

Prayer has the power to change us. We can change as we see God's power
work in someone who has cursed and/or hurt us and make that person into
a better person. Seeing their change helps us to continue our changing to be
more like Jesus. However, even when folks don't change, prayer changes us as
we offer ourselves to God for his service. In this case, it is praying for those for
whom we wouldn't naturally want to pray. Such prayer is an act of faith and
submission: "Father, may what is accomplished be what you will and not what
I want." While such prayer is unnatural, we are called to be unnatural! We are
God's spiritual children. Redeeming those lost in hate, bitterness, rage, and
malice is important to us. Our goal is to have those who mistreat us ultimately
find their way into the Kingdom and become our brother or sister in Christ.
We must pray!

TODAY'S PRAYER

*Father, I know of several people who do not wish me well. They love it when I stumble.
They rejoice when I hurt. They delight in my failures. Father, I first ask that they
can come to know Jesus and have your Spirit minister to their deepest hurts and
transform them into your children. Help me release all vindictiveness, desires for
vengeance, and cultivated bitterness and malice. In Jesus' name I pray. Amen.*

CONTEXT: LUKE 6:27-36
Related Passages: Luke 22:46; Galatians 5:18-26; 1 Peter 3:9

Day 95

TURN THE OTHER CHEEK?

Luke 6:29

[Jesus said] "If someone hits you on the side of your face, let them hit the other side too. If someone takes your coat, don't stop them from taking your shirt too."

KEY THOUGHT

This doesn't make sense to us if we look at it only on a human level. We don't want people to run all over us. We don't want to be doormats so people can stomp all over us. We don't want folks taking advantage of us. Clearly in Scripture, there comes a time to stop enabling people to be evil and to stop allowing them to continue their evil behavior because of our fear and compliance. On the other hand, Jesus' followers ARE to offer conflicted situations the opportunity to de-escalate instead of "upping the ante" with destructive and vindictive behavior. This should not be a compliance of fear or powerlessness. Instead, it should be a Kingdom commitment to honor God and do what he says to help bless and redeem others.

TODAY'S PRAYER

Give me strength, O God, to turn the other cheek and not to be embittered. Give me courage, O God, so that I do not lose my heart or my head when others take advantage of me by misusing my help. Give me a generous heart, O Father, so that others can find their way back to you because of my influence and behavior. In Jesus' name I pray. Amen.

CONTEXT: LUKE 6:27-36
Related Passages: Romans 12:9-21; 1 Timothy 2:2; Ephesians 6:23

Day 96

GENEROUS TO A FAULT

Luke 6:30
[Jesus said] "Give to everyone who asks you for something. When someone takes something that is yours, don't ask for it back."

KEY THOUGHT

Our stuff often owns us. We can even get more attached to our stuff than to the people in our lives. When our things are taken from us, we can be more concerned about the things than we are about the heart of the person who took them. God wants us to be generous with others, just as he is generous with us. God poured out his grace lavishly. Do some people abuse that grace? Absolutely! Is God sorry he offered us his grace? Absolutely not! Some people will abuse us financially or take advantage of us in a "deal." Rather than destroying the reputation of the church and bringing ruin on ourselves through bitterness, let us forgive and let go of what anchors us to the world.

TODAY'S PRAYER

O Father, give me open hands and an open heart to deal with those around me generously. Please help me from becoming bitter toward those who take advantage of me. Help me control my desire for "my justice" and seek after your grace, mercy, and generosity. In Jesus' name I ask for this grace. Amen.

CONTEXT: LUKE 6:27-36
Related Passages: Philemon 1:6; 2 Corinthians 9:6-8; Ephesians 4:28

Day 97

OUR GOLD STANDARD

Luke 6:31
[Jesus said] "Do for others what you want them to do for you."

KEY THOUGHT

Some principles are the center around which other principles turn. They capture the truth in a succinct yet profound way. The "Golden Rule" is one of those principles. It is the gold standard of relationship principles. This short principle defines what it means to love our neighbors as ourselves and opens our motives and behaviors up to self-scrutiny. Now, if we will only go live this principle in every area of life—like when we drive, or when we talk to family members, or when we are asked to forgive someone, or when we are ready to gossip or to condemn another's motives, or when we . . . .

TODAY'S PRAYER

Father, may my understanding of this profound principle be matched by my practice of it in my daily life. Move through your Holy Spirit in me to conform me more completely into the embodiment of this principle your Son both taught and lived. In Jesus' name I pray. Amen.

CONTEXT: LUKE 6:27-36
Related Passages: Luke 10:25-28; John 13:12-17; Ephesians 4:31-32

Day 98

BEYOND OUR CIRCLE OF FRIENDS

Luke 6:32

[Jesus said] "If you love only those who love you, should you get any special praise for doing that? No, even sinners love those who love them!"

KEY THOUGHT

Jesus has just given us the golden rule (see previous verse). Now he wants to make clear that this principle is not just a principle to practice with people we like and people who treat us nicely. This is a principle to use with all people, even our enemies! Just as God loves all people, he calls on us, his children, to do the same.

TODAY'S PRAYER

Holy and righteous Father, the True and Living God of all nations, mold my heart by your Holy Spirit and fashion it into a vessel filled with your love for all peoples. Break down the walls of prejudice, pride, bitterness, arrogance, malice, and ethnocentrism that can produce unholy barriers to your love that is operating through me. In Jesus' name I pray. Amen.

CONTEXT: LUKE 6:27-36
Related Passages: John 3:16-17; Matthew 5:43-45; 2 Peter 3:9

Day 99

OUTSIDE OUR CIRCLE

Luke 6:33-34

[Jesus said] "If you do good only to those who do good to you, should you get any special praise for doing that? No, even sinners do that! If you lend things to people, always expecting to get something back, should you get any special praise for that? No, even sinners lend to other sinners so that they can get back the same amount!"

KEY THOUGHT

Almost all of us have a circle of "nice folks" or "familiar folks" with whom we associate and for whom we extend a special grace. Jesus reminds us that even sinners have that kind of circle and are nice to people who fit in their special circle of friendships. However, his followers, those who are true children of God, open their circles to folks other than their close friends. Why? Because we are called to be redemptive; we are placed in relationship with those people to make an eternal difference in their lives. Our goal is not to get what we deserve out of social relationships, but it is to help others get to God's grace. That principle, that kind of heart, changes everything . . . especially us!

TODAY'S PRAYER

Loving Father, give me the courage to extend my kindness outside the limits of my comfort zone so that others can revel in your grace and become a part of your family. In Jesus' name I pray for your help to be more like your Son in this way. Amen.

CONTEXT: LUKE 6:27-36
Related Passages: Ephesians 2:1-10; Psalm 145:17; Proverbs 3:3

Day 100

BE LIKE YOUR FATHER

Luke 6:35

*[Jesus said] "I'm telling you to love your enemies and do good to them. Lend
to people without expecting to get anything back. If you do this, you will have
a great reward. You will be children of the Most High God. Yes, because
God is good even to the people who are full of sin and not thankful."*

KEY THOUGHT

"I have my Father's eyes," Amy Grant sang years ago. While that may be
good, God wants us to have his heart as well. Most of us mortals have a tight
clutch on what we feel we have earned and are skeptical of sharing any of that
with those who might not be grateful or might want to take advantage of us.
God, however, is not only rich in goods and power, he is also rich in mercy,
kindness, and grace. He asks us to be the same. Our Father even promises to
help us have the power to love in this way through the Holy Spirit (Rom. 5:5).
So let's be open to being generous, gracious, and merciful. If we are, we'll not
only have our Father's eyes, but we'll also have our Father's heart.

TODAY'S PRAYER

*O God, my glorious and almighty Abba Father, make my heart generous,
gracious, and merciful like yours. Use my kindness to help others know
your love and find your grace. In Jesus' name I ask this. Amen.*

CONTEXT: LUKE 6:27-36
Related Passages: Galatians 5:22-23; Psalm 112:5; Proverbs 11:25

Day 101

COMPASSIONATE CHILDREN

Luke 6:36
[Jesus said] "Give love and mercy the same as your Father gives love and mercy."

KEY THOUGHT

We *must* be compassionate. We *must* show love and mercy to others! Hmm, that doesn't leave any wiggle room, does it? God is serious about us being compassionate. Why is showing compassion to others such an important principle to our Father in heaven? Because he has been so gracious, forgiving, loving, merciful, and compassionate with us. How can we take the love and mercy he has shown us and not be willing to share it with others? It is unthinkable! If we are going to be children of God, he is adamant that we reflect this area of his holy character.

TODAY'S PRAYER

Thank you, dear Father, that even though you are the only true and living God, the Lord God Almighty, you are also the God of compassion and grace. Without your example, dear Father, and without your generous compassion shared with me, I know that I would not have the conviction, the desire, or the power to be as compassionate with others as they need me to be. Please empower me to be more like you in this area of my life. In Jesus' name I pray. Amen.

CONTEXT: LUKE 6:27-36
Related Passages: Ephesians 4:30-32; Isaiah 49:13; Philippians 1:8

Day 102
QUIT IT!

Luke 6:37

[Jesus said] "Don't judge others, and God will not judge you. Don't condemn others, and you will not be condemned. Forgive others, and you will be forgiven."

KEY THOUGHT

Jesus isn't talking hypothetically. He is talking about a problem that has plagued the petty human race for centuries. God doesn't want us judging people's motives. Only he can see inside another person's heart. He loathes the all-too-human practice of judging other's intentions and motives. We have no right to judge God's servant! If someone's actions are good and kind, we are to accept them as genuine. Jesus reminds us that the spirit of judgment with which we treat others will also be the spirit of judgment that becomes the standard used to judge us. We are to be a forgiving people because we know the transforming power of God's forgiveness!

TODAY'S PRAYER

Father of glory, I want to intentionally and specifically pray for the forgiveness of those who have wronged me, taken advantage of me, wounded me, or wounded those I love. Please receive with grace each name that I give to you and do not hold their offenses against them. In Jesus' name I pray for you to extend your mercy to those who have wounded me. Amen.

CONTEXT: LUKE 6:37-42
Related Passages: Luke 22:32-34; Acts 7:-59; James 4:11

Day 103

THE PRINCIPLE OF GENEROSITY

Luke 6:38

[Jesus said] "Give to others, and you will receive. You will be given much. It will be poured into your hands—more than you can hold. You will be given so much that it will spill into your lap. The way you give to others is the way God will give to you."

KEY THOUGHT

The two areas where many of us can be the stingiest are money and forgiveness. So after all that Jesus taught us in the previous statements about graciousness and generosity, he now sums it up with these two summary principles: 1) our blessings will be based upon our willingness to bless others, and 2) our measure of treating and judging others will be the basis used for measuring and treating us. In other words, God has been gracious with us; we can either share that graciousness or abuse it. Grace is wonderful and free until we take it off the market and out of circulation in our relationships. If we stymie, hold, or remove God's grace from circulation, it becomes damaged and lost to us. This stern warning reminds us again how seriously God takes our generosity with others.

TODAY'S PRAYER

Father God, forgive my miserly forgiveness in the past. Forgive my previous condemning attitude toward others. Open my heart to share your generosity. Open my heart to give others the benefit of the doubt instead of judging them. Use me as a conduit of your generosity and grace. In Jesus' name I pray. Amen.

CONTEXT: LUKE 6:37-42
Related Passages: Matthew 7:1-5; Galatians 6:7-10; 2 Corinthians 9:6-10

Day 104

BECOMING LIKE OUR TEACHER

Luke 6:39-40

Jesus told them this story: "Can a blind man lead another blind man? No. Both of them will fall into a ditch. Students are not better than their teacher. But when they have been fully taught, they will be like their teacher."

KEY THOUGHT

Who is the greatest embodiment of generosity, forgiveness, and grace who has ever lived? It is Jesus, of course. So Jesus becomes our example. To follow lesser examples is to be led into a trap. Our goal isn't to be good, but to be godly. Our goal isn't to be the best of our peers, but to be like Jesus in front of our peers. So let's set our sights on Jesus as our example, especially in the way he extended grace and dealt generously with the people around him.

TODAY'S PRAYER

O Lord God Almighty, my precious Abba Father, when this day is done, may you find me more closely conformed to the character of your Son and my Savior. In Jesus' name I pray. Amen.

CONTEXT: LUKE 6:37-42

Related Passages: Colossians 1:28-29; 2 Corinthians 3:17-18; 1 Corinthians 10:31-11:1

Day 105

BLIND TO OUR FAULTS

Luke 6:41-42

*[Jesus said] "Why do you notice the small piece of dust that is in your friend's eye,
but you don't see the big piece of wood that is in your own eye? You say to your friend,
'Let me get that little piece of dust out of your eye.' Why do you say this? Can't you see
that big piece of wood in your own eye? You are a hypocrite. First, take the wood out
of your own eye. Then you will see clearly to get the dust out of your friend's eye."*

KEY THOUGHT

The problem with sin and forgiveness, the problem with inconsistency, the
problem with questionable motives, and the problem with unjust criticism
are problems of our heart—not the problems of others and their actions
against us. We must look inwardly at ourselves. We must look critically at
ourselves. We must look correctively at ourselves. God holds us responsible
for ourselves. Jesus wants us to see that our primary job is to deal with our
own problems, sins, weaknesses, mistakes, inconsistencies, wrong motives,
and other faults. Only after we've begun to address these problems in our own
lives can we dare begin to help others address the sin in their lives—and even
then, we must approach them with humility, love, and grace, knowing that
we're sinners saved by grace.

TODAY'S PRAYER

*O God my heavenly Father, please forgive me for my sins. I know that I fall short of what
I want to be. I do not want to use someone else's weaknesses or stumbling to be an excuse
for my shortcomings. In addition, Father, please open my eyes so that I do not avoid my
own shortcomings by pointing to the deficiencies of another. In Jesus' name I pray. Amen.*

CONTEXT: LUKE 6:37-42
Related Passages: Romans 12:3; Romans 14:4; Galatians 6:1-5

Day 106

LOOK AT YOUR HEART

Luke 6:43-45

[Jesus said] "A good tree does not produce bad fruit. And a bad tree does not produce good fruit. Every tree is known by the kind of fruit it produces. You won't find figs on thorny weeds. And you can't pick grapes from thornbushes! Good people have good things saved in their hearts. That's why they say good things. But those who are evil have hearts full of evil, and that's why they say things that are evil. What people say with their mouths comes from what fills their hearts."

KEY THOUGHT

Ultimately, all the principles Jesus talks about in Luke 6 are heart issues. Our hearts, not just our actions, need to be conformed to God's will. Yes, our actions are crucial. Yes, obedience is necessary. However, that obedience needs to be heartfelt and heart-driven. When it is, then our hearts determine the fruit we bear. So let's ask God to guard our hearts, cleanse our hearts, and conform our hearts to his own.

TODAY'S PRAYER

Holy God, purify my heart. Remove from it all bitterness and rivalry. Get rid of self-interest and evil. Fill my heart with your love by the power of your Holy Spirit. In Jesus' name I pray. Amen.

CONTEXT: LUKE 6:43-49
Related Passages: Titus 2:11-15; Hebrews 9:14; James 4:8

Day 107

JUST DO IT!

Luke 6:46
[Jesus said] "Why do you call me, 'Lord, Lord,' but you don't do what I say?"

KEY THOUGHT

Jesus has one simple point: if I am your Lord, then you will obey what I tell you. If you don't, then I'm not your Lord. It's that simple. It's that clear. So why have we grown so passionless about obeying what he says? After all, if we have trouble with obedience, our fundamental problem is really a lack of love for Jesus. He said "If anyone loves me, he will obey my teaching" (John 14:23). So as our passion for the Lord grows, so also should our obedience. If we love the Lord, then we'll do what he says!

TODAY'S PRAYER

Abba Father, give me a passion to obey your will just as you have filled my heart with your love through the Holy Spirit. In Jesus' name I request this grace. Amen.

CONTEXT: LUKE 6:43-49
Related Passages: Matthew 7:21-23; Mark 3:31-35; Matthew 28:18-20

Day 108

HOW ARE WE GOING TO BUILD?

Luke 6:47-49

[Jesus said] The people who come to me, who listen to my teachings and obey them—I will show you what they are like: They are like a man building a house. He digs deep and builds his house on rock. The floods come, and the water crashes against the house. But the flood cannot move the house, because it was built well.

"But the people who hear my words and do not obey are like a man who builds a house without preparing a foundation. When the floods come, the house falls down easily and is completely destroyed."

KEY THOUGHT

In modern Western culture, intention often counts for more than action and emotion often means more than effort. Into our self-absorbed culture, Jesus comes and weds intention with action and emotion with effort. Simply being moved by Jesus' words, simply being convicted of the truth, or simply intellectually accepting what Jesus says is destructive. Jesus says that passion, conviction, and faith without life-change, obedience, and action are futile. This vain faith, emotion, and conviction aren't merely shortsighted or lacking; they are self-destructive, wasteful, and disastrous. Faith that doesn't call us to act, emotion that doesn't move us to effort, and conviction that doesn't motivate us to change are empty and vain. Such religion becomes an inoculation against holiness, godly character, and redemptive action. I believe with all of my heart that Jesus would say that our greatest need today is to learn to obey our Father, humbly and thankfully.

TODAY'S PRAYER

Forgive me, Father. Forgive us, dear Father, for our attention to words, emotions, and passions while ignoring your call to obey. Through the power of your Spirit, please, dear Father, move me to conform my emotions, convictions, and beliefs to your will and obey you in my actions. In Jesus' name I pray. Amen.

CONTEXT: LUKE 6:43-49
Related Passages: James 1:21-25; James 2:14-18; Galatians 5:6

Day 109

A LOVE FOR THE CITY!

Luke 7:1

Jesus finished saying all these things to the people. Then he went into Capernaum.

KEY THOUGHT

I've lived in the country. I've lived in the city. I've lived in the suburbs. Each has its own rhythm. Each has its own advantages. Each has its own drawbacks. Jesus chose the cities. Yes, a good bit of his ministry occurred on the mountainsides or along the lake, but he felt a call to the city. That's where the most people lived. That's where the need was greatest. So after his ministry of teaching in the countryside, he goes back to the city to share himself with those in need of God's good news of hope and salvation. As Luke tells us Jesus' story—first through his earthly ministry in the Gospel of Luke and then through his heavenly ministry through the Spirit in the early church (in the book of Acts)—he reminds us of Jesus' love for the cities and his desire to save the masses. So no matter where we find ourselves living, I can't help but believe that the Master will place the lost of the cities on our hearts, calling those of us in cities to share hope and salvation with those who do not yet know it and calling the rest of us to support efforts to reach city-dwellers.

TODAY'S PRAYER

O Lord, God of the nations and lover of the people who inhabit the great cities of the world, please move me to be more selfless as I look at where I invest my time and my energies. Open my heart to the needs of those in the great cities and teach me how to reach them more effectively with your message of grace, hope, and salvation. In Jesus' name I pray. Amen.

CONTEXT: LUKE 7:1-10
Related Passages: Jonah 4:9-11; Luke 13:34; Mark 1:33-39

Day 110

KINDNESS DISPLAYED

Luke 7:2-5

In Capernaum there was an army officer. He had a servant who was very sick; he was near death. The officer loved the servant very much. When he heard about Jesus, he sent some older Jewish leaders to him. He wanted the men to ask Jesus to come and save the life of his servant. The men went to Jesus. They begged Jesus to help the officer. They said, "This officer is worthy to have your help. He loves our people and he built the synagogue for us."

KEY THOUGHT

In a world of prejudice and rank, this is one story that warms our hearts and points us to our better selves. While Jews plead the case of a non-Jew to Jesus, an officer of rank pleads the case of his servant. Of course for Jesus, these distinctions didn't make a difference, but they did to the people of his day. This is a great reminder that in the presence of Jesus, race, rank, and reputation pale in comparison to his desire to save and bless all people who will come to him as Lord.

TODAY'S PRAYER

O Lord God Almighty, please forgive me for the barriers and the labels that I allow to be erected between others and me. I know that those "others" are your precious creations who so desperately need your grace. Use me to help make your children more open to all peoples so that our earthly reality can more perfectly mirror the complete racial and social diversity that exists in the presence of your glory in heaven. In Jesus' name I pray. Amen.

CONTEXT: LUKE 7:1-10
Related Passages: Galatians 3:26-4:7; Ephesians 2:14-18; Revelation 7:9-10

Day 111

TRUST IN AUTHORITY

Luke 7:6-8

So Jesus went with them. He was coming near the officer's house when the officer sent friends to say, "Lord, you don't need to do anything special for me. I am not good enough for you to come into my house. That is why I did not come to you myself. You need only to give the order, and my servant will be healed. I know this because I am a man under the authority of other men. And I have soldiers under my authority. I tell one soldier, 'Go,' and he goes. And I tell another soldier, 'Come,' and he comes. And I say to my servant, 'Do this,' and my servant obeys me."

KEY THOUGHT

It takes someone of authority to truly and fully appreciate someone else who exercises authority. Here is a man of authority who shows his faith in Jesus' authority and shows his own humility, a humility that was most unexpected for his position. He trusted in the power of Jesus and the power of Jesus' will and word. His faith is exemplary. Do we have that same faith? Do we believe in Jesus' promises and trust in his word with the same humility?

TODAY'S PRAYER

Father, I believe, but help my faith grow and mature. Help my actions match Jesus' word more fully as I learn to trust Jesus' promises more completely. I ask this in Jesus' name. Amen.

CONTEXT: LUKE 7:1-10
Related Passages: Matthew 28:18-20; Acts 2:33-36; Luke 4:36

Day 112

EXAMPLES FROM THE OUTSIDE

Luke 7:9

*When Jesus heard this, he was amazed. He turned to the people following him and
said, "I tell you, this is the most faith I have seen anywhere, even in Israel."*

KEY THOUGHT

Jesus loved to shock those who heard him into listening. He sometimes did
this by making outsiders the heroes of stories. As in the stories of the Good
Samaritan (10:30-37), Zacchaeus (19:1-10), the widow of Zerephath, and
Naaman the Syrian (4:24-30), the Roman soldier is the hero in this episode,
as Jesus turns the attention away from himself. He wants the people to see the
importance of faith that trusts in his authority to act redemptively and bring
salvation. For those of us who have been Christians awhile, new Christians,
especially those who have come from outside our social circle and our range of
experience, have much to teach us about the joy of salvation. The freshness of
their faith, the new-found joy of knowing Jesus, and the challenges they face
of living for Jesus can renew our faith and increase our joy as we encourage
them in their walk with the Lord.

TODAY'S PRAYER

*Father, thank you for the new children in your spiritual family and the fresh joy they have
in being your children. Please use those who have been Christians longer to encourage
these newer Christians in their walk with Jesus. Please use the newer Christians as a
powerful example of faith and trust for those who have been Christians longer. Help each
of us to see our deep need to love and appreciate each other. In Jesus' name I pray. Amen.*

CONTEXT: LUKE 10:30-37
Related Passages: 7:1-10; Luke 19:5-10; Luke 4:24-30

Day 113

COMPLETELY HEALED!

Luke 7:10
*The group that was sent to Jesus went back to the house.
There they found that the servant was healed.*

KEY THOUGHT

The Roman soldier's trust in Jesus' power was more than warranted. His servant was completely healed—not partially healed, not temporarily healed, not incrementally healed, but completely healed! When we open our lives to the authority of Jesus, when we trust him at his word and do what he says, Jesus can do amazing things to bring us to complete healing. The issue isn't his authority or his power or his grace, but our willingness to take him at his word and trust in his work. Even if we never experience the complete healing on this side of eternity, we will ultimately go to his house and find ourselves complete in every way.

TODAY'S PRAYER

Dear Almighty God, I do anticipate the day that you make me complete in every way. Until that day, I commit to take Jesus at his word and show my trust in him with my whole-hearted obedience. I know that I am made of dust, mortal in every way. However, dear Father, I trust that you have adopted me as your child and that I will experience my relationship with you in perfection when Jesus comes to bring me home in glory. Give me strength to live out this trust with passion and conviction. In Jesus' name I pray. Amen.

CONTEXT: LUKE 7:1-10
Related Passages: John 14:1-4; Romans 8:18-24; Philippians 3:12

Day 114

COMPASSION FOR THOSE WHO GRIEVE

Luke 7:11-13

The next day Jesus and his followers went to a town called Nain. A big crowd was traveling with them. When Jesus came near the town gate, he saw some people carrying a dead body. It was the only son of a woman who was a widow. Walking with her were many other people from the town. When the Lord saw the woman, he felt very sorry for her and said, "Don't cry."

KEY THOUGHT

Jesus heart went out to this woman left all alone. While many mourn with her, Jesus longed to comfort her. His heart was full of compassion. He could say what no one else could say, "Don't cry!" We can only cry with those who have lost loved ones. Only Jesus can wipe away our tears. Jesus is touched by our loss and by our mortal limitations. That's why he came. We can be assured that he feels our loss in the same way. When we cry in grief, we do not cry alone.

TODAY'S PRAYER

Thank you, Father, for sending Jesus as the answer for our death sentence. I am profoundly touched by his empathy and concern for those who lost loved ones. Use me to bless those touched by death and share your grace with them. In Jesus' name I pray. Amen.

CONTEXT: LUKE 7:11-17
Related Passages: Hebrews 2:14-15; 1 Thessalonians 4:13-18; Revelations 7:17

REUNION!

Luke 7:14-15

He walked to the open coffin and touched it. The men who were carrying the coffin stopped. Jesus spoke to the dead son: "Young man, I tell you, get up!" Then the boy sat up and began to talk, and Jesus gave him back to his mother.

KEY THOUGHT

Jesus speaks to the dead young man and makes him alive. Then Luke says it so simply and beautifully: "And Jesus gave him back to his mother." Despite death, Jesus brings reunion! Despite the sorrow, Jesus brings back the joy. This one event is a preview of our future in Christ. One day, all those who are dead in Christ will hear his voice and rise from the dead with immortal bodies and join Jesus. Those believers who are still alive when Christ comes will also be changed and go to be with the Lord forever (1 Cor. 15:51-53). This event will be a day of great rejoicing as all Christians are reunited with each other and with their Lord.

TODAY'S PRAYER

Father, thank you for the promise of reunion with those I love who have died before me. Thank you for their faith and Jesus' power over death that insures our reunion. I thank you in Jesus' name. Amen.

CONTEXT: LUKE 7:14-15
Related Passages: 1 Corinthians 15:50-57; 2 Timothy 4:6-8; 1 Thessalonians 4:16-17

Day 116

FEAR AND PRAISE

Luke 7:16-17

Everyone was filled with fear. They began praising God and said, "A great prophet is here with us!" and "God is taking care of his people."

This news about Jesus spread all over Judea and to all the other places around there.

KEY THOUGHT

Talk about a mind-blowing experience: seeing this dead boy raised from the dead was unbelievable. Naturally, there was a holy fear of Jesus and his power by those who witnessed this event. They recognized that this was not a trick, but the power and presence of God himself on display. Praise and confession of God's greatness were the proper responses to such an event. They realized they were seeing the work and care of God. They also felt it was important to share this news with others. Holy fear, praise, recognition of God's greatness, and evangelism were the proper responses. These are also the proper responses to the mighty work of God in our times.

TODAY'S PRAYER

O holy God, give me the eyes of faith to see and the spiritual discernment to know how best to honor and praise you for your great acts of blessing, mercy, and grace. You are holy God, so teach me reverence. You are concerned with my daily wounds and struggles, so teach me discernment so that I can better see your hand at work. As you show your presence in my life, use me to spread the story of your grace and deliverance to others. In Jesus' name I ask for you help in these important ways. Amen.

CONTEXT: LUKE 7:11-17
Related Passages: John 1:14-18; 1 John 1:1-4; Luke 24:47-48

Day 117

SECOND THOUGHTS

Luke 7:18-19

John's followers told him about all these things. John called for two
of his followers. He sent them to the Lord to ask, "Are you the one we
heard was coming, or should we wait for someone else?"

KEY THOUGHT

We sometimes exalt key figures in the Scriptures to the legendary status of "Bible characters." We don't allow them to have bad days, bouts with doubt, lapses of passion, or dilemmas with faith. Jesus is the only flesh and blood "Bible character" who was sinless. All the others had feet of clay. Even John the Baptizer, with all his passion and integrity, wanted to know for sure that Jesus was who John claimed him to be. Jesus' demonstration of what John prophesied was different, at least from the distance from which John viewed him. (Remember Herod had John in prison and would soon execute him.) The crucial thing about John is that he kept seeking the truth, even in his moments of confusion and doubt. When we have doubts, we can let the doubts overtake us and grow silent and afraid to seek the truth. Jesus never discouraged truth seekers! Jesus was not afraid to answer questions from his critics, the skeptics, or even his followers who had doubts. We will pass through a valley or two of doubt and confusion. Let's refuse to be afraid! Let's be honest with Jesus about our struggles. So often, that is exactly where we find the Lord—there waiting for the seeker who honestly comes to him with questions.

TODAY'S PRAYER

Father, please help me never be afraid to bring my honest questions to you as
I seek to know the truth. Give me wisdom and faith as I seek you, for I know
that in finding you, I will find the truth. In Jesus' name I pray. Amen.

CONTEXT: LUKE 7:18-35
Related Passages: Luke 11:9-13; John 7:16-17; 8:31-32; John 20:24-29

Day 118

THE PROOF IS IN THE PREACHER

Luke 7:20-23

So the men came to Jesus. They said, "John the Baptizer sent us to you with this question: 'Are you the one who is coming, or should we wait for someone else?'" Right then Jesus healed many people of their sicknesses and diseases. He healed those who had evil spirits and made many who were blind able to see again. Then he said to John's followers, "Go tell John what you have seen and heard: The blind can see. The crippled can walk. People with leprosy are healed. The deaf can hear. The dead are brought back to life. And the Good News is being told to the poor. Great blessings belong to those who don't have a problem accepting me."

KEY THOUGHT

I have reminded preaching students, "God could use a donkey to speak his will, so simply having a message from God doesn't make us all that important." I was referring to Balaam's donkey, of course (Numbers 22). God wants his messengers to have their message and their lives line up. Jesus reaches back and uses this less-known prophetic description of the Messiah to remind John that he, Jesus, is the Christ of God. To help reinforce his claim, he asks John's followers to report to him what they have seen him do and heard him say. Jesus has been doing what the prophets proclaimed he would do. John's words were right, even if his personal expectations of the Messiah do not line up with reality. In our weaker moments, we may want a Messiah who is a little different from Jesus—not so straight talking about obedience and not so demanding about discipleship. But, it is not Jesus who needs to change to fit our expectations; it is our expectations and our behaviors that need to fit who Jesus is and what he taught.

TODAY'S PRAYER

Holy God, thank you for lovingly sending your Son to be my Savior. Please open my mind and my heart to better understand who Jesus is and who he wants me to be. In the name of your Son, Christ Jesus my Lord, I pray. Amen.

CONTEXT: LUKE 7:18-35
Related Passages: Isaiah 61:1-3; Isaiah 49:5-6; John 7:16-18

Day 119

MORE THAN A PROPHET

Luke 7:24-26

When John's followers left, Jesus began talking to the people about John: "What did you people go out into the desert to see? Someone who is weak, like a stem of grass blowing in the wind? Really, what did you expect to see? Someone dressed in fine clothes? Of course not. People who wear fancy clothes and live in luxury are all in kings' palaces. So what did you go out to see? A prophet? Yes, John is a prophet. But I tell you, he is more than that.

KEY THOUGHT

John the Baptizer had changed everything! The voice of God through the prophets had been silent for hundreds of years. When John bursts onto the scene, they heard the human voice of John; but through that voice they experienced the power and presence of God. John was a prophet who pointed others to Jesus. But, John was much more than a prophet; he was a trailblazer. He made the way ready for the Messiah and opened the hearts of the people to the Savior who was the Lamb of God. He was known by his godly character, his passionate preaching of God's message, and his unquenchable passion to make people ready for the Messiah. He was Jesus' cousin, forerunner, and servant. Yes, John was much more than a prophet!

TODAY'S PRAYER

O God Almighty, the great God who keeps his promises and is faithful to his people, thank you for sending John. I appreciate his example of service to Jesus. I am convicted by the integrity and clarity of his message regardless of his audience. Help me to be more like John in my service to your King, Jesus, in whose name I pray. Amen.

CONTEXT: LUKE 7:18-35
Related Passages: John 1:19-29; John 3:27-30; Luke 1:17

NONE GREATER!

Luke 7:27-28

[Jesus said] "This Scripture was written about him: 'Listen! I will send my messenger ahead of you. He will prepare the way for you.' I tell you, no one ever born is greater than John. But even the least important person in God's kingdom is greater than John."

KEY THOUGHT

John was incredible! The voice of God through the prophets had not been heard for hundreds of years in Israel. When John the Baptizer came on the scene, people flocked to hear him. They recognized in the clarity of his words something that can only come from God. He lived his life and used his ministry to serve Jesus and open the hearts of people for the coming of the Christ. John spoke the truth regardless of who listened or who cared. This integrity and godly character were what got John in trouble with Herod. As great as John was, Jesus says that those in God's Kingdom are greater still—not because of what those in the Kingdom have done or will do, but because of God's gift of salvation, the resurrection power of Jesus, and the indwelling presence of the Holy Spirit.

TODAY'S PRAYER

Father, thank you for the incredible example of John the Baptizer. Use me to be a servant for the message of Jesus. Help me to have the integrity of John as I speak your truth. Give me the courage to do your will, even under threat and opposition. Thank you for receiving me as your child and a part of your Kingdom. In Jesus' name I pray. Amen.

CONTEXT: LUKE 7:18-35
Related Passages: Luke 3:15-18; John 3:26-30; Revelation 11:15

Day 121

REJECTING GOD'S PLAN

Luke 7:29-30
(When the people heard this, they all agreed that God's teaching was
good. Even the tax collectors agreed. These were the people who were
baptized by John. But the Pharisees and experts in the law refused to accept
God's plan for themselves; they did not let John baptize them.)

KEY THOUGHT

"Some are last who will be first, and some are first who will be last" (Luke
13:30 RSV). Luke helps us see the great reversals that God's justice brings.
Those who had all the advantages of being religious insiders often rejected
Jesus because he called them to repent—to change their hearts and lives.
Those who were outsiders, who knew they were sinners and were looking for
a way out of their sinful bondage, repented and let Jesus completely reorient
their lives. Even today, many of us who have had all the advantages of being
raised around faith can find it hard not to tone down Jesus' call to change our
lives and follow him as Lord. Let's use their failure as our warning! We are all
saved by grace and are called to follow Jesus with our all.

TODAY'S PRAYER

Abba Father, please help me never let my familiarity with faith blind me
to true and whole-hearted belief in Jesus. I don't want anything to dilute
my devotion to your Son as my Lord or to turn my heart away from his
sacrifice; so please give me the discernment I need when Satan tries to use
my weaknesses to blind me to your truth. In Jesus' name I pray. Amen.

CONTEXT: LUKE 7:18-35
Related Passages: John 5:39-44; Colossians 1:19-21; John 12:42-43

Day 122

NO WAY TO WIN THEIR HEARTS

Luke 7:31-35

[Jesus said] "What shall I say about the people of this time? What can I compare them to? What are they like? They are like children sitting in the marketplace. One group of children calls to the other children and says,' We played flute music for you, but you did not dance; we sang a sad song, but you did not cry.' John the Baptizer came and did not eat the usual food or drink wine. And you say, 'He has a demon inside him.' The Son of Man came eating and drinking. And you say, 'Look at him! He eats too much and drinks too much wine! He is a friend of tax collectors and other sinners!' But wisdom is shown to be right by those who accept it."

KEY THOUGHT

Jesus was not going to win the hearts of those who had decided not to believe. Jesus and John were very different in demeanor and style, yet those who refused to believe rejected each of them, oftentimes using their "style" as the excuse. Jesus confronts them and basically says, "You're not going to believe because you don't want to believe!" As Jesus so often did, he reminds anyone who will listen that the real proof of character is seen in the fruit a person produces. When you look at the fruit of their lives, both John and Jesus show they are from God, regardless of their differing styles.

TODAY'S PRAYER

Holy God, please forgive me for judging others based on their personal style and demeanor. I don't want to reject, judge, or be unsupportive of any of your servants. In addition, dear Father, help my life consistently bear fruit for you. In Jesus' name I ask this. Amen.

CONTEXT: LUKE 7:18-35
Related Passages: John 7:16-17; Luke 6:43-49; Galatians 5:22-26

Day 123

OPEN TO ALL PEOPLE

Luke 7:36
*One of the Pharisees asked Jesus to eat with him. Jesus went into
the Pharisee's house and took a place at the table.*

KEY THOUGHT

Even though many Pharisees had rejected Jesus, opposed his every move, and demonstrated an unwillingness to believe, Jesus went to the Pharisee's home because he loved all people—even those who opposed him and were critical of him. He didn't rule out anyone or any group from being exposed to God's grace. Let's not let our prejudices, or the prejudices of others who appear to oppose us, keep us from the opportunity of sharing the good news of God's grace found in Jesus!

TODAY'S PRAYER

Father, I admit that I have assumed someone's negative attitude toward your Word, your Son, or your people because of the way they talked or dressed, or because of my past experiences with others like them. Please forgive me for underestimating the power of the gospel and for my prejudice. I want to love all people just as you have loved me. In Jesus' name I pray, fervently asking for your grace to change me to be more like Jesus. Amen.

CONTEXT: LUKE 7:36-50
Related Passages: John 3:16-17; 2 Peter 3:9; Luke 24:47-49

Day 124

EXTRAVAGANT LOVE

Luke 7:37-38

There was a sinful woman in that town. She knew that Jesus was eating at the Pharisee's house. So the woman brought some expensive perfume in an alabaster jar. She stood at Jesus' feet, crying. Then she began to wash his feet with her tears. She dried his feet with her hair. She kissed his feet many times and rubbed them with the perfume.

KEY THOUGHT

This event occurs in the house of a certain Pharisee. This woman was the antithesis of the Pharisee. He was a man. She was a woman. He was scrupulously and legalistically religious in his behavior. She was a sinner from the city. He would have been very conservative and appropriate in his demeanor. She was extravagant and bold in showing her love and appreciation for Jesus. The key message, however, is that Jesus is open to both of them and longs to show love and share God's grace with each of them. Are we like Jesus in this way? How would we respond to the presence of Jesus among us? Isn't he present with us when we are with other believers? Hmm . . . . I wonder about the extravagance of our display of love when Jesus is present among us. Even more revealing, how would we respond to the presence of someone like the woman among us who is so extravagant in her display of love?

TODAY'S PRAYER

Holy and Almighty God, my Abba Father, thank you for your overwhelming display of grace in Jesus. Jesus, thank you for being the extravagant sacrifice for my sins. While I have nothing that compares in value to the gifts you have given me, please receive my heartfelt praise, thanks, appreciation, and adoration. I offer them freely with all of my heart in thanks for all that you have done to save me, to give me your Spirit, to bless me with a spiritual gift to serve your people, and to make my character more like yours. Please remove from my heart anything that keeps me from appropriately displaying my love for you. In the name of Jesus, I offer my praise and eternal thanks. Amen.

CONTEXT: LUKE 7:36-50
Related Passages: 1 Peter 1:8-9; Romans 7:24-25; Revelation 4:9-11

Day 125

SPEAKING TO OUR THOUGHTS!

Luke 7:39-40

When the Pharisee who asked Jesus to come to his house saw this, he thought to himself, "If this man were a prophet, he would know that the woman who is touching him is a sinner!"

In response, Jesus said to the Pharisee, "Simon, I have something to say to you." Simon said, "Let me hear it, Teacher."

KEY THOUGHT

Jesus heard and answered the Pharisee's thoughts. I don't want Jesus answering my thoughts in front of a room full of important guests. I have some thoughts that aren't as righteous as I would like. I'm trying to "take every thought captive" (2 Cor. 10:5). Unfortunately my intentions and my performance aren't always congruent. How about yours? Since we are led by the Spirit, Jesus does answer our thoughts. All too often we are not open to hearing his voice because it comes in forms less direct than the words this Pharisee is about to receive. Jesus can answer our thoughts in the sermon on Sunday or by stray comments in it. Jesus can answer our thoughts through the books we read, songs we hear, and conversations we have. Sometimes it takes a boatload of these messages to get through to us, but they are there if we are listening. If we begin each day with intending to walk with the Lord and be led by the Holy Spirit, then God is shaping us through the events, conversations, and messages we receive. Jesus still knows our thoughts! He still speaks to them through his Word and through his Spirit. Let's tear down the wall between the secular and the sacred and let Jesus be Lord of all of life. Let's begin each day with the words of Simon, "Let me hear it, Teacher."

TODAY'S PRAYER

O precious and majestic Father, God of all the universe and my Abba Father, awaken my mind and open my heart to hear all that you are seeking to say to me through your Word, through your world, and through your people. Open my heart to your messages in my everyday life. In Jesus' name I pray. Amen.

CONTEXT: LUKE 7:36-50
Related Passages: Psalm 19:1-4, 9-14; Philippians 2:12-13; Romans 8:28-30

Day 126

FORGIVEN THE GREATER DEBT

Luke 7:41-43

Jesus said, "There were two men. Both men owed money to the same banker. One man owed him 500 silver coins. The other man owed him 50 silver coins. The men had no money, so they could not pay their debt. But the banker told the men that they did not have to pay him. Which one of those two men will love him more?"

Simon answered, "I think it would be the one who owed him the most money."

Jesus said to him, "You are right."

KEY THOUGHT

Have you been forgiven much? That's the whole issue with our Christian walk. Joy, appreciation, and thanksgiving are the heartfelt responses to a deep realization that in Jesus Christ, God has forgiven us of everything! We have been forgiven of more than "much"; we've been forgiven of everything! How can we not love much? How can we not show that love extravagantly?

TODAY'S PRAYER

Holy and righteous God, thank you so much for sending Jesus to pay the price for my sin so that you could forgive me of everything. How can I ever express my appreciation appropriately? I'm not sure, dear Father, but I offer you my life, my love, and my all in deepest appreciation. In Jesus' name I pray. Amen.

CONTEXT: LUKE 7:36-50
Related Passages: Psalm 103:1-5; Romans 5:6-11; Ephesians 1:7

Day 127

WHAT ARE YOU SHOWING?

Luke 7:44-47

Then he turned to the woman and said to Simon, "Do you see this woman? When I came into your house, you gave me no water for my feet. But she washed my feet with her tears and dried my feet with her hair. You did not greet me with a kiss, but she has been kissing my feet since I came in. You did not honor me with oil for my head, but she rubbed my feet with her sweet-smelling oil. I tell you that her many sins are forgiven. This is clear, because she showed great love. People who are forgiven only a little will love only a little."

KEY THOUGHT

What are you showing the Lord about your appreciation for what he has done for you? Is it merely what is required or expected by religious convention? Is it less than that? Or is it extravagant and heartfelt? Is it driven by obligation, religious convention, or deep appreciation—propelled by love? This woman's display of love convicts me. Jesus said that her sins were forgiven and it was clear "because she showed great love." Do I show Jesus great love? Or do I only show a little?

TODAY'S PRAYER

Father, thank you! Thank you a million times over! May my words of praise, my gifts of thanksgiving, and my life of service be the beginning of thanks to you which I anticipate sharing with you in a fuller way when I stand before you face to face and share in the joy of my coming home. In Jesus' name, and by his gift of grace, I pray. Amen.

CONTEXT: LUKE 7:36-50
Related Passages: 1 Peter 1:3-9; 1 John 3:1-2; Ephesians 2:1-10

Day 128

THREE PHRASES THAT MEAN EVERYTHING

Luke 7:48-50
Then Jesus said to her, "Your sins are forgiven."

The people sitting at the table began to think to themselves, "Who does this man think he is? How can he forgive sins?"

Jesus said to the woman, "Because you believed, you are saved from your sins. Go in peace."

KEY THOUGHT

Jesus, our Savior, says, "Your sins are forgiven . . . . Because you believed, you are saved from your sins. Go in peace." Can you think of anything sweeter? Three sentences that mean everything! We can even abbreviate them to three words: forgiven, saved, peace. Do these words describe me? What about you? How could we not be extravagant in our response to these three incredible gifts of grace? And when the woman responds to these gifts with extravagant love, Jesus affirms her in front of her critics.

TODAY'S PRAYER

Thank you, Father, for receiving my gifts of thanks and appreciation. Thank you, Lord Jesus, for affirming those gifts given in your honor by reminding me and the hosts of heaven that I'm forgiven, saved, and given the gift of peace. Even in returning my thanks, you bless me! All praise to the Father for his sacrificial love! All thanks to the Lord Jesus for his saving gift! All thanks to the Holy Spirit for filling my heart with joy! Amen.

CONTEXT: LUKE 7:36-50
Related Passages: Mark 2:1-12; Luke 8:43-48; Luke 19:5-10

Day 129

SUPPORTING THE SAVIOR

Luke 8:1-3

The next day, Jesus traveled through some cities and small towns. Jesus told the people a message from God, the Good News about God's kingdom. The twelve apostles were with him. There were also some women with him. Jesus had healed these women of sicknesses and evil spirits. One of them was Mary, who was called Magdalene. Seven demons had come out of her. Also with these women were Joanna, the wife of Chuza (the manager of Herod's property), Suzanna, and many other women. These women used their own money to help Jesus and his apostles.

KEY THOUGHT

Many Bible students have never thought about how Jesus and his followers paid for the ministry needs. Luke lets his readers know. Women who accompanied him and the twelve, along with others, helped fund the Savior and his closest followers. Today, many ministries and mission efforts that do the work of Christ go wanting because they cannot find financial support. Others that do continue to minister have to give up valuable time and energy to keep their work supported. Please, think about helping keep the Lord's work on track by offering your support to the Lord's work today.

TODAY'S PRAYER

Father, please bless the following ministries that need your power and grace to continue doing your work . . . Father, please bless all who are giving themselves in sharing the life and love of Jesus with people all over the world. In Jesus' name I ask this. Amen.

CONTEXT: LUKE 8:1-3
Related Passages: 2 Corinthians 9:6-10; Philippians 1:3-6; Philippians 4:10-14

Day 130

A STORY FOR THE CROWD

Luke 8:4
*A large crowd came together. People came to Jesus from
every town, and he told them this story:*

KEY THOUGHT

Jesus used stories to help drive home his message, to plant a seed to help people remember a biblical truth, or to help give his hearers insight. Stories are an essential part of the Master's ministry. Stories are powerful and stick in our hearts. Much of the Bible is written in stories. The four Gospels tell the story of Jesus' earthly ministry and the book of Acts tells the story of Jesus' ministry through the early church. One of the great ways for you to gain a firm grasp of the New Testament, or even the whole Bible, is to keep a notebook with a list of the Bible's stories in it, the references where each story can be found, and a one-sentence summary of the lesson it teaches. If Jesus used stories to communicate God's truth, then let's learn those stories and let them come to life in us!

TODAY'S PRAYER

Father, thank you for the story of your love and grace found in the Bible. Thank you that Jesus used stories to communicate many of your truths. Please help me to learn these stories and have the Holy Spirit open my mind and heart to understand and apply them to my life. In Jesus' name I pray. Amen.

CONTEXT: LUKE 8:4-15
Related Passages: Mark 1:35-38; Luke 15:11; Luke 18:1

Day 131

TOO MANY STORIES?

Luke 8:5-10

[Jesus said] "A farmer went out to sow seed. While he was scattering the seed, some of it fell beside the road. People walked on the seed, and the birds ate it all. Other seed fell on rock. It began to grow but then died because it had no water. Some other seed fell among thorny weeds. This seed grew, but later the weeds stopped the plants from growing. The rest of the seed fell on good ground. This seed grew and made 100 times more grain."

Jesus finished the story. Then he called out, "You people who hear me, listen!"

Jesus' followers asked him, "What does this story mean?"

He said, "You have been chosen to know the secret truths about God's kingdom. But I use stories to speak to other people. I do this so that, Jesus' Followers See His Power 'They will look, but they will not see, and they will listen, but they will not understand.'"

KEY THOUGHT

"Too many people today just want to be entertained with stories. What I like is just good ol' plain, Bible-based preaching!" I've heard that a time or two. Yet God's greatest preachers, Jesus included, made frequent use of stories and illustrations in their preaching and prophecies. Can a person use too many stories? Probably not if the stories are used like Jesus used them—to help his listeners gain insight and have visual cues to help them remember the main point of his message. Jesus sometimes used stories to make things clear to his followers while making them confusing to his critics. Stories can be used frivolously or to manipulate the emotions of people. But they can be used powerfully to drive home important spiritual truths.

TODAY'S PRAYER

Father, thank you for the power of stories to illustrate your truth and to help me remember that truth more easily. Thank you for giving me the Bible, which is full of all sorts of stories that tell of your work in the world and your love for your people. Bless me as I take time each day to open my heart to that story. In Jesus' name I thank you. Amen.

CONTEXT: LUKE 8:4-15
Related Passages: Matthew 13:9-13; Luke 13:9-13; Mark 12:12

Day 132

WE DON'T SHARE THE MESSAGE IN A VACUUM

Luke 8:11-12

[Jesus said] "This is what the story means: The seed is God's teaching.
Some people are like the seed that fell beside the path. They hear God's
teaching, but then the devil comes and causes them to stop thinking
about it. This keeps them from believing it and being saved."

KEY THOUGHT

As we share the message of Jesus, we need to know that there are all sorts
of forces, powers, and people who will seek to destroy, corrupt, and negate
that message in the hearts of those who are open to God's Kingdom. Sharing
the message of Jesus Christ is far more than sharing our religious opinions;
it is spiritual warfare against the evil one and all of his forces. He does not
want Jesus' name honored or God's Kingdom to rule in the hearts of men
and women. That's why the apostle Paul solicited prayers for his efforts to
share the gospel. That's why he was sometimes met with fierce opposition and
persecution. Those who share the message of God's grace in Jesus take on, not
just the power of closed-minded, hard-hearted, and bigoted people, but the
powers of hell. It will sometimes not be easy, but we can always be assured of
ultimate and eternal victory!

TODAY'S PRAYER

Father, may your will be done on earth as completely as it is in heaven. Please guard me
as I seek to live and to share your truth with those around me. Protect your servants who
share your good news with others. Please guard the hearts of those who are deciding about
the gospel right now. Help them see the radical choice they are facing. Give me boldness to
declare this message clearly and courageously. In Jesus' name I ask for this grace. Amen.

CONTEXT: LUKE 8:4-15
Related Passages: Ephesians 6:10-12; Colossians 1:11-13; 2 Thessalonians 3:1-3

Day 133

WILTING UNDER FIRE

Luke 8:13

[Jesus said] "Others are like the seed that fell on rock. That is like the people who hear God's teaching and gladly accept it. But they don't have deep roots. They believe for a while. But when trouble comes, they turn away from God."

KEY THOUGHT

Sometimes the gospel starts up in people's hearts, but things get too tough. The evil one brings his times of testing. Difficulties in life mount. Friends reject us now that our values have changed. Suddenly, it seems that we are under attack from every corner. Those who don't criticize, shun and avoid us. Will we hold onto faith? Even more, will those who are mature help rescue those who get pulled away? All of us will go through periods of testing in our lives. The real issue is whether we have friends who love us enough to encourage us and to help us not "cave in" to the pressures of testing and temptation. So let's be that kind of friend to new Christians. Let's not let the overwhelming changes in their lifestyle, friends, and values make them vulnerable to isolation and abandonment!

TODAY'S PRAYER

Father, forgive me for not paying more attention to your new children in the faith. Open my eyes, help me see where they are in their journeys with you, and encourage them in ways that are a blessing. I know that even your Son went through a period of temptation and testing shortly after he was baptized. I fully expect that new Christians will face similar challenges. Please use me to bless, encourage, and strengthen them. In Jesus' name I pray. Amen.

CONTEXT: LUKE 8:4-15
Related Passages: Hebrews 3:12-14; Galatians 6:1-2; James 5:19-20

Day 134

THE THREAT OF TOO MUCH

Luke 8:14

[Jesus said] "What about the seed that fell among the thorny weeds? That is like the people who hear God's teaching, but they let the worries, riches, and pleasures of this life stop them from growing. So they never produce a crop."

KEY THOUGHT

We have more things than most people who have lived could ever imagine. However, rather than making things so much better, they tend to crowd out our allegiance to and passion for the Lord. Too many voices are competing for our attention and Jesus' voice gets drowned out. We become stunted in our growth—anemic believers who do not develop in our discipleship as we should. We face a huge battle with complacency, passion, commitment, and allegiance simply because we have too much.

TODAY'S PRAYER

O gracious and Almighty Lord, the God and Father of Jesus Christ, thank you for your powerful deliverance. I now ask that you deliver me from the threat of having my eyes diverted away from you by the things I possess. Through your Holy Spirit, instill a new heart within me. Turn me in faith to your Son with passion and devotion. In Jesus' name I pray. Amen.

CONTEXT: LUKE 8:4-15
Related Passages: 1 Timothy 6:6-10; Luke 18:24-28; Luke 16:13

Day 135

READY TO PRODUCE FRUIT

Luke 8:15

[Jesus said] "And what about the seed that fell on the good ground?
That is like the people who hear God's teaching with a good, honest
heart. They obey it and patiently produce a good crop."

KEY THOUGHT

Good soil! That's what the message of Jesus, the gospel of the Kingdom of God, is looking to find. What is that good soil? It is a heart that is open, honest, and good—a heart that is genuinely searching for truth. Is that your heart? Fruitfulness is the natural spiritual result of a heart that is open to God and that clings to the message of God's good news. How's your heart?

TODAY'S PRAYER

O Father, may the words of my mouth and the meditations of my heart be
pleasing to you. Guard my heart from evil. Protect my heart from pettiness.
Use your Spirit to cleanse my heart of every residue of evil, unrighteousness,
and ungodliness. Purify my heart and make it ready to produce the fruit
of your character, grace, and love. In Jesus' name I pray. Amen.

CONTEXT: LUKE 8:4-15
Related Passages: Luke 10:1-2; James 3:13-18; Proverbs 4:23; Luke 6:45

Day 136

OPEN TO JESUS' TEACHING

Luke 8:16-18

[Jesus said] "No one lights a lamp and then covers it with a bowl or hides it under a bed. Instead, they put the lamp on a lampstand so that the people who come in will have enough light to see. Everything that is hidden will become clear. Every secret thing will be made known, and everyone will see it. So think carefully about what you are hearing. The people who have some understanding will receive more. But those who do not have understanding will lose even what they think they have."

KEY THOUGHT

Are you open to what Jesus says? It isn't hidden. It is said to bring light to your darkness. The real issue is whether you and I are willing to pay attention to what he says and long to know and to live what we hear. We may not grasp all of what he says at first, but over time, as our hearts are open, more understanding comes. As the Holy Spirit works in our hearts, as our hearts yearn to know more of Jesus, and as we put into practice what we have already heard and understood, deeper insight and a more productive life follow. Let's open our hearts to Jesus' teaching and open our lives to be the place where his light is seen.

TODAY'S PRAYER

Father, I ask for your Spirit of knowledge so that I can know you better. I pray that out of your glorious riches, you open my heart to the deeper things of your truth. I recognize, dear Father, that my part in this dance of grace is to put into practice today, and each day, the truth that I understand. So I offer my day, my future, and myself to you. I trust that as I receive and obey the words of Jesus, you will open my heart to know you, your Son, and your truth more fully. In Jesus' name I pray. Amen.

CONTEXT: LUKE 8:16-21
Related Passages: Ephesians 1:15-17; 1 Corinthians 2:6-14; John 8:31-32

Day 137

TRUE FAMILY—LUKE 8:19-21

Jesus' mother and brothers came to visit him. But they could not get close to him, because there were so many people. Someone said to Jesus, "Your mother and your brothers are standing outside. They want to see you."

Jesus answered them, "My mother and my brothers are those who listen to God's teaching and obey it."

KEY THOUGHT

We can be a part of Jesus' true family! We can be Jesus' brother or sister! God presented this gift to us as his way of grace. The word grace actually has two meanings wrapped up into one word. Grace means an undeserved gift as well as having in mind the thankful response to that gift. We become God's children by God's grace, and our initial response of faith is demonstrated through our baptism (Gal. 3:26-29). Then, we are to be obedient to what God has taught us in Jesus, showing we are God's children by our behavior—this is Jesus' point in this statement. It is God's grace, not our obedience that makes us God's children. We obey out of genuine appreciation for his grace; and then the character we reveal shows we are part of the family. So what does your life show? Are you living out the grace you have received? Does the character of the Father shine through your behavior? Do you show you are part of Jesus' family by how you live?

TODAY'S PRAYER

Father of mercy and grace, how can I thank you enough for the incredible gift of grace you have given me in Jesus? I can never fully show my appreciation, but please accept my heartfelt intention to joyously obey the teachings of your Son and my heartfelt desire to reflect your holy character and compassion in all that I do and say. In Jesus' name I pray. Amen.

CONTEXT: LUKE 8:16-25
Related Passages: Galatians 3:26-29; Ephesians 2:8-10; James 2:19-23

Day 138

THE POWER OF HIS WORD

Luke 8:22-24

One day Jesus and his followers got into a boat. He said to them, "Come with me across the lake." And so they started across. While they were sailing, Jesus slept. A big storm blew across the lake, and the boat began to fill with water. They were in danger. The followers went to Jesus and woke him. They said, "Master! Master! We will drown!"

Jesus got up. He gave a command to the wind and the waves.
The wind stopped, and the lake became calm.

KEY THOUGHT

Jesus has been teaching about the power of his words and how we must obey them. Now, we see a powerful demonstration of Jesus' authority and just how powerful his words are. Jesus speaks and the elements obey him. He rules over nature! His words have power over the storm! Since Jesus' words are so powerful, shouldn't we obey them, too?

TODAY'S PRAYER

Wow! Father, your Son Jesus is awesome and glorious. His words can calm the raging storm simply by speaking and it is so. My prayer is that his words will have that same impact on me. May the words Jesus speaks produce immediate results in my life. As I obey, I truly believe that those very words will calm the restlessness of my soul. In the mighty name of Jesus, I pray. Amen.

CONTEXT: LUKE 8:16-25
Related Passages: Hebrews 1:3; Colossians 1:15-17; 2 Peter 3:3-9

Day 139

WHO IS THIS MAN?

Luke 8:24-25

The followers went to Jesus and woke him. They said, "Master! Master! We will drown!"

Jesus got up. He gave a command to the wind and the waves. The wind stopped, and the lake became calm. He said to his followers, "Where is your faith?"

They were afraid and amazed. They said to each other, "What kind of man is this? He commands the wind and the water, and they obey him."

KEY THOUGHT

The question Jesus' followers ask answers itself. Only the Creator controls creation. No human can. Only God can bring calm to the storm and order out of chaos. This Jesus they follow is much more than a mere mortal; he is the Creator in human flesh! His words must be met with faith and obedience. His words bring grace, mercy, and peace!

TODAY'S PRAYER

Almighty God, the Father of all, I praise you for your creation. I confess that my mind cannot adequately grasp all that it means for Jesus to be fully you and yet to have come in the limitations of human flesh. Yet I praise you for that grace and I offer you my life in obedience to your gift. In Jesus' name I offer you my praise. Amen.

CONTEXT: LUKE 8:16-25
Related Passages: John 1:1-4, 10-14, 17-18; Ephesians 3:14-15; 1 Corinthians 8:5-6

Day 140

WHEN SATAN ENTERS A LIFE

Luke 8:26-29

Jesus and his followers sailed on across the lake. They sailed to the area where the Gerasene people live, across from Galilee. When Jesus got out of the boat, a man from that town came to him. This man had demons inside him. For a long time he had worn no clothes. He did not live in a house but in the caves where the dead are buried.

The demon inside the man had often seized him, and he had been put in jail with his hands and feet in chains. But he would always break the chains. The demon inside him would force him to go out to the places where no one lived. Jesus commanded the evil spirit to come out of the man. When the man saw Jesus, he fell down before him, shouting loudly, "What do you want with me, Jesus, Son of the Most High God? Please, don't punish me!"

KEY THOUGHT

Never lose sight of the underlying truth in this event: when Satan enters a life, this is his ultimate goal—isolation, self-inflicted pain, anguish, death, and loss of human identity. While temptations are presented as alluring shortcuts to things we want, the evil one uses them as traps to ensnare us and deceive us into letting him take control. His alluring bait comes at first with a host of pleasures. In the end, however, they lead to all that we see in the man's tormented life in today's story. Remember this man the next time temptation knocks. Understand, this is Satan's desire for you, and surrendering to his power through sin is the open door for him to enter and take control.

TODAY'S PRAYER

Father, open my eyes so that I am not blind to the deceptive tricks and the alluring temptations of Satan. Banish him, I ask in the mighty name of Jesus, from any control in my life. Remove, through your Holy Spirit, any broken and mangled thinking that sin's residue has left in my life. Keep me in my right mind and give me a pure heart to distinguish your truth from Satan's lies. In Jesus' name I ask for this spiritual wisdom. Amen.

CONTEXT: LUKE 8:26-39
Related Passages: John 8:42-47; 2 Corinthians 2:9-11; Ephesians 6:10-11

Day 141

RECLAIMING IDENTITY

Luke 8:30-33
Jesus asked him, "What is your name?"

The man answered, "Legion." (He said his name was "Legion" because many demons had gone into him.) The demons begged Jesus not to send them into the bottomless pit. On that hill there was a big herd of pigs eating. The demons begged Jesus to allow them to go into the pigs. So he allowed them to do this. Then the demons came out of the man and went into the pigs. The herd of pigs ran down the hill into the lake, and all were drowned.

KEY THOUGHT

God made us in our mother's womb, carefully putting us together in a wonderful way for his very purpose (Psalm 139:13-16). We were designed to do something wonderful. Satan, however, tries to destroy our identity and rob us of God's purpose. This man had lost his name and was known only by the evil powers that controlled him. But, just as Jesus has power over the storm, his words have power over Satan and his hordes of evil. Jesus' presence, power, and words judge and destroy the work of Satan that had kept this man in bondage and on the edge of death. Jesus gives the man back himself as he drives away the evil by his command. He can do the same with you, if you will ask him.

TODAY'S PRAYER

Father, today I praise you for the power in Jesus' name and the authority of Jesus' words. With deep reverence and respect, I ask Jesus to drive out every vestige of evil in my life. I believe that only by his power can I find lasting peace. So Lord Jesus, take control of my life. In Jesus' name I pray and I also order every spirit of deception and destruction to cease its ugly influence in my life. I ask for you to send the Holy Spirit to cleanse what I already know he inhabits—my very soul. Amen.

CONTEXT: LUKE 8:26-39
Related Passages: Luke 11:13; 1 John 4:4; Colossians 2:11-15

Day 142

HE WILL GO AWAY AND LEAVE YOU ALONE

Luke 8:34-37

The men who were caring for the pigs ran away and told the story in the fields and in the town. People went out to see what had happened. They came to Jesus and found the man sitting there at the feet of Jesus. The man had clothes on and was in his right mind again; the demons were gone. This made the people afraid. The men who saw these things happen told the others all about how Jesus made the man well. All those who lived in the area around Gerasa asked Jesus to go away because they were afraid.

So Jesus got into the boat to go back to Galilee.

KEY THOUGHT

Jesus' power can be quite threatening to those who do not know him and are not looking for God's work in their lives. While what Jesus did to liberate this man is amazing, it is also threatening. Someone who can command thousands of demons to obey him certainly will have some clean up work to do in other lives, even mine. So let's be very honest with ourselves today. Do we want Jesus to be in control, or do we want to play the religious game? Jesus will leave us alone to fend for ourselves against the forces of evil if we choose to ignore, dismiss, or reject him. While he longs to save, he will not force himself on us. True deliverance comes to those who are willing to fully and wholeheartedly surrender to his grace and find their freedom and peace in him.

TODAY'S PRAYER

Father, my prayer is that the commitment reflected by the words of the old hymn is truly reflected in my life: "All to Jesus, I surrender; all to him I freely give." Today I surrender my will to your Son. In Jesus' name I pray. Amen.

CONTEXT: LUKE 8:26-39
Related Passages: Revelation 3:20-22; Romans 1:1-5; 14:9; Philippians 2:5-11

Day 143

GO AND TELL

Luke 8:38-39

The man he had healed begged to go with him. But Jesus sent him away, saying, "Go back home and tell people what God did for you."

So the man went all over town telling what Jesus had done for him.

KEY THOUGHT

Unlike so many others to whom Jesus gives the opposite instruction, Jesus commands this man to go tell what has happened in his life. Why? Probably because this man wasn't Jewish and the people in his family didn't have expectations of the Messiah. We can't be sure. But we can be sure of this: Jesus has asked us to tell others what he has done to bless us. So let's take him seriously. Sit down and write out a page of what all Jesus has done to bless your life. Then rehearse it enough to be able to share it with others when God gives you the chance. Then, begin to pray for God to open your eyes to the people around you who are waiting to hear this good news!

TODAY'S PRAYER

Father, open my eyes to the people around me who are aching to receive the good news of your grace in Jesus. Please give me the words and the wisdom to share Jesus in a loving way. I pray today especially for the following people and ask you to be at work in each of their lives so they can come to know Jesus . . . . In Jesus' name I ask for this grace. Amen.

CONTEXT: LUKE 8:26-39
Related Passages: 1 Peter 3:15-16; Matthew 28:18-20; Colossians 1:28-29

Day 144

WAITING FOR JESUS

Luke 8:40-42

*When Jesus went back to Galilee, the people welcomed him. Everyone was waiting
for him. A man named Jairus came to him. He was a leader of the synagogue.
He had only one daughter. She was twelve years old, and she was dying. So
Jairus bowed down at the feet of Jesus and begged him to come to his house.*

While Jesus was going to Jairus' house, the people crowded all around him.

KEY THOUGHT

If the folks on the other side of the lake were afraid of Jesus (the final
reaction of the pig herders in the previous story), on the Capernaum side
they were waiting for him. The crowds longed to be with Jesus because they
expected him to work miracles for them. One man, an important man in the
community, was particularly anxious for Jesus' return. His only daughter
was very ill and he wanted Jesus to come heal her. However, the crowds
mobbed Jesus. On the other side of the Sea of Galilee, Jesus had faced
demonic opposition and misunderstanding that led to rejection. On this side,
he faced the problems of popularity and acceptance that were based upon
misunderstanding. In many ways, these stories are opposites. Even the final
command in each story is an opposite. However, these stories represent the
wide-ranging styles of attack that Satan uses to try to ruin the work of God –
popularity and rejection. Jesus, however, ensures that God's work is done no
matter the circumstance.

TODAY'S PRAYER

*Give me faith, O God, that you will work in all of my life's situations
for your glory and my good. I believe you can help me overcome any
obstacle, problem, or temptation that Satan throws my way. Please
show your victory in my life. I pray this in Jesus' name. Amen.*

CONTEXT: LUKE 8:40-56
Related Passages: Romans 8:28-30; Philippians 1:6; 2:13; Jude 24-25

Day 145

A SECOND DESPERATE PERSON

Luke 8:43-44
A woman was there who had been bleeding for twelve years. She had spent all her money on doctors, but no doctor was able to heal her. The woman came behind Jesus and touched the bottom of his coat. At that moment, her bleeding stopped.

KEY THOUGHT

Jairus wasn't the only person desperate for Jesus' help. A woman was equally desperate. Jairus was the ruler of the synagogue, with money to use to influence people, and had many who would plead his case for him. Here was a woman who was kept from the synagogue because she was considered unclean under the Jewish Law because of her hemorrhaging, and she was all alone and without money. However, these people from opposite extremes had two things in common: first, they had a great need, and second, they both had faith that Jesus could do something miraculous for them. In each case, as the two stories tell us, they received their miracle and much more. So what is the message for us? No matter who we are or where we come from, Jesus loves us and will help us if we will come to him in faith.

TODAY'S PRAYER

Father, I believe, but help my belief to grow stronger. In Jesus' name I ask you for this grace and growth in my faith. Amen.

CONTEXT: LUKE 8:40-56
Related Passages: John 3:16-17; 1 John 2:1-2; Matthew 28:18-20

Day 146

AFFIRMING HER FAITH TO GIVE HER PEACE

Luke 8:45-48
Then Jesus said, "Who touched me?"

*They all said they had not touched him. And Peter said, "Master,
people are all around you, pushing against you."*

*But Jesus said, "Someone touched me. I felt power go out from me." When the
woman saw that she could not hide, she came forward, shaking. She bowed
down before Jesus. While everyone listened, she told why she touched him. Then
she said that she was healed immediately when she touched him. Jesus said to
her, "My daughter, you are made well because you believed. Go in peace."*

KEY THOUGHT

This woman comes for healing. She receives much more than that. Jesus
refuses for the woman to receive an anonymous miracle. Instead, he has her
come forward and then praises her faith and dismisses her to live in peace. She is
not only healed; she is praised! In her fear and isolation she ventures out in faith
and receives a double blessing. Jesus not only healed her disease, but he restores
her back to a place in society with his words of praise. He didn't call her out to
embarrass her, but to restore her! Jesus longs to heal us and make us whole.

TODAY'S PRAYER

*O Lord God, my Abba Father, may my faith be as bold and as
unrelenting as this woman's faith. Stir me to courage and action. I
ask for this boldness and passion in Jesus' name. Amen.*

CONTEXT: LUKE 8:40-56
Related Passages: Matthew 21:21; Luke 7:4-9; Mark 6:5

Day 147

THE HARD MOMENT OF TRUST

Luke 8:49-50

While Jesus was still speaking, someone came from the house of the synagogue leader and said, "Your daughter has died! Don't bother the Teacher anymore."

Jesus heard this and said to Jairus, "Don't be afraid!
Just believe and your daughter will be well."

KEY THOUGHT

For nearly all of us, there will come a time of crisis when everything we hold dear appears to be lost. Faith may not have been hard for us in the past, but this will be the moment of truth. Will our faith hold? Is what we believe true? Can we trust Jesus in our crisis, even when we can't see a positive outcome? When all seems lost and everyone else has doubts, Jesus comes to us and says, "Don't be afraid. Just trust me!" In some of my life's worst moments, I heard the Savior. In some of them, I wasn't even listening. I am so thankful that Jesus not only notices the seeking heart, but that he runs to the retreating and broken-hearted.

TODAY'S PRAYER

Holy God, the Lord Almighty, please help my faith hold firm in the worst of times and keep me pure and undistracted in the best of times. And in those times when I've lost my way, please come find me. I cannot make it through life without the love of Jesus, in whose name I pray. Amen.

CONTEXT: LUKE 8:40-56
Related Passages: Mark 9:20-24; John 6:16-24; Luke 12:29-32

Day 148
JUST A FEW

Luke 8:51-53

Jesus went to the house. He let only Peter, John, James, and the girl's father and mother go inside with him. Everyone was crying and feeling sad because the girl was dead. But Jesus said, "Don't cry. She is not dead. She is only sleeping."

The people laughed at him, because they knew that the girl was dead.

KEY THOUGHT

Just a few well-chosen people witness the miracle that is described in the verses that follow—mom, dad, Peter, James, and John. Why? The answer is really quite simple. Jesus didn't do miracles to show out, to raise money, or to garner a following. Jesus did his miracles to demonstrate God's love for broken, wounded, and grieving people. This was a moment of grief and heartbreak. It was also a moment of incredible joy and wonder. Jesus was not about to let the crowd hijack this moment from Jairus and his wife and daughter. For these chosen few, and for those of us who get to read this beautifully sensitive account of an incredible miracle, Jesus reveals that, when he is present, death becomes only sleep.

TODAY'S PRAYER

Heavenly Father, give me faith to believe that, because of my faith in your Son, death becomes a brief parting and not a permanent separation. In Jesus' name I ask. Amen.

CONTEXT: LUKE 8:40-56
Related Passages: 1 Thessalonians 4:13-18; 1 Corinthians 15:51-53; 2 Corinthians 5:6-9

Day 149

HER LIFE RETURNED

Luke 8:54-56

But Jesus held her hand and called to her, "Little girl, stand up!" Her spirit came back into her, and she stood up immediately. Jesus said, "Give her something to eat." The girl's parents were amazed. He told them not to tell anyone about what happened.

KEY THOUGHT

I have a good friend who lost his hearing when he was just a boy. He talks about the first words he will ever hear. At the coming of the Lord, Jesus will say to him, "Lloyd, it's time to get up and go home with me!" Each of us who belongs to the Lord will one day hear that same voice, and everything will change, including us! Just as in this encounter with a dead girl, death is no match for the touch of Jesus and the lovingly strong command of his voice. He has power over death. Those who belong to him will hear his voice and death will be overcome forever!

TODAY'S PRAYER

Father, thank you for the victory that is mine in Jesus Christ my Lord. I praise you for overcoming death through Jesus' resurrection from the dead and sharing that victory with me. Thank you for giving me a reminder each week of this victory as I greet each Sunday and remember the Lord's victory over death. In his name I thank you. Amen.

CONTEXT: LUKE 8:40-56
Related Passages: John 5:25-26; Romans 8:18-25; 1 Corinthians 15:51-57

Day 150

AUTHORITY!

Luke 9:1-2

Jesus called his twelve apostles together. He gave them power to heal sicknesses and power to force demons out of people. He sent them to tell about God's kingdom and to heal the sick.

KEY THOUGHT

The word translated "power" literally means "that authoritative power to act." This authority is something that really belongs only to God, Jesus, and the Holy Spirit. Jesus created and now sustains the universe. He has authoritative power to act! This power to act is also his because of his loving obedience and sacrifice to redeem us on the cross. It is his because of his resurrection from the dead. All authority is his—to use, to command, and to give. Any authority we have is based on the Lord Jesus' gracious giving of it to us. We should have no sense of selfish pride or arrogance. The glory belongs to Jesus for any good thing accomplished by us and any debilitating thing removed from us. In honoring him, we will find ourselves empowered to be a blessing to others.

TODAY'S PRAYER

Father God, thank you for your Son. To you and to your Son belong all honor, glory, wisdom, authority, and power. I offer myself to you as your servant. Use me in whatever way most brings you glory and most blesses your work and your people. In Jesus' name I pray. Amen.

CONTEXT: LUKE 9:1-9
Related Passages: Colossians 1:15-20; Philippians 2:5-11; Romans 1:3-4

Day 151

SHAKE THE DUST FROM YOUR FEET

Luke 9:3-5

He said to them, "When you travel, don't take a walking stick. Also, don't carry a bag, food, or money. Take for your trip only the clothes you are wearing. When you go into a house, stay there until it is time to leave. If the people in the town will not welcome you, go outside the town and shake the dust off your feet as a warning to them."

KEY THOUGHT

Some folks are determined to reject the message of Jesus. There are many reasons why this is true, but they all boil down to one truth: Satan has poisoned their hearts to the good news of God's Kingdom. Rather than keep beating our heads against a wall that the evil one has erected in the heart of someone, God calls us to move on in our efforts to reach others. If we are in the same family or office or neighborhood and have regular proximity to them and can't move on, then we are called to live our faith before them and pray that our actions will demonstrate the faith we profess and win them before the day of Christ.

TODAY'S PRAYER

Father, give me wisdom to know the best way to share the message of Jesus with all those that I know who are not yet Christians. Father, I recognize that only you can break down the barriers Satan erects in their hearts. Help me know when it is best to move on and leave that work to you. In the lives of those near and dear to me, please use my daily faithfulness as one of the influences used to win their hearts for Jesus, in whose name I pray. Amen.

CONTEXT: LUKE 9:1-9
Related Passages: 2 Corinthians 4:4; Acts 13:46-52; 1 Peter 3:1-4

Day 152

PREACHING AND HEALING

Luke 9:6
So the apostles went out. They traveled through all the towns.
They told the Good News and healed people everywhere.

KEY THOUGHT

Like Jesus' preaching, the preaching of the good news by the twelve involved an effort to reach both heart and body. I believe we should take away two important understandings from this. First, we are called to walk in the footsteps of Jesus and serve others as the Body of Christ. Together, as we all use our gifts, we are the physical presence of Jesus to the world. Second, authentic outreach involves both proclaiming the message of Christ and showing the compassion of Christ. One without the other is lacking and is less than the presence of Jesus to the broken of our world.

TODAY'S PRAYER

Holy and righteous Father, please give us the courage and the conviction to preach the good news and to serve the needs of those around us. God, I confess that doing both preaching and serving seems hard for us, so let this kind of authentic ministry be both active and effective through me. In Jesus' name I ask this. Amen.

CONTEXT: LUKE 9:1-9
Related Passages: Matthew 4:23-25; Luke 5:15; Ephesians 4:11-16

Day 153

FASCINATION WITH THE SAVIOR

Luke 9:7-9

Herod the ruler heard about all these things that were happening. He was confused because some people said, "John the Baptizer has risen from death." Others said, "Elijah has come to us." And some others said, "One of the prophets from long ago has risen from death." Herod said, "I cut off John's head. So who is this man I hear these things about?" Herod continued trying to see Jesus.

KEY THOUGHT

Jesus didn't do his miracles to impress people. However, Jesus' miracles were impressive. They were so impressive that Herod learned about them. He was curious and fascinated. Herod and the people speculated that Jesus might be connected to John the Baptizer, Elijah, and the prophets. These people were all impressive. However, Jesus isn't trying to be impressive; he wants to serve people and be the Savior of all people. He isn't trying to be fascinating, but Jesus is determined to be liberating. He came to set people free from all that held them back and kept them in bondage—diseases, demonic powers, and personal failures. He didn't come to gain a reputation as a great miracle worker. Like our Savior, let us work to bless others rather than trying to be impressive; let us serve rather than trying to be superstars.

TODAY'S PRAYER

Holy Father, I'm glad that Jesus didn't settle for an impressive reputation among the crowds. Thank you that he didn't work for popularity with the politically important. I am so thankful that he chose to invest himself in the lives of all sorts of people to make your grace known to folks like me. Thank you! In Jesus' name I pray. Amen.

CONTEXT: LUKE 9:7-9
Related Passages: Matthew 16:13-20; Mark 10:42-45; Luke 7:18-23

Day 154

SLIPPING QUIETLY AWAY!

Luke 9:10

*When the apostles came back, they told Jesus what they had done
on their trip. Then he took them away to a town called Bethsaida.
There, he and his apostles could be alone together.*

KEY THOUGHT

Jesus often worked to give his followers some quiet, down time, to be alone
with him. With the pressures of the crowd, the stress of their own experiences
in ministry, the challenges the Jesus' teaching gave them, and the pressures of
everyday living, Jesus knew that they needed rest. So do we! As the remainder
of this chapter reveals, sometimes that rest has to wait till more pressing
people-concerns pass, but Jesus makes clear that he does want us to rest and
recuperate. Our Lord and Savior, Jesus, wants us to rest so we are ready to
return to useful service and also to give us time alone in his presence.

TODAY'S PRAYER

*Father, please help me balance my work, opportunities, and rest in a more spiritually
responsible way. Please use me mightily, but also convict me when I'm focused too much
on being busy and not focused enough on being with you. In Jesus' name I ask this. Amen.*

CONTEXT: LUKE 9:1-9
Related Passages: Luke 5:15-16; John 6:14-15; Mark 6:31-32

Day 155

CALLED TO THE IMPOSSIBLE

Luke 9:11-14

But the people learned where Jesus went and followed him. He welcomed them and talked with them about God's kingdom. He healed the people who were sick.

Late in the afternoon, the twelve apostles came to Jesus and said, "No one lives in this place. Send the people away. They need to find food and places to sleep in the farms and towns around here."

But Jesus said to the apostles, "You give them something to eat."

They said, "We have only five loaves of bread and two fish. Do you want us to go buy food for all these people?" There are too many! (There were about 5000 men there.)

Jesus said to his followers, "Tell the people to sit in groups of about 50 people."

KEY THOUGHT

"You feed them." Don't you wish you could have seen their expressions when Jesus told them to feed the crowd? "Impossible!" they honestly replied. Their reply was correct, of course, based on standard human limitations. This realization was exactly what Jesus wanted them to confront. He was calling them to the impossible. Yet that is precisely what Jesus did through them and their meager resources. You may be hearing that same call from the Lord in your life today. While it isn't a call to feed 5,000 people out in the middle of nowhere, it still seems impossible. It may be a call to give up some secret sin or relationship, it may be a call to persevere under painful and difficult circumstances, it may be to keep loving someone who is unloving, or a host of other seemingly impossible challenges. Jesus does the impossible through ordinary folks like us!

TODAY'S PRAYER

Holy God, I'm not sure why I can believe in the resurrection of Jesus yet have problems believing you can do incredible, even impossible, things through me. Father, I need courage to believe that you can do your work through me even when it seems beyond my strength, and resources. So please, dear Lord, minister to my heart through this story of the feeding of the 5,000 and renew my faith that your Spirit can empower me to do more than I can even imagine. In Jesus' name I request this grace. Amen.

CONTEXT: LUKE 9:11-17
Related Passages: Ephesians 3:20-21; Luke 1:34-38; Luke 18:23-26

Day 156

NEAT, ORDERLY, AND MIRACULOUS

Luke 9:14-16

*(There were about 5000 men there.) Jesus said to his followers,
"Tell the people to sit in groups of about 50 people."*

*So the followers did this and everyone sat down. Then Jesus took the five loaves
of bread and two fish. He looked up into the sky and thanked God for the food.
Then he broke it into pieces, which he gave to the followers to give to the people.*

KEY THOUGHT

For those of us who have read this story, there is a bizarre element that
we often miss because of our familiarity. Jesus goes about his task in an
orderly and planned way. Then, right in the middle of executing his orderly
plan, he interjects the miraculous. It is like the creation story in Genesis 1,
told with such order and precision until you look at what is really happening
and then it is simply miraculous beyond description. We have a tendency to
segment people into the empirical, orderly, and predictable or the emotional,
expressive, and excitable. However, the Lord brings both together with a
prayer of blessing to provide a picnic for over 5,000. Jesus reminds us that
we need both types of approaches and people. Maybe this is an even more
powerful reminder that we need to be open and respectful to both approaches
in the same event. God brings order out of chaos and provides blessing out of
potential disaster and he does it in a neat, orderly, and astonishing way.

TODAY'S PRAYER

*Thank you, dear God, for being bigger than my stereotypes. Thank you for
calling me to be more than just my preferences. Thank you for bringing order
out of chaos. Thank you for providing order and symmetry. Thank you for
doing what defies description. Thank you for being sovereign and gracious,
as well as orderly and miraculous. In Jesus' name I thank you. Amen.*

CONTEXT: LUKE 9:11-17
Related Passages: Romans 12:6-8; 1 Corinthians 12:12-21; Ephesians 4:16

Day 157

HOLDING THE MIRACLE IN THEIR HANDS

Luke 9:17

They all ate until they were full. And there was a lot of food left. Twelve baskets were filled with the pieces of food that were not eaten.

KEY THOUGHT

Our story began with Jesus telling his followers to feed the 5,000 themselves. "Impossible!" was their reply. Yet when all is said and done, the twelve apostles picked up twelve baskets of leftovers. Each of them got to hold a bit of the miracle in his own hands. Jesus didn't want a single apostle to miss the point. Jesus was preparing them for what would follow in their ministry. One day soon, Jesus would not be physically present to help them, yet they would be called to do the impossible. He wants them to know that with his blessing, they can do it. Now he wants you and me to believe the same thing. If we will offer what we have to Jesus for him to bless and use, he can do incredible and miraculous things. The issue isn't Jesus' power, but our willingness to bring him what we have and who we are and let him do amazing things with us and through us.

TODAY'S PRAYER

Father, thank you for the twelve baskets of leftovers. As I offer myself to your service, please use me to bring you glory in big or small ways. Selfishly, dear Father, I ask that occasionally you let me find a "basketful of leftovers" to remind me of your powerful work. But please help me serve you faithfully even if I never get to hold those "leftovers" in my hand. In Jesus' name I pray. Amen.

CONTEXT: LUKE 9:11-17
Related Passages: John 1:43-51; Matthew 21:21; Ephesians 1:19-20

Day 158

INSIGHTS FROM TIMES OF PRAYER!

Luke 9:18-19

*One time Jesus was praying alone. His followers came together
there, and he asked them, "Who do the people say I am?"*

*They answered, "Some people say you are John the Baptizer. Others say you are Elijah.
And some people say you are one of the prophets from long ago that has come back to life."*

KEY THOUGHT

The Gospel of Luke reminds us that many great moments in Jesus' life and ministry are tied to prayer. Sometime soon, get a colored highlighter and read the Gospel of Luke and underline every time prayer occurs or is the subject of Jesus' teaching. Then go back and make an outline of key events tied to those prayer sessions. You will be amazed at how important prayer is to the unfolding of Jesus' ministry. Peter's confession of Jesus as the Christ follows this prayer time and the discussion that follows it. This is just another one of the Holy Spirit's reminders that fresh insights for life and faith often occur during our times of prayer. This was true for Jesus and his first followers and it will no doubt be true of us.

TODAY'S PRAYER

Father in heaven, God Almighty, thank you for providing me the great avenue and opportunity of prayer. To know that you listen to my words, my thoughts, and my heart is simply overwhelming. Help me to hunger more for these special times in your presence. Give me wisdom and understanding as I pray and seek your will. Do your will in my life as I seek your presence. In Jesus' name I pray. Amen.

CONTEXT: LUKE 9:18-27
Related Passages: James 1:5-6; Acts 4:31; Romans 8:26-27

YOU ARE ...!

Luke 9:20

Then Jesus said to his followers, "And who do you say I am?"

Peter answered, "You are the Christ from God."

KEY THOUGHT

No matter what the world might think of him—whether it is Herod or the crowd or the his enemies—Jesus' real concern was that his closest followers know his true identity. He would leave his mission in their hands. They would be called upon to put their lives on the line. They would be called to move from being merely followers to becoming followers who were leaders, mentors, and guides for thousands of others. Peter answers for them: "You are the Christ from God." Who is Jesus to you? Is he your Christ, your Messiah, the gift sent from God to save you? If not, what stands in your way?

TODAY'S PRAYER

Loving Father, full of mercy and compassion but altogether holy and righteous, thank you for sending Jesus. I truly believe that Jesus is your promised Messiah, sent by you to save me from my sins and to give me the assurance of an eternal home with you. So I praise and thank you in the name of Christ Jesus, my Lord. Amen.

CONTEXT: LUKE 9:18-27
Related Passages: Acts 2:; Romans 1:2-6; Matthew 26:62-64

Day 160

I MUST SUFFER!

Luke 9:21-22

Jesus warned them not to tell anyone. Then Jesus said, "The Son of Man must suffer many things. He will be rejected by the older Jewish leaders, the leading priests, and teachers of the law. And he will be killed. But after three days he will be raised from death."

KEY THOUGHT

Once the apostles had the right title for Jesus—the Christ from God—they needed to have that term redefined. While Jesus would have to repeat this reminder to them several times, they had to get it through their hard heads that God's servant, the Christ, would have to suffer and rise from the dead. Jesus would redefine everyone's expectations of the Christ. This was not because he was powerless to do it in another way, but because it was God's will that the Christ would suffer in an effort to reach all peoples and fulfill all the promises.

TODAY'S PRAYER

Dear Lord God Almighty, please give me courage to truly follow Jesus as Christ, my Messiah and Savior, all the way to the cross! In Jesus' name I pray. Amen.

CONTEXT: LUKE 9:18-27
Related Passages: Luke 24:44-48; Acts 8:29-38; 1 Peter 2:4

CRUCIFIED!

Luke 9:23
Jesus continued to say to all of them, "Any of you who want to be my follower must stop thinking about yourself and what you want. You must be willing to carry the cross that is given to you every day for following me."

KEY THOUGHT

If we are going to be one of Jesus' followers, one of his true disciples, we're going to have to be willing to walk in the way of the cross. That means giving up our selfish ambition and pride. That means we live to honor Christ and to bless others in his name. And it means that our trip to the cross must occur every day.

TODAY'S PRAYER

Father, may I never claim glory except for the glorious grace you have given me in the cross of Jesus upon which I have crucified my selfish desires and committed to trust in the salvation that is found in Jesus alone. In the Lord Jesus' name I pray. Amen.

CONTEXT: LUKE 9:18-27
Related Passages: Philippians 2:3-11; Galatians 2:20; Galatians 5:24-25

Day 162

WHAT'S IT WORTH?

Luke 9:24-25

[Jesus said] "Any of you who try to save the life you have will lose it. But you who give up your life for me will save it. It is worth nothing for you to have the whole world if you yourself are destroyed or lost."

KEY THOUGHT

We only get one lifetime on this earth. That's it. No more and no less. What we do in this life influences how we will spend eternal life. So if we live our lives trying to bring fulfillment to ourselves and to gain achievement that brings honor only to us, we're going to end up losing everything. They don't put trailer hitches on hearses for a reason: all we take with us into the next life is our relationship with Jesus and those who love him. So let's not pursue what is insignificant, inconsequential, and ultimately what is perishable. The only lasting investment for our lives is Jesus!

TODAY'S PRAYER

Clear my clouded vision, O God, so that I can see your will more clearly and not be distracted by my own selfishness and self-seeking. In Jesus' name I pray. Amen.

CONTEXT: LUKE 9:18-27
Related Passages: Haggai 1:3-6; Matthew 6:19-21; Philippians 3:7-9

Day 163

ASHAMED?

Luke 9:26-27

*[Jesus said] "Don't be ashamed of me and my teaching. If that happens,
I will be ashamed of you when I come with my divine greatness and that
of the Father and the holy angels. Believe me when I say that some of
you people standing here will see God's kingdom before you die."*

KEY THOUGHT

Many of us live in cultures that ridicule faith. Oh sure, some give passing
reference to Jesus, but their hearts don't belong to him and they might as
easily use his name in vain as they do in honor. I don't know about you, but I
sure don't want to make the Lord ashamed because of my behavior or my lack
of courage. I want to be bold and courageous with my faith in Jesus. Why?
Because he left heaven and went to the cross to boldly identify with me and
reclaim me as God's child! (See Hebrews 2:16-18)

TODAY'S PRAYER

*Give me courage and boldness, O God, that I might always demonstrate my allegiance
and my love for the Lord Jesus and for the sacrifices he made to claim me as your
child and his fellow heir of all that heaven offers. I ask this in Jesus' name. Amen.*

CONTEXT: LUKE 9:18-27
Related Passages: Romans 1:16-17; 2 Timothy 1:7-14; Philippians 1:20

Day 164

FULFILLING GOD'S PLAN

Luke 9:28-31

About eight days after Jesus said these things, he took Peter, James, and John and went up on a mountain to pray. While Jesus was praying, his face began to change. His clothes became shining white. Then two men were talking with Jesus. The men were Moses and Elijah. Moses and Elijah were shining bright too. They were talking with Jesus about his death that would happen in Jerusalem.

KEY THOUGHT

The glorious appearance of Moses and Elijah happens while Jesus is praying. Their mission appears to be one of affirmation. They are there to reinforce Jesus' conviction that he must go to Jerusalem and face rejection and death. This was not a new plan, but was the fulfillment of something God had planned much earlier. Jesus is not delusional. Jesus does not have a death wish. Jesus is not blindly ambitious and unaware of what awaits him. Jesus is headed to Jerusalem to do the will of God and fulfill the promises God had made over the centuries through his prophets. Jesus is the great reminder that God keeps his promises!

TODAY'S PRAYER

Thank you, dear Father, for your constant faithfulness to your promises. I am not used to people who scrupulously keep their word. Thank you for setting such a clear standard. Help me remember your faithfulness in those times when my life is hard and things are not going well. Sustain me as I seek to be faithful during difficult times. In Jesus' name I pray. Amen.

CONTEXT: LUKE 9:28-43
Related Passages: Luke 24:44-48; 1 Thessalonians 5:23-24; 2 Corinthians 1:20

Day 165

A TIME FOR SILENCE

Luke 9:32-34

Peter and the others were asleep. But they woke up and saw the glory of Jesus. They also saw the two men who were standing with him. When Moses and Elijah were leaving, Peter said, "Master, it is good that we are here. We will put three tents here—one for you, one for Moses, and one for Elijah." (He did not know what he was saying.)

While Peter was saying these things, a cloud came all around them. Peter, John, and James were afraid when the cloud covered them. A voice came from the cloud and said, "This is my Son. He is the one I have chosen. Obey him."

KEY THOUGHT

I can identify with Peter, can't you? He wakes up and sees this once-in-a-lifetime event and does not know what to do or say. Humility and awe would suggest that he remain silent and take his cue from Jesus. Instead, Peter talks when it is really a time for silence. However, his impertinent and shallow comments are put in their place as the event humbles him into silent terror. Reverence, awe, and listening are the proper responses to a glorious glimpse of Jesus in all of his glory!

TODAY'S PRAYER

O gracious heavenly Father, please forgive my compulsion to speak when I should be reverently silent. Humble me gently and help me see my proper response in the presence of your glorious Son with whom there is no equal, rival, or comparison. In Jesus' name I pray. Amen.

CONTEXT: LUKE 9:28-43
Related Passages: Ecclesiastes 5:1-6; James 1:19; Proverbs 17:28

Day 166

ONLY ONE

Luke 9:35-36
A voice came from the cloud and said, "This is my Son.
He is the one I have chosen. Obey him."

When the voice stopped, only Jesus was there. Peter, John, and James said nothing.
And for a long time after that, they told no one about what they had seen.

KEY THOUGHT

The Law and the Prophets were revered in Israel. They represented the
heart of God's communication with his people, Israel. Yet God has spoken to
us most clearly through his Son (Heb. 1:1-3) and we must listen to Jesus. Peter,
James, and John help us realize what we must do. As in awe as they were to see
Moses and Elijah, God's ultimate spokesman, Jesus the Christ, stood before
them. They must listen to Jesus. He is God's Son, the Christ, the Lord and
Savior, God's chosen messenger. Moses and Elijah pale in comparison with
Jesus. We, too, must listen and obey Jesus!

TODAY'S PRAYER

Holy God, help me look to Jesus as your Supreme Messenger and my
Savior. I recognize Jesus as the one who can most completely and fully
reveal you and your will to me. Lead my heart to honor him as my Lord
without rival. In Jesus' name, and for Jesus' glory, I ask it. Amen.

CONTEXT: LUKE 9:28-43
Related Passages: Hebrews 1:1-3; John 1:14-18; John 14:6

Day 167

MOUNTAINS AND VALLEYS

Luke 9:37-43a

The next day, Jesus, Peter, John, and James came down from the mountain.
A large group of people met Jesus. A man in the group shouted to him, "Teacher, please
come and look at my son. He is the only child I have. An evil spirit comes into him,
and then he shouts. He loses control of himself and foams at the mouth. The evil spirit
continues to hurt him and almost never leaves him. I begged your followers to make the
evil spirit leave my son, but they could not do it."

Jesus answered, "You people today have no faith. Your lives are all wrong. How long must
I be with you and be patient with you?" Then Jesus said to the man, "Bring your son here."

While the boy was coming, the demon threw the boy to the ground. The boy lost control of
himself. But Jesus gave a strong command to the evil spirit. Then the boy was healed, and
Jesus gave him back to his father. All the people were amazed at the great power of God.

KEY THOUGHT

Although Jesus' mountain peak experience (the transfiguration experience
with Moses and Elijah and God's blessing) was a great moment, he comes down
from the mountain to a great disappointment. A father says, "I begged your
followers . . . but they could not do it." After their great mission trip where they
preached and healed and after their experience in helping feed 5000 people, once
again they are reminded that on their own, they are limited and lacking. Just as
Jesus' closest followers often disappointed him, other Christian servants are likely
going to disappoint us. However, Jesus didn't give up on his followers and we
must not give up on each other when we let each other down. While he rebuked
them, he remained faithful to them. His goal was to make them into God's men.
He would not let his discouragement with them keep him from his task.

TODAY'S PRAYER

Father God, please help me not to be overly discouraged when other Christians
don't measure up to what I think they ought to be. Help me be gracious
with them just as you are. Guard my heart from bitter discouragement and
cynicism about the failure of other believers. In Jesus' name I pray. Amen.

CONTEXT: LUKE 9:28-43
Related Passages: Luke 6:42; 2 Corinthians 7:6; Galatians 6:9

Day 168

STAYING ON TASK

Luke 9:43-44
*The people were still amazed about all the things Jesus did. He said
to his followers, "Don't forget what I will tell you now: The Son of
Man will soon be handed over to the control of other men."*

KEY THOUGHT

Sometimes discouragement can derail us from our mission. Sometimes it
is pride that comes from praise—we sometimes call it "resting on our laurels."
Jesus, however, was not diverted. He stayed on task. He remembered his
mission. This was possible because of his daily walk with God in quiet prayer
time and his commitment to finish his Father's mission. Yesterday we focused
on not letting difficulties and disappointments, especially those that center
upon people, keep us from continuing in our mission for God. Today, we are
reminded not to let success and praise derail us through pride. While others
talked about all the wonderful things Jesus was doing, Jesus stayed focused on
developing his followers.

TODAY'S PRAYER

*Father, please help me not be diverted from my mission because of the praise
of others. While I genuinely appreciate the affirmation, I know my heart
can sometimes swell with pride. Thank you for the encouragement and keep
me on the path of honoring you. I ask this in Jesus' name. Amen.*

CONTEXT: LUKE 9:43-50
Related Passages: Acts 20:24; John 4:34; John 12:42-43

Day 169

A TRAITOR IN OUR MIDST

Luke 9:43-45

[Jesus said] "Don't forget what I will tell you now: The Son of Man will soon be
handed over to the control of other men." But the followers did not understand
what he meant. The meaning was hidden from them so that they could not
understand it. But they were afraid to ask Jesus about what he said.

KEY THOUGHT

At this moment of glory in his ministry—Jesus has just been transfigured,
has shown his healing power, and is being praised—Jesus reminds his
closest followers that treachery and betrayal lie ahead. While they could not
understand this, they could remember it. Failure, even horrible and colossal
failure, on the part of those we hold dear is always a possibility. We are flawed
human beings who often fail each other. We must not let the total failure of
those whom we admire destroy our faith. Jesus warned his closest followers
that his betrayal and death lay ahead and even though they could not
understand it, they could remember and not be destroyed in their faith. Such
things must not destroy us either.

TODAY'S PRAYER

Father, the failure of those whom I love and trust hurts so badly. Please don't let that
keep me from the joy you have given me in Christian fellowship and the hope I have
in you. Help me remember that many of Jesus' greatest servants failed at one time or
another, and were redeemed and used powerfully by you. In Jesus' name I pray. Amen.

CONTEXT: LUKE 9:43-50
Related Passages: Luke 22:31-32; John 21:15-21; 2 Corinthians 2:5-8

Day 170

JUST NOT GETTING IT!

Luke 9:46

Jesus' followers began to have an argument about which one of them was the greatest.

KEY THOUGHT

Jesus had just warned his closest followers that he was going to be betrayed (see verses 43-45). Instead of questioning if they might be the offender, they wrestled with their own delusions of grandeur. Rather than following Jesus in the way of the cross, they were looking for their own place in glory. Our pride and desire to be noticed can blind us to our own potential for failure. Rather than being faithful through this time of difficulty, these followers would all let Jesus down during his most difficult time. When we feel ourselves striving for recognition and are frustrated because we don't get recognized as prominently as someone else, let's remember these early followers and their spiritual blindness so we can avoid a case of our own spiritual blindness.

TODAY'S PRAYER

Give me eyes to see, O Lord God, so that I will not be deceived by own lust for recognition. Please help me see my weaknesses and draw close to you for wisdom, strength, and perseverance. In Jesus' name I ask for this grace. Amen.

CONTEXT: LUKE 9:43-50
Related Passages: Proverbs 16:18; 1 Corinthians 10:12-13; 1 Timothy 3:6

Day 171

WELCOME THEM IN!

Luke 9:47-48

Jesus knew what they were thinking, so he took a little child and stood the child beside him. Then he said to the followers, "Whoever accepts a little child like this in my name is accepting me. And anyone who accepts me is also accepting the one who sent me. The one among you who is the most humble—this is the one who is great."

KEY THOUGHT

Jesus turns the whole discussion of greatness upside down. Instead of greatness being determined by status, position, and having others wait upon you, greatness is determined by serving those whom others don't view as important. In Jesus' day, important people considered associating with children a waste of time. The child in Jesus' story becomes a symbol of those viewed as unimportant. However, Jesus says that a great person is going to find the left out, the forgotten, and the neglected rather than avoid them. The truly great person is going to welcome and serve these left out, forgotten, and neglected ones rather than trying to name-drop and hang around with the "in crowd." Greatness is about serving, not about appearances or what the world regards as status.

TODAY'S PRAYER

Father, give me a heart to welcome those who are left out, overlooked, and forgotten in my world. Please humble me gently so that I am not so full of myself that I won't help others in need and associate with those whom the world might not value. Make me more like your Son. I pray this in Jesus' name. Amen.

CONTEXT: LUKE 9:43-50
Related Passages: Luke 22:24-27; Romans 15:7; Romans 12:16

Day 172

GROUP PRIDE

Luke 9:49-50

John answered, "Master, we saw someone using your name to force demons out of people. We told him to stop because he does not belong to our group."

Jesus said to him, "Don't stop him. Whoever is not against you is for you."

KEY THOUGHT

So often our pride shows itself in group pride. The attitude is "if we don't do it, then it must not be important." The apostles want their little band of "Jesus followers" to be the primary bunch. Their thinking seems to be something like this: "Jesus chose us, so surely there couldn't be anyone else as important as us!" But Jesus is not about building prideful little cliques. Instead, he wants to build groups of welcoming followers who are thankful for all who are helping to build the Kingdom of God. Jesus' point is very simple: if they're not against us, then they're for us! Imagine what would happen if all who love Jesus had this attitude today.

TODAY'S PRAYER

Forgive us, humble us, and correct us, O Father, for our rivalry, pettiness, divisiveness, pride, and arrogance. We have split your church into so many subgroups it is unconscionable. Work in us, all of your people, with your Spirit. Bring us back to a more forgiving, generous, and faithful unity. In Jesus' name I pray. Amen.

CONTEXT: LUKE 9:43-50
Related Passages: John 17:20-21; 1 Corinthians 1:10; 1 Corinthians 14:36

Day 173

SOME FOLKS WON'T SEE

Luke 9:51-56

The time was coming near when Jesus would leave and go back to heaven. He decided to go to Jerusalem. He sent some men ahead of him. They went into a town in Samaria to make everything ready for him. But the people there would not welcome Jesus because he was going toward Jerusalem. James and John, the followers of Jesus, saw this. They said, "Lord, do you want us to call fire down from heaven and destroy those people?"

But Jesus turned and criticized them for saying this. Then he and his followers went to another town.

KEY THOUGHT

As hard as it is to accept, some folks just aren't ready to meet Jesus. They will simply reject him because of his race, his gender, his time in history, or because of their prejudices against his followers. Our response shouldn't be anger and hostility—these attitudes use up too much energy and damage our hearts. Instead, our response should be doing good things when and where we can, and when we are rejected, we just move on to the next open door. Some day, the closed door may open and many may come to know Jesus when the time in their hearts is right—just as it happened at a later time with the Samaritans (see John 4 and Acts 8).

TODAY'S PRAYER

Father, please help my attitude when I see folks rejecting Jesus before even giving him a chance. Please keep me patient and hopeful. Ban resentment from my heart. Help me to see the open doors you have placed before me. In Jesus' name I ask this. Amen.

CONTEXT: LUKE 9:51-62
Related Passages: Luke 9:5; John 4:39-42; Acts 8:25

Day 174

FOLLOWING IS HARD

Luke 9:57-58
*They were all traveling along the road. Someone said to
Jesus, "I will follow you anywhere you go."*

*He answered, "The foxes have holes to live in. The birds have nests.
But the Son of Man has no place where he can rest his head."*

KEY THOUGHT

Put in plain English: following Jesus is hard! Following Jesus basically means giving up our comforts and pursuing him with our whole hearts. He may give us some of those conveniences back to use for his cause, but to follow Jesus means giving up our claim to everything in our life and offering it to him as Lord.

TODAY'S PRAYER

*Father, please don't let anything stand in the way of me following Jesus.
Help me see those things in my life I have not yielded to his lordship
and surrender them. Please use whatever I have to bring you glory. I
request for your help in these areas in Jesus' name. Amen.*

CONTEXT: LUKE 9:51-62
Related Passages: Luke 14:33; Luke 9:23-25; 2 Corinthians 9:10

Day 175

FIRST PRIORITY: FOLLOWING

Luke 9:59-60

Jesus said to another man, "Follow me!"

But the man said, "Lord, let me go and bury my father first."

But Jesus said to him, "Let the people who are dead bury their own dead. You must go and tell about God's kingdom."

KEY THOUGHT

Following Christ is our first priority. Nothing should stand in our way. Does that mean abandoning our responsibility to our families? Certainly not! God makes clear that how we live in our families is crucial to our discipleship and to our leadership. However, we so often use family concerns as excuses for not following rather than reconciling family matters with Kingdom values and priorities. Jesus must come first. God and his Kingdom must be THE priority in our families. Our families must see honoring God as the primary value lived out in our own lives.

TODAY'S PRAYER

Give me wisdom, O God, to make you and your Kingdom THE primary value of my home. I want to demonstrate your compassion and your holy character in my interactions with my loved ones. Help them see me as loyal, faithful, and supportive of them while knowing that my heart's first allegiance is to you. In Jesus' name I pray. Amen.

CONTEXT: LUKE 9:51-62
Related Passages: 1 Timothy 5:8; Matthew 10:37; Ephesians 6:1-4

Day 176

NO TURNING BACK

Luke 9:61-62

*Another man said, "I will follow you, Lord, but first
let me go and say goodbye to my family."*

*Jesus said, "Anyone who begins to plow a field but looks
back is not prepared for God's kingdom."*

KEY THOUGHT

Again, Jesus is emphasizing the importance of Kingdom commitment.
Nothing, absolutely nothing, can stand in the way of the all-surpassing call
to follow Jesus. We press on, full speed ahead. When we get diverted—when
we lose our way and when we stumble and fall—we point our hearts back
in the direction of Christ and the Kingdom of God, and continue on. Ours
is a Kingdom calling, a forward calling, an upward calling—it is not a call
to return to the old ways, the old values, and the old answers. No turning
back! Full steam ahead! Sin, death, and defeat are in our rear view mirror. No
turning back, for we are bound for glory as we live out the Kingdom.

TODAY'S PRAYER

*Keep me focused, dear God, on the Kingdom call of Christ Jesus. I want to
live with the focus of your Kingdom and its righteousness filling my heart,
providing my dreams, and calling me to share in your glory. Help me notice
the needs of others and bless them with your grace as I press on to fulfill the
Kingdom call you have given me. In Jesus' name I ask this. Amen.*

CONTEXT: LUKE 9:51-62
Related Passages: Matthew 6:32-33; Philippians 3:12-14; 2 Peter 2:2

Day 177

TEAMWORK!

Luke 10:1

After this, the Lord chose 72 more followers. He sent them out in groups of two. He sent them ahead of him into every town and place where he planned to go.

KEY THOUGHT

The Lord didn't send his followers out solo. He sent them out in pairs. Pairs were more than twice as effective as a single person in accomplishing the work of preparing people's hearts for the Kingdom of God. Several Jewish principles were behind this. First, testimony needed to be at the hands of two or three witnesses (Deut. 19:15). Second, two are stronger and more effective than one (Eccles. 4:9-12). To this, Jesus adds a third principle of his own: where two or three gather, there he is present (Matt. 18:20). No matter how strong we are, we need a partner. Even the incredibly committed apostle Paul needed his co-workers and friends (see 2 Tim.). We need each other to do God's work and accomplish God's mission. Let's make a commitment not to do life or ministry solo!

TODAY'S PRAYER

Father, I confess that there have been times when other brothers and sisters in Christ have let me down and this has caused me to try to do too much on my own. I also confess that it is easy to give into the cultural assumptions about self-reliance and quit depending upon you. I want to open up more of myself to others in your family. Please use me along with others to advance the work of your Kingdom. In Jesus' name I pray. Amen.

CONTEXT: LUKE 10:1-20
Related Passages: Ecclesiastes 4:9-12; Deuteronomy 19:15; Matthew 18:20

Day 178

PRAY FOR HARVESTERS

Luke 10:2

*He said to them, "There is such a big harvest of people to bring in. But
there are only a few workers to help harvest them. God owns the harvest.
Ask him to send more workers to help bring in his harvest."*

KEY THOUGHT

So often we wring our hands when messages about how all Christians
should be evangelistic don't seem to make much difference. At times, we can
get frustrated when so few people sign up for evangelism training classes.
However, we often neglect the approach Jesus commanded: we need to pray
for harvester workers. Why do we have so few reaching out to the lost? Could
it be that we have not fervently and consistently prayed for the Lord to send
out workers into his harvest fields?

TODAY'S PRAYER

*Holy and gracious God, please stir your people's hearts and open up our eyes to the need
of reaching the lost. Send out workers for the harvest. I ask for this in Jesus' name. Amen.*

CONTEXT: LUKE 10:1-20
Related Passages: John 4:34-38; John 12:23-26; Galatians 6:8

Day 179

LEARN TO DEPEND UPON GOD

Luke 10:3-7

[Jesus said] "You can go now. But listen! I am sending you, and you will be like sheep among wolves. Don't carry any money, a bag, or sandals. Don't stop to talk with people on the road. Before you go into a house, say 'Peace be with this home.' If the people living there love peace, your blessing of peace will stay with them. But if not, your blessing of peace will come back to you. Stay in the peace-loving house. Eat and drink what the people there give you. A worker should be given his pay. Don't leave that house to stay in another house."

KEY THOUGHT

These specific commands about going out to reach the people of Israel are interesting, but they are more than just a novelty from long ago and far away. These commands are the great reminder that our outreach efforts begin with a dependence upon God to do what he has promised. We must trust him and his grace, not our own cunning and ingenuity. In fact, we must go a step further: we should seek the help of other people. Things won't get done without the grace of God and the partnership of people who feel a call to his word and work.

TODAY'S PRAYER

Father, I know you are trying to help me realize that I can't live my Christian life alone. I need your power and your direction to be what you want me to be. I need the help and encouragement of your people to fulfill your plans in me. Please give me patience to trust in your timing to bring these things about. In Jesus' name I pray. Amen.

CONTEXT: LUKE 10:1-20
Related Passages: Luke 24:44-49; Acts 1:6-8; Acts 28:28-30

Day 180

THE URGENCY OF GOD'S KINGDOM

Luke 10:8-11

"If you go into a town and the people welcome you, eat the food they give you. Heal the sick people who live there, and tell them, 'God's kingdom is coming to you soon!'

"But if you go into a town, and the people don't welcome you, then go out into the streets of that town and say, 'Even the dirt from your town that sticks to our feet we wipe off against you. But remember that God's kingdom is coming soon.'"

KEY THOUGHT

God's Kingdom drew near with the coming of Jesus. He sent his followers to prepare the people's hearts. The announcement of the Kingdom was not only urgent; it was also eternally important. Jesus' instructions were given to help them know that importance. In a time when so few accept any standards for truth or morality, we can easily lose our sense of urgency about the Kingdom of God. Let's be open to the strong language Jesus uses in Luke 10 to shake us from our lethargy and remember that accepting Jesus' truth about God's Kingdom is eternally important.

TODAY'S PRAYER

Father, forgive my lethargy toward those whose lives are not yet yielded to the Lordship of Jesus. Renew my passion to share your grace and to declare your Kingdom. In Jesus' name I pray. Amen.

CONTEXT: LUKE 10:1-20
Related Passages: Luke 9:1-5; Acts 13:48-52; John 12:48

Day 181

WORSE THAN SODOM?

Luke 10:12
*[Jesus said] "I tell you, on the judgment day it will be worse for
the people of that town than for the people of Sodom."*

KEY THOUGHT

Jesus is trying to help his closest followers understand the dire
consequences for those who reject his message. For those from the Jewish
heritage, there is no worse example of evil than the city of Sodom. Nor is there
any more powerful example of God's judgment on wickedness than Sodom.
Jesus wants it made clear: to reject him, his messengers, and his message is to
be worse than Sodom and to choose a fate worse than Sodom. This sobering
truth should make us realize how precious the message of Jesus is to the lost
world's salvation . . . and our own!

TODAY'S PRAYER

*Father, in a world of relativism where the only value seems to be to despise those with
values, please help me know with both my mind and heart the importance of the
gospel of Jesus Christ. Never let me take it lightly. Never let me take for granted the
need others have to know your Son as their Lord. Instead, help me to do something
to lead others to know your Son as their Savior. In Jesus' name I pray. Amen.*

CONTEXT: LUKE 10:1-20
Related Passages: Genesis 19:12-25; Isaiah 1:9; Lamentations 4:6

Day 182

JESUS PRONOUNCES JUDGMENT

Luke 10:13-15

[Jesus said] "It will be bad for you, Chorazin! It will be bad for you, Bethsaida! I did many miracles in you. If those same miracles had happened in Tyre and Sidon, then the people in those cities would have changed their lives and stopped sinning a long time ago. They would have worn sackcloth and sat in ashes to show that they were sorry for their sins. But on the judgment day it will be worse for you than for Tyre and Sidon. And you, Capernaum, will you be lifted up to heaven? No, you will be thrown down to the place of death!"

KEY THOUGHT

Jesus seldom pronounces judgment so sternly and so clearly. Yet here, he does so with great passion and clarity. He had done great miracles and taught God's truth. Yet the people refused to believe in him and change their lives. Jesus is the embodiment of God's love. However, part of love is being upset, concerned, and yes, even angry, when those we love choose destruction. By rejecting Jesus, these cities chose death and destruction over deliverance. Let's understand the stakes in the choices that people make and work for deliverance in the lives of those we influence.

TODAY'S PRAYER

O God, I am shocked and motivated by Jesus' sharp words and deep frustration. I know he left heaven to bring salvation and that his goal was not judgment. Yet I am constantly amazed at how often people I know choose their own way, the way of destruction, over Jesus' grace and deliverance. Stir me to such deep concern and help me find ways to communicate that concern to the lost with passion and love. I pray this in Jesus' name. Amen.

CONTEXT: LUKE 10:1-20
Related Passages: John 3:16-21; Colossians 1:19-22; 1 John 5:12

Day 183

NOT A PERSONAL REJECTION

Luke 10:16

[Jesus said] "When anyone listens to you my followers, they are really listening to me. But when anyone refuses to accept you, they are really refusing to accept me. And when anyone refuses to accept me, they are refusing to accept the one who sent me."

KEY THOUGHT

As Jesus' followers, let's not take the rejection or the acceptance of the message of Christ too personally. Yes, we should be passionate about sharing that message. Yes, we must understand the eternal implications of accepting or rejecting that message. But the message is about Jesus. People aren't choosing or rejecting us; they are choosing or rejecting Jesus. And when they choose or reject Jesus, they are choosing or rejecting God. Let's remember that this is not about us, but about God, his message, his Son, his Kingdom, and his desire to save the lost. Jesus is Savior, and we must keep our hearts and our efforts focused on him!

TODAY'S PRAYER

Father, I confess that when people reject my attempts at sharing your good news about Jesus, I take it too personally. I know deep in my heart that it is not a personal rejection, but those feelings do often get in my way. Help me see the issue more clearly. Help me see it as the acceptance or rejection of you and your grace. Help me see it as the coming into your light out of the grip of darkness on the hearts of others. In Jesus' name I pray. Amen.

CONTEXT: LUKE 10:1-20
Related Passages: Matthew 13:23; John 1:5-14; John 5:24

Day 184

THE POWER OF JESUS' NAME

Luke 10:17

When the 72 followers came back from their trip, they were very happy. They said, "Lord, even the demons obeyed us when we used your name!"

KEY THOUGHT

Jesus' name is so frequently used in vain today that we often forget how powerful that name is. We pray in Jesus' name because he intercedes for us with authority. We call upon Jesus power and authority to work in our lives and the lives of those we love—to help them, to heal them, to renew them, to comfort them—when we pray in Jesus' name. Jesus has authority over all powers and forces. They cannot stand up to his authority and truth. Both Jesus' presence in us and his love for us assure us that we have overcome the world because the one in us is greater than the one in the world. Even though many may reject Jesus, we rejoice because of the liberating power over sin and death that Jesus' presence brings us!

TODAY'S PRAYER

I praise you, Father, for displaying your mighty power in the resurrection of Jesus from the dead. I thank you for making that power work in my life as I yield myself to Jesus' authority and trust in his grace. I praise you for hearing my heart when I pray because of the authority of Jesus' name. Amen.

CONTEXT: LUKE 10:1-20
Related Passages: Acts 4:12; Philippians 2:5-11; John 16:23

Day 185

EYES ON THE PRIZE!

Luke 10:18-20

Jesus said to them, "I saw Satan falling like lightning from the sky. He is the enemy, but know that I have given you more power than he has. I have given you power to crush his snakes and scorpions under your feet. Nothing will hurt you. Yes, even the spirits obey you. And you can be happy, not because you have this power, but because your names are written in heaven."

KEY THOUGHT

If you are at all like me, you find yourself distracted from your ultimate goal by all sorts of temporary opportunities, achievements, and victories. However, I've come to realize that Satan lets few victories stand without counter-attack. Unfortunately, I often let my guard down after a major victory. While Jesus is thrilled about the followers' successes, he also knows their vulnerabilities and wants to keep them focused on the ultimate blessing— eternity with God in heaven. Let's "keep our eyes on the prize" while we rejoice that Jesus does his great work through us!

TODAY'S PRAYER

Father, I confess that I let the world, and those moments of glory that I find in the world, distract me from my ultimate goal of spending eternal life with you in heaven. Keep my hope focused on the glory yet to be revealed in me at Jesus' coming. At the same time, Father, please work through me to do your work and to bring you praise. In Jesus' name I pray. Amen.

CONTEXT: LUKE 10:1-20
Related Passages: John 14:1-4; 1 John 3:1-2; Philippians 3:13-14

Day 186

THE JOY OF THE HOLY SPIRIT

Luke 10:21

Then the Holy Spirit made Jesus feel very happy. Jesus said, "I praise you, Father, Lord of heaven and earth. I am thankful that you have hidden these things from those who are so wise and so smart. But you have shown them to people who are like little children. Yes, Father, you did this because it's what you really wanted to do."

KEY THOUGHT

Joy is a sign of the Spirit's presence (see Rom. 14:17; Gal. 5:22; 1 Thes. 1:6). It was in Jesus' day and it is in our day. For Jesus, the basis of this joy has to do with God's plan to reveal his truth, grace, and hope to the childlike—not to those the world classifies as wise and clever. Our understanding of God's truth is very much like spiritual joy; it is a gift from the Spirit's work in our lives and it is something the Father wants to share with us.

TODAY'S PRAYER

Holy and loving Father, God of all grace, thank you for giving me your truth and your joy as gifts with the presence of your Spirit in my life. May I never take these gifts for granted! For all of your many blessings and all the varied nuances of your grace, I praise and thank you in Jesus' name. Amen.

CONTEXT: LUKE 10:21-24
Related Passages: Acts 15:32; Romans 14:17; 1 Corinthians 2:13-15

Day 187

AUTHORITY TO REVEAL THE FATHER

Luke 10:22

[Jesus said] "My Father has given me all things. No one knows who the Son is—only the Father knows. And only the Son knows who the Father is. The only people who will know about the Father are those the Son chooses to tell."

KEY THOUGHT

Jesus reveals God. You want to know God? You need to look to Jesus! Jesus is God's ultimate expression in human form (Heb. 1:1-3). He is God's Living Word—God's message spoken through the life of Jesus (John 1:1-18). Jesus has authority over everything. He knows and reveals the Father. So, if you really want to know God, get to know Jesus! Jesus, God's Son, reveals the Father and his will to us!

TODAY'S PRAYER

Father, thank you for revealing yourself in Jesus, your Son and my Savior. In his name I offer you my praise and thanksgiving. Amen.

CONTEXT: LUKE 10:21-24
Related Passages: John 1:18; John 14:6-7; Matthew 28:18-20

BLESSED EYES!

Luke 10:23-24

Then Jesus turned to his followers. They were there alone with him. He said, "It is a great blessing for you to see what you now see! I tell you, many prophets and kings wanted to see what you now see, but they could not. And they wanted to hear what you now hear, but they could not."

KEY THOUGHT

The apostles were common men given an incredible blessing. They were blessed to be able to see God's ultimate promise delivered, fulfilled, and embodied in Jesus. We have received their testimony to this Word, this fulfillment to God's promises, in the four Gospels (Mathew, Mark, Luke, and John). We are incredibly blessed. Jesus is the tuning fork of all revelation and the fulfillment of all of God's plans (2 Cor. 1:20). If we are going to understand Scripture and God's plan for salvation, we begin with Jesus. Let's rejoice at the privilege of living in the light of the glory of Christ.

TODAY'S PRAYER

Father, how can I ever thank you properly for the incredible grace of knowing Jesus, and in knowing Jesus, understanding your incredible love and grace? Never let me lose my sense of wonder at knowing Jesus, in whose name I offer my devotion, thanks, and praise. Amen.

CONTEXT: LUKE 10:21-24
Related Passages: 1 Peter 1:10-12; John 17:6-8; Hebrews 1:1-3

Day 189

REMEMBERING THE HEART OF THE MATTER

Luke 10:25-28

Then an expert in the law stood up to test Jesus. He said,
"Teacher, what must I do to get eternal life?"

Jesus said to him, "What is written in the law? What do you understand from it?"

The man answered, "'Love the Lord your God with all your heart, all your soul, all your
strength, and all your mind.' Also, 'Love your neighbor the same as you love yourself.'"

Jesus said, "Your answer is right. Do this and you will have eternal life."

KEY THOUGHT

A couple of observations are worth making about this interchange. A
critic, called an expert of the law, was testing Jesus. However, Jesus didn't just
brush him off, but instead engaged him in honest and meaningful teaching.
Second, Jesus affirms the expert for his insight into the truth and affirms that
loving God and our neighbor is a great summary of God's Law given through
Moses. However, Jesus reminds the expert (and us as well) that the heart of
God's truth is not knowing it, but doing it. God's blessing comes when we put
God's truth into practice.

TODAY'S PRAYER

God, help me know your will and treasure it. Even more, dear God, give me the conviction,
courage, and the compassion to put your truth into practice. In Jesus' name I pray. Amen.

CONTEXT: LUKE 10:25-37
Related Passages: Matthew 7:24-27; James 1:21-25; John 17:12-17

Day 190

TRYING TO JUSTIFY OURSELVES

Luke 10:29

But the man wanted to show that the way he was living was right. So he said to Jesus, "But who is my neighbor?"

KEY THOUGHT

When the conviction of God's word strikes our hearts, we often try to justify ourselves. We do this instead of throwing ourselves on the mercy of God and changing our hearts and lives. If the expert who had come to test Jesus had honest motives, Jesus' question, affirmation, and reply would have been enough. But the expert wanted to look righteous more than he wanted to be righteous. How many times does this pattern of behavior reflect our own attitudes? Let's realize that we cannot justify ourselves. We will find righteousness only in trusting in God's grace given to us in Jesus Christ. Our job is to go out and share that grace with the world as we are supplied by the power of his Holy Spirit.

TODAY'S PRAYER

God, my heavenly Father, forgive me for trying to make myself look righteous when that gift comes only from you. Forgive me for my religious posturing that has kept me from opening my heart up completely to your grace and from living my life in honor of that grace. In Jesus' name I pray. Amen.

CONTEXT: LUKE 10:25-37
Related Passages: Romans 3:22-27; Romans 8:1-4; Galatians 5:6

Day 191

WHEN RELIGION STUMBLES

Luke 10:30-35

To answer this question, Jesus said, "A man was going down the road from Jerusalem to Jericho. Some robbers surrounded him, tore off his clothes, and beat him. Then they left him lying there on the ground almost dead.

"It happened that a Jewish priest was going down that road. When he saw the man, he did not stop to help him. He walked away. Next, a Levite came near. He saw the hurt man, but he went around him. He would not stop to help him either. He just walked away.

"Then a Samaritan man traveled down that road. He came to the place where the hurt man was lying. He saw the man and felt very sorry for him. The Samaritan went to him and poured olive oil and wine on his wounds. Then he covered the man's wounds with cloth. The Samaritan had a donkey. He put the hurt man on his donkey, and he took him to an inn. There he cared for him. The next day, the Samaritan took out two silver coins and gave them to the man who worked at the inn. He said, 'Take care of this hurt man. If you spend more money on him, I will pay it back to you when I come again.'"

KEY THOUGHT

Jesus wanted the expert in the Old Testament who had asked, "Who is my neighbor?" to realize that the key to God's truth was not knowing it, but putting it into practice. To shock and jar the truth into this Jewish religious expert, he makes the hero of the story a despised Samaritan. This Samaritan does just as God wants his children to do for those in need. He was the one who saw the need and acted. And that is what God wants of us: not a hollow religion of words, arguments, and nuances, but a faith that is vibrantly and compassionately lived out in the real world.

TODAY'S PRAYER

O Lord, my Abba Father, please forgive me for letting my fascination with religious arguments take my heart off the truth you want me to live with character and compassion. Open my eyes to see the opportunities you give me each day so that I can put my faith into redemptive action in my world. In Jesus' name I pray. Amen.

CONTEXT: LUKE 10:25-37
Related Passages: James 2:14-21; James 4:17; Luke 6:31

Day 192

TRUE NEIGHBORS!

Luke 10:36-37

Then Jesus said, "Which one of these three men do you think was really a neighbor to the man who was hurt by the robbers?"

The teacher of the law answered, "The one who helped him."

Jesus said, "Then you go and do the same."

KEY THOUGHT

Who is our neighbor? Not someone who can do something FOR us, but the one who has a need that Jesus can meet THROUGH us. Let's be that neighbor today!

TODAY'S PRAYER

Open my eyes, Lord, to the person who needs me to be his or her neighbor today. In Jesus' name I pray. Amen.

CONTEXT: LUKE 10:25-37
Related Passages: Matthew 5:43-47; Leviticus 19:18; Zechariah 7:9

Day 193

REVOLUTIONARY PRIORITIES!

Luke 10:38-42

While Jesus and his followers were traveling, he went into a town, and a woman named Martha let him stay at her house. She had a sister named Mary. Mary was sitting at Jesus' feet and listening to him teach. But her sister Martha was busy doing all the work that had to be done. Martha went in and said, "Lord, don't you care that my sister has left me to do all the work by myself? Tell her to help me!"

But the Lord answered her, "Martha, Martha, you are getting worried and upset about too many things. Only one thing is important. Mary has made the right choice, and it will never be taken away from her."

KEY THOUGHT

In an age when Rabbis didn't even talk to women in public—much less teach them and enter into Bible study with them—Jesus broke all the rules. In John 4, he visits publicly with a woman who was also a despised Samaritan, and through her, Jesus reaches her whole village. In Luke 10, Jesus not only discusses and teaches God's word with a woman, but he emphasizes that this is the one crucial thing about which she should be concerned. Women are not only given the opportunity to associate with and learn from Jesus, but they are also told that this is the primary concern—to know Jesus, his words, and his Kingdom.

TODAY'S PRAYER

Father, please let nothing hinder me from placing Jesus first in my life. Please use me to influence all those in my family to see that this should be their primary concern. In Jesus' name I pray. Amen.

CONTEXT: LUKE 10:38-42
Related Passages: Matthew 6:31-33; Luke 8:1-3; 2 Timothy 1:5; 3:14-15

Day 194

LORD, TEACH ME TO PRAY!

Luke 11:1

One time Jesus was out praying, and when he finished, one of his followers said to him, "John taught his followers how to pray. Lord, teach us how to pray too."

KEY THOUGHT

Many books have been written about prayer. Many of us have attended classes that chose prayer as their subject matter. Yet, when was the last time you gave serious time to looking in the Gospels and studying prayer? Have you noticed Jesus as he prayed? Do you know what he taught about prayer? Have you listened to what Jesus said about the importance of prayer? Why don't we commit to spending several months with a highlighter reading the Gospels? As we read, let's ask Jesus each day, "Lord, teach me to pray!" While we pray in the power and authority of Jesus' name every day, let's also commit to learning to pray as Jesus prayed.

TODAY'S PRAYER

Holy God and Almighty Father, thank you for giving me the avenue of prayer to speak with you, to seek you, and to come into your presence. I recognize that prayer is a gift from you, ensured and assisted by the intercession of your Son and the Holy Spirit. Please, dear Father guide me in my efforts to learn to pray as your Son prayed and as he taught his followers to pray. I long to draw nearer to you, to honor you more completely with all of my being, and to open my will up to your will. In the mighty name of Jesus I pray. Amen.

CONTEXT: LUKE 11:1-13
Related Passages: Matthew 6:7-13; Ephesians 3:14-21; Revelation 8:1-6

FATHER!

Luke 11:2

Jesus said to the followers, "This is how you should pray: 'Father, we pray that your name will always be kept holy. We pray that your kingdom will come.'"

KEY THOUGHT

Prayer begins with two realities. The first reality is that the Almighty God, holy and majestic, eternal and all powerful, longs for us to enter into relationship with him as his children. He is our Father! The second reality is that God our Father calls us to let his will and his way set the direction and the meaning for our lives. We voluntarily offer ourselves as subjects to his rule and to live for his Kingdom. This means that our hearts' deepest yearnings are to come into the presence of our Father and to see the dawning of his unrestrained and untainted rule over all things. Prayer is the perfect place to experience his presence and to anticipate the great day of his complete reign over all things. Prayer is also the place where we affirm that God is our Father, that we want his name and character to be honored in all the earth, and that we live in anticipation of the day when Christ brings all his glory to full view. Such few words to express awesome truth; yet these words, this relationship, and this future, are ours in Jesus!

TODAY'S PRAYER

Holy and tender Father, it breaks my heart to hear your name violated by profanity and by flippant exclamations. Please bring about a deeper reverence for your name by bringing the rule of your Kingdom into full and glorious view with the return of your Son. Until that day, dear Father, empower your church, your outpost for your Kingdom, to powerfully display her reverence for your name, her desire to draw close to you, and her passion for the day of your Son's return. In Jesus' name I pray. Amen.

CONTEXT: LUKE 11:1-13
Related Passages: Leviticus 22:32; 1 Samuel 7:12-13; Revelation 11:16

Day 196

DAILY FOOD

Luke 11:3
[Jesus taught them to pray] "'Give us the food we need for each day.'"

KEY THOUGHT

One of the great blessings of Israel's wilderness wanderings was the lesson of daily dependence. They had to trust God for their daily food. They couldn't gather too much and store it or it would spoil and become a putrid mass of worms. They never suffered from having too little. They were reminded daily that the Lord is gracious, faithful, and practical. The prayer of our hearts is that we, too, may experience the Lord as gracious, faithful, and practical. We want to know beyond theory that the Lord provides and blesses. So we pray in humble recognition that today's food is not the work of our hands, but the blessing of God. We won't store up for ourselves, but we will depend upon his graciousness and use our overabundance to share his blessings. The food we have today is a reminder of the eternal faithfulness and generosity of our Father.

TODAY'S PRAYER

Almighty God, Abba Father, thank you for the food you have given me today. Please supply it day by day and never let me think that it is mine because of my power or the work of my hands. In Jesus' name I thank you for your daily grace. Amen.

CONTEXT: LUKE 11:1-13
Related Passages: 1 Timothy 6:6-8; Matthew 6:25-34; Philippians 4:11-13

Day 197

THE PERVASIVENESS OF OUR PROBLEM

Luke 11:4

[Jesus taught them to pray] "Forgive our sins, just as we forgive everyone who has done wrong to us. And don't let us be tempted."

KEY THOUGHT

Sin is our problem. We bring it into the world of those around us and unleash the power of Satan to damage others. Others bring sin into our lives, leaving us wounded, battered, disillusioned, and angry. Satan knows how to seduce us with just the right combination of circumstances and temptations to take advantage of sin's power on us. How can we pray and not acknowledge our sin and our vulnerability to temptation? How can we pray and not be reminded that to be forgiven means that we must be forgiving?

TODAY'S PRAYER

Father God, please forgive me of my sins. Give me wisdom to see your escape path out of temptation. Use my knowledge of your gracious forgiveness to motivate me to extend that graciousness to others. Most of all, by the power of your Spirit, help me conquer sin's power in all of its forms and to overcome Satan's schemes to trap me by his temptations. In Jesus' name I ask for these gifts. Amen.

CONTEXT: LUKE 11:1-13
Related Passages: 1 John 1:8-2:2; Hebrews 3:12-14; Genesis 4:6-7

Day 198

MORE THAN ONCE

Luke 11:5-6

Then Jesus said to them, "Suppose one of you went to your friend's house very late at night and said to him, 'A friend of mine has come into town to visit me. But I have nothing for him to eat. Please give me three loaves of bread.'"

KEY THOUGHT

Jesus didn't just teach about prayer once, but many times. Jesus didn't pray just once, but the Son consistently went to his Father in prayer. Prayer is not something that we master, but it is a grace by which God gains mastery over us. So Jesus stressed its importance, demonstrated his dependence upon it, and often made it the subject of his teaching. Here, to emphasize the importance of persistence, he uses an illustration from the real world in which they lived. This not only made his teaching memorable, but anchored the importance and meaning of prayer in real, everyday living.

TODAY'S PRAYER

Father, thank you for Jesus' repeated emphasis on the importance of prayer, both in his teaching and with his example. Teach me to value prayer the way your Son did. Give me daily reminders of prayer's importance to me and to you. In Jesus' name I pray. Amen.

CONTEXT: LUKE 11:1-13
Related Passages: 1 Thessalonians 5:17; James 5:16-18; Ephesians 6:18

Day 199

EVEN MORE!

Luke 11:5-8

Then Jesus said to them, "Suppose one of you went to your friend's house very late at night and said to him, 'A friend of mine has come into town to visit me. But I have nothing for him to eat. Please give me three loaves of bread.' Your friend inside the house answers, 'Go away! Don't bother me! The door is already locked. My children and I are in bed. I cannot get up and give you the bread now.' I tell you, maybe friendship is not enough to make him get up to give you the bread. But he will surely get up to give you what you need if you continue to ask."

KEY THOUGHT

One of the ways the rabbis often reasoned with people in Jesus' day was by comparing a lesser thing with a greater one. In this example, Jesus uses this same practice. He uses a principle of human perseverance with a neighbor and emphasizes that if this is true among human neighbors, how much more will it be true of our perseverance in requesting the action of God? If someone keeps asking, the person may grant the request just to avoid the embarrassment of not helping. If that is true of sinful people, how much more will we receive gracious things from our heavenly Father who longs to give good gifts to his children!

TODAY'S PRAYER

Thank you, Lord God Almighty, for your generous grace that comes from your heart of love. In those times when prayer is hard and my frustrations mount, help me persevere in prayer—especially when nothing seems to be happening, prayer doesn't seem very exciting, and I am discouraged. Give me the courage and conviction to keep praying. In Jesus' name I pray. Amen.

CONTEXT: LUKE 11:1-13
Related Passages: Luke 18:1-8; Colossians 4:2; Hebrews 5:7

Day 200

KEEP ON KEEPIN' ON!

Luke 11:9-10

*[Jesus said] "So I tell you, continue to ask, and God will give to you. Continue
to search, and you will find. Continue to knock, and the door will open for you.
Yes, whoever continues to ask will receive. Whoever continues to look will find.
And whoever continues to knock will have the door opened for them."*

KEY THOUGHT

"Don't quit!" Jesus says this repeatedly. "Don't give up! Keep on knocking,
seeking, and asking! Keep on keepin' on because God will answer you!" Rather
than spending a lot of words on what we're supposed to do, let's just hear
Jesus tell us to keep on doing it! Keep on searching. Keep on knocking. Keep
on asking. Keep on keepin' on!

TODAY'S PRAYER

*Father, you know that I have had several things on my heart. I now ask that
you hear me once again and act in your great might and for your glory and
accomplish your will in the following areas and for the following special
people: _____. I ask all this in Jesus' name. Amen.*

CONTEXT: LUKE 11:1-13
Related Passages: Psalm 28:1-7; Hebrews 4:14-16; Matthew 6:7

Day 201

THE GREATEST ANSWER TO PRAYER?

Luke 11:11-13

[Jesus said] "Do any of you have a son? What would you do if your son asked you for a fish? Would any father give him a snake? Or, if he asked for an egg, would you give him a scorpion? Of course not! Even you who are bad know how to give good things to your children. So surely your heavenly Father knows how to give the Holy Spirit to the people who ask him."

KEY THOUGHT

What's the greatest answer to our prayers? The gift of God's cleansing, justifying, sanctifying, saving, empowering, and indwelling Holy Spirit! If fathers know how to give good gifts, don't you think the Father will give us his Holy Spirit? So let's ask to receive and expect to receive this great from God!

TODAY'S PRAYER

Father, I know when I was saved you cleansed me by your Holy Spirit and that you came to live in me and make my body your temple through your Spirit. Now I ask that the Spirit's presence and power be more real to me, not just to sense your presence, but also so that I can be like Christ in every way. In Jesus' name I ask for this promised gift. Amen.

CONTEXT: LUKE 11:1-13
Related Passages: 1 Corinthians 6:9-11; Romans 8:12-14, 26-27; Acts 4:31

Day 202

CONSTANT AND UNFAIR ATTACK

Luke 11:14-15
*One time Jesus was sending a demon out of a man who could not talk.
When the demon came out, the man was able to speak. The crowds
were amazed. But some of the people said, "He uses the power of Satan
to force demons out of people. Satan is the ruler of demons."*

KEY THOUGHT

One of the ways Satan tries to discourage God's workers is through the constant badgering and attack of tenaciously unfair opponents. While Jesus cast out a demon and Satan knew his power was no match for Jesus, the devil made sure the voices of Jesus' opponents were heard. In the deceptive mode as the "Father of Lies" (i.e., Satan—see John 8:44), the opponents of Jesus directly turn around the truth of this exorcism. They claimed Jesus' power to cast out demons came from Satan. Of course, we can easily see the lie from our distance. However, be warned, dear Christian servant! Don't be discouraged or defeated if the good you do is attributed to false motives or to the power of evil. If they did it to our Savior, they are going to do it to us. But, if Jesus could stand firm, then by his power, we can stand firm as well.

TODAY'S PRAYER

Holy God, I confess that the unfair criticism of my motives and my actions is discouraging. Thank you for showing me that this happened to your Son. If Satan could turn around the truth of his own defeat and attribute Jesus' power to evil, then I know the opposition that I face should not be surprising. Help me to keep the ultimate victory of Jesus over sin, death, and Satan in my head and in my heart so that these unfair attacks do not discourage, derail, or defeat me. In Jesus' name I pray. Amen.

CONTEXT: LUKE 11:14-28
Related Passages: Colossians 2:6-15; 1 Corinthians 15:57; 1 John 5:4

Day 203

NEVER ENOUGH

Luke 11:16
*Some others there wanted to test Jesus. They asked
him to do a miracle as a sign from God.*

KEY THOUGHT

When someone is determined to oppose us, we will never be able to do enough to satisfy that person. Jesus' involvement with his opponents here reminds us of this. The request for Jesus to do a sign to prove himself wasn't a genuine request. It was just another test from opponents who refused to be satisfied by anything he did. Jesus shows us what we should do in such impossible situations: tell the truth and do the next right thing. We must not let such tests divert us from the work of God.

TODAY'S PRAYER

*Give me courage, O Lord my Father, to continue your work no matter the
criticisms or attacks that are launched against me. Please, dear Father, help
me determine whether the questions posed to me are from genuine hearts or
from the hearts of those who oppose your truth and who will never be satisfied
until your work is halted. Please give me the insight and the courage to be your
person of integrity when under such attacks. In Jesus' name I pray. Amen.*

CONTEXT: LUKE 11:14-28
Related Passages: Philippians 3:12-16; Psalm 17:9; Psalm 109:28

Day 204

UNDIVIDED!

Luke 11:17-18

But he knew what they were thinking. So he said to them, "Every kingdom that fights against itself will be destroyed. And a family that fights against itself will break apart. So if Satan is fighting against himself, how will his kingdom survive? You say that I use the power of Satan to force out demons."

KEY THOUGHT

Jesus takes the criticisms of his opponents and destroys them by a simple statement of truth. We recognize this truth. Many of us have also experienced or witnessed this truth: a divided house does indeed collapse. We also have seen the opposite demonstrated: an undivided house is hard to defeat. We need to stick close together and to speak the simple truth.

TODAY'S PRAYER

Holy God, help my church to resist being divided by the distractions of evil and sin. Help us stick close together and live out the purpose of Jesus. And, dear Father, please give me the wisdom to know when NOT to respond to false accusations and when I should respond. In Jesus' name I pray. Amen.

CONTEXT: LUKE 11:14-28
Related Passages: John 17:13-21; 1 Corinthians 1:13; Ezekiel 37:22

Day 205

YOU'RE ASKING FOR TROUBLE!

Luke 11:19

[Jesus said] "But if I use Satan's power to force out demons, then what power do your people use when they force out demons? So your own people will prove that you are wrong."

KEY THOUGHT

Jesus had been accused of casting out demons by the power of demons. The response to their accusation is very simple. If they are going to explain that his power is coming from Satan, then where does the power of other Jewish exorcists come from? Jesus wants them to understand that if they are going to make that accusation against him, then they are implicating their fellow Jewish teachers who do similar things. While Jesus clearly has power over demons, Satan, and evil, he also has to battle the opponents who accuse him. To communicate effectively, he must use their own logic and law to help the true seekers understand him. While he will never convince these "dyed in the wool" opponents, he can bring those who are genuinely interested closer to himself by using terms they understand and their own forms of rhetoric. We can learn from Jesus how to speak to others more effectively. Let us speak in ways others can understand so they can find their way to the truth!

TODAY'S PRAYER

Father, help me as I seek to communicate your grace and truth to those who look at the world differently than I do. Help me find wise and effective ways to share your message based on the way others understand and evaluate truth. In Jesus' name I pray. Amen.

CONTEXT: LUKE 11:14-28
Related Passages: 1 Corinthians 9:20-23; Acts 17:22-28; 2 Corinthians 4:5

Day 206

THE KINGDOM'S ARRIVAL!

Luke 11:20-22

[Jesus said] "But I use the power of God to force out demons.
This shows that God's kingdom has come to you.

"When a strong man with many weapons guards his own house, the things in his
house are safe. But suppose a stronger man comes and defeats him. The stronger
man will take away the weapons that the first man trusted to keep his house safe.
Then the stronger man will do what he wants with the other man's things."

KEY THOUGHT

Jesus' power is God's power demonstrated in human flesh. Jesus' power is
Kingdom power on arrival. Jesus' power is stronger than Satan's power and
enables the Son of God to triumph. Jesus' power is our assurance of ultimate
victory, deliverance, and salvation. Satan's most treasured "belongings" are
stripped from him and carried away to glory. Those treasures are us!

TODAY'S PRAYER

Thank you, dear Father, for the victory that you won for me in Jesus. Thank
you for Jesus' triumph over sin and death. Thank you for rescuing me from
the hands of the evil one. Now, dear Father, please give me the courage and
the will to stand up to his temptations and assaults knowing that the victory
is mine through Christ Jesus my Lord, in whose name I pray. Amen.

CONTEXT: LUKE 11:14-28
Related Passages: 1 Corinthians 15:51-56; Revelation 19:11-16; Romans 8:35-39

Day 207

DECISION TIME!

Luke 11:23
*[Jesus said] "Whoever is not with me is against me. And anyone
who does not work with me is working against me."*

KEY THOUGHT

There is no way to be neutral about Jesus. He challenges us to decide
if we are going to follow and help his cause or not. Simply ignoring Jesus,
putting off a decision about him, treating him lightly, or looking at him as just
another good religious person is not an option. We help and work with him
or we oppose him. Neutrality is opposition. Disinterest is opposition. He asks
us to decide to follow him, help him, and work with him. It is time for us to
decide: are we for Jesus or not?

TODAY'S PRAYER

*Father, forgive me when I've placed my discipleship and the work of the Lord
Jesus on the back burner of my life. Today, I realize again that your Son is calling
me to actively follow and serve in his work, not just stand by passively watching.
In Jesus' name I pray for courage and passion as I follow him. Amen.*

CONTEXT: LUKE 11:14-28
Related Passages: Revelation 3:15-16; Joshua 24:14-15; Luke 9:23-26

Day 208

MORE THAN GETTING RID OF THE BAD

Luke 11:24-26

[Jesus said] "When an evil spirit comes out of someone, it travels through dry places, looking for a place to rest. But it finds no place to rest. So it says, 'I will go back to the home I left.' When it comes back, it finds that home all neat and clean. Then the evil spirit goes out and brings back seven other spirits more evil than itself. They all go and live there, and that person has even more trouble than before."

KEY THOUGHT

Many people look at religion and see it as a litany of "thou shalt not" commands. Others look at the problems in their lives and want to be rid of the problems, focusing primarily on what they should not do. Jesus is reminding us, however, that getting rid of bad things is not the complete answer. There must be something good, vital, powerful, and real to put in place of the bad. If all we do is stop doing what is wrong and just get rid of what is bad, sooner or later something even worse will fill the void of the old sinfulness. We must replace the old, bad things with God's presence, power, and purpose in our lives. Let's pursue Jesus. Let's pursue the character and concerns of his kingdom, letting the Holy Spirit fill and empower us. Let's truly be instruments of Jesus' grace as we seek to expand God's Kingdom.

TODAY'S PRAYER

Holy and righteous Father, I want to be a person of character. I know that simply getting rid of the bad things in my life is not the answer in and of itself. I know, dear God, that you must fill my life with your presence, power, and purpose. In Jesus' name I pray. Amen.

CONTEXT: LUKE 11:14-28
Related Passages: Romans 8:9-14; Matthew 6:32-33; Philippians 3:12-14

Day 209

THE REAL BLESSING

Luke 11:27-28

As Jesus was saying these things, a woman with the people there called out to him, "Blessings from God belong to the woman who gave birth to you and fed you!"

But Jesus said, "The people who hear the teaching of God and obey it—they are the ones who have God's blessing."

KEY THOUGHT

Jesus never passed up an opportunity to help people move to a higher truth. Yes, there were those who criticized him. Yes, there were those who idolized him. He came, however, to bring God's message of salvation and the Kingdom to people who had just about lost hope. He came to share God's truth with folks normally left out of the religious discussion. So Jesus uses both criticism and praise as an opportunity to lead people to greater truth. The real blessing doesn't have to do with the physical ties to Jesus. No, the real blessing is given to those who put the Word of God into practice.

TODAY'S PRAYER

Holy and Almighty Father, thank you for helping me clearly see my need to obey your Word. Please give me the strength to obey it through the power of your Spirit. Forgive me for getting so wrapped up in the nuances of religious discussion that I forget the profound simplicity of obeying your truth from my heart. In Jesus' name I pray. Amen.

CONTEXT: LUKE 11:14-28
Related Passages: Luke 8:19-20; Matthew 7:21; 1 Samuel 15:22-23

Day 210

SIGN SEEKERS

Luke 11:29-30

The crowd grew larger and larger. Jesus said, "The people who live today are evil. They ask for a miracle as a sign from God. But no miracle will be done to prove anything to them. The only sign will be the miracle that happened to Jonah. Jonah was a sign for those who lived in Nineveh. It is the same with the Son of Man. He will be a sign for the people of this time."

KEY THOUGHT

Jesus does not conduct his ministry as a "proof show" for doubters or a "miracle spectacular" for the interested. For those demanding signs, there would be none. Jesus plants a seed that can fully germinate only after his death, burial, and resurrection—the sign of Jonah. The bigger challenge is to believe before we see "our sign." The faith hurdle is to trust when all looks hopeless and the miracle we desire does not happen before our eyes and on our time schedule. If we need a miraculous sign to believe, then we have the formula backwards. Let's believe, trusting that what Jesus promises is true and expectantly wait on the Lord to act!

TODAY'S PRAYER

Father, I believe, but sometimes in the middle of my most difficult trials, I need help with a stronger and more stable faith. I believe, but help my unbelief! Through your Spirit, give me the courage to walk in faith in moments of crisis, trial, and hardship, trusting that even if I do not receive my earthly miracle I can know I will receive my heavenly one. In Jesus' name I ask for your help. Amen.

CONTEXT: LUKE 11:29-35
Related Passages: John 20:24-29; 1 Peter 1:8-9; Mark 9:17-24

Day 211

GREATER THAN

Luke 11:31-32

[Jesus said] "On the judgment day, you people who live now will be compared with the Queen of the South, and she will be a witness who shows how guilty you are. Why do I say this? Because she traveled from far, far away to listen to Solomon's wise teaching. And I tell you that someone greater than Solomon is right here, but you won't listen!

"On the judgment day, you people who live now will also be compared with the people from Nineveh, and they will be witnesses who show how guilty you are. I say this because when Jonah preached to those people, they changed their hearts and lives. And you are listening to someone greater than Jonah, but you refuse to change!"

KEY THOUGHT

There were far greater leaps of faith made in the past than Jesus was asking people to take in his day. The Queen of Sheba traveled a long way to learn from Solomon. The people of Nineveh repented at the preaching of a hated enemy, Jonah. Jesus was far greater than either of them, yet his own people often refused to believe. Their refusal, however, will not go unnoticed in heaven. But do I really believe in Jesus? He challenges us to believe that he is greater than any other earthly teacher. No fence straddling allowed. No lukewarm position-takers included. No middle ground-holders allowed. We must believe that Jesus is both Savior and Lord!

TODAY'S PRAYER

Thank you, dear heavenly Father, for calling me to get off the fence and place my faith in Jesus. I know that my values, my hope, my character, my morals, my code of life, and my closest friendships all depend on this one crucial choice. So, dear Father, I proclaim to you and to all who know me that I believe that Jesus Christ is your Son, my Lord and Savior. I believe that because of Jesus' death, burial, and resurrection I will stand before you forgiven and cleansed, one of your holy children. I thank you in Jesus' name. Amen.

CONTEXT: LUKE 11:29-35
Related Passages: John 1:9-12; John 20:30-31; Galatians 3:26-29

Day 212

WHEN LIGHT IS DARKNESS

Luke 11:33-36

[Jesus said] "No one takes a light and puts it under a bowl or hides it. Instead, they put it on a lampstand so that the people who come in can see. The only source of light for the body is the eye. When you look at people and want to help them, you are full of light. But when you look at people in a selfish way, you are full of darkness. So be careful! Don't let the light in you become darkness. If you are full of light, and there is no part of you that is dark, then you will be all bright, as though you have the light of a lamp shining on you."

KEY THOUGHT

Not all religion is the same. Despite the claims of many in today's culture, simply choosing a religion is not the issue. The issue has to do with choosing a Savior. Only one Savior has already chosen you. He has already paid for your sins. He has already set in motion the power to make you a child of God and bring you home to himself as a fellow heir of heaven's riches. This Savior warns about false lights that are really just another form of darkness.

TODAY'S PRAYER

Father, please give me eyes to see and a heart that is open to your truth. I do not want to put my faith in something simply because I have a deep-seated need to be religious. I want the true light, the eternal light, and the saving light to illuminate my soul. I seek your truth. Lead me to an authentic faith in what is true. In Jesus' name I pray. Amen.

CONTEXT: LUKE 11:29-35
Related Passages: Proverbs 14:12; John 7:16-18; Luke 11:9-10

Day 213

TAKE A LOOK INSIDE!

Luke 11:37-41

After Jesus had finished speaking, a Pharisee asked Jesus to eat with him. So he went and took a place at the table. But the Pharisee was surprised when he saw that Jesus did not wash his hands first before the meal. The Lord said to him, "The washing you Pharisees do is like cleaning only the outside of a cup or a dish. But what is inside you? You want only to cheat and hurt people. You are foolish! The same one who made what is outside also made what is inside. So pay attention to what is inside. Give to the people who need help. Then you will be fully clean."

KEY THOUGHT

In the previous verses, Jesus warned about the light in us actually being darkness. Now, he is asking those who invited him over for a meal to take a look inside. They were spending a great deal of time, energy, and worry over being clean outside. While there is nothing wrong with that, the bigger issue was on the inside clean hearts. Knowing them and their values, he challenges them to do something that would reveal just who they were, inside and out. He spoke to their greed. While they may look religious and righteous on the outside, he knew that greed was consuming them on the inside. In our age, Jesus' challenge still stands—take a look on the inside. And the monster on the inside for a lot of us today is still the same: greed.

TODAY'S PRAYER

Father, forgive me for my greed. I know that many of your children live with joy in the midst of poverty. I know many of them are far more generous than I am. Open my heart and cleanse me through and through. Make me more generous with others, just as you have been generous with me. Thank you for all of my blessings, in Jesus' name. Amen.

CONTEXT: LUKE 11:37-44
Related Passages: Isaiah 56:11; Luke 12:15; Ephesians 5:5

Day 214

TITHING THE HEART

Luke 11:42

"But it will be bad for you Pharisees! You give God a tenth of the food you get, even your mint, your rue, and every other little plant in your garden. But you forget to be fair to others and to love God. These are the things you should do. And you should also continue to do those other things."

KEY THOUGHT

Jesus reminds the Pharisees that tithing is important. They shouldn't neglect their tithes. However, tithing down to the tiny details isn't the ultimate issue in giving. Working to insure that justice and God's love are a part of our personal lives and lived out in our world are crucial to be people of integrity. The reason we are to be generous is because our Father is generous. The reason we are to act in love is because God has loved us. The reason we work for justice is because God has blessed us with his merciful justice. We want to be about our Father's business and living out our Father's character. Tithing is one aspect of that. Love and justice are the heart of it!

TODAY'S PRAYER

Father, I confess that I sometimes get so caught up in my personal responsibilities to give that I lose sight of why you call me to be generous and loving. Give me a heart that works for justice for the oppressed, downtrodden, forgotten, and marginalized. In Jesus' name I pray. Amen.

CONTEXT: LUKE 11:37-44
Related Passages: Amos 5:14-15, 21-24; Malachi 3:5; Isaiah 1:17

Day 215

THE FLEETING VALUE OF THE PRAISE OF OUR PEERS

Luke 11:43

[Jesus said] "It will be bad for you Pharisees because you love to have the most important seats in the synagogues. And you love for people to show respect to you in the marketplaces."

KEY THOUGHT

Whose approval matters most? The praise of our peers drives many of us. While we often talk about the peer pressure that influences our teens, we fail to acknowledge that adults are equally as controlled by it. Christian leaders are not immune to this temptation. If the approval of others is what matters most, Satan will find a way to use that adulation, approval, and need for affirmation to corrupt our message. We must know why we do what we do and say what we say. We must not "spin" things just so that we look good. We are not to do what we do to be accepted. What should matter most to us? God's approval, appreciation, and affirmation must matter most!

TODAY'S PRAYER

Father, help me live to honor you with pure motives. While I know you will send others to encourage and affirm me when I need it most, I also do not want to "sell out" my faith for the approval and acceptance of others. Keep my heart, my motives, and my life pure of any contaminant that would rob you of your glory and your place of preeminence in my life. I ask for this grace in Jesus' name. Amen.

CONTEXT: LUKE 11:37-44
Related Passages: John 7:18; John 12:42-43; Galatians 1:10

Day 216

RECOGNIZE HOW BAD IT IS!

Luke 11:44
*[Jesus said] "It will be bad for you, because you are like hidden
graves. People walk on them without knowing it."*

KEY THOUGHT

Many of us look at our sins and shortcomings, and then dismiss them as
less sinful than other people's sin. Jesus is confronting the Pharisees about
their sin. The Pharisees were generally considered to be some of the most
righteous living people in Jesus' day. Yet Jesus calls on them (see the previous
verses in Luke 11) to look past their outward demonstrations of righteousness
and to look at their hearts—to deal with their inner greed, their outward show
of generosity coupled with their lack of passion for social justice, and their
desire to be treated with special honor. Jesus wants them to know that their
sin is just as bad as those to whom they feel righteously superior. If we are
willing, we will also hear him knock on the door of our hearts and challenge
us not to settle for outward righteous appearances, but to pursue the things
that are genuinely righteous. Let us pursue these from the heart, knowing that
our inner attitudes matter most to God.

TODAY'S PRAYER

*Help me, O God my Abba Father, to pursue what is to your glory and honor. Forgive
me for my sins. Help me to understand the guilt of those sins as I confess them.
Help me to understand that you have forgiven me of those sins and cleansed me
of their guilt. However, help me to honestly see my sins as you have and to be as
repulsed by them as I am repulsed by the sins of others. Don't let the shame of my
sins destroy me, but use my awareness of my sins and my appreciation of your
grace to motivate me away from sin in the future. In Jesus' name I pray. Amen.*

CONTEXT: LUKE 11:37-44
Related Passages: James 1:14-16; 1 John 1:5-2:2; Luke 6:41-42

Day 217

THE PROBLEM OF RELIGIOUS PRETENSE

Luke 11:45-49
One of the experts in the law said to Jesus, "Teacher, when you say these things about the Pharisees, you are criticizing our group too."

Jesus answered, "It will be bad for you, you experts in the law! You make strict rules that are very hard for people to obey. You try to force others to obey your rules. But you yourselves don't even try to follow any of those rules. It will be bad for you, because you build tombs for the prophets. But these are the same prophets your ancestors killed! And now you show all people that you agree with what your ancestors did. They killed the prophets, and you build tombs for the prophets! This is why God in his wisdom said, 'I will send prophets and apostles to them. Some of my prophets and apostles will be killed by evil men. Others will be treated badly.'"

KEY THOUGHT

Religious pretense is damnable. That's not my opinion or society's opinion. It's Jesus' verdict! Rather than seeking the character and the heart of God, religious pretense looks for forms and ignores character; it looks for self-justifying laws and crushes people. Let's seek the heart of God and hunger and thirst for his righteousness rather than settling for some man-made collection of legal requirements that make us look good. Let's use God's truth to bless and enable people to be what God calls them to be rather than setting impossible standards and then criticizing them when they fail. Jesus calls us to righteousness. Yet his standard of righteousness is displayed in his own compassion, mercy, grace, truth, and love.

TODAY'S PRAYER

Father, please prevent me from being a self-justifying religious legalist who is full of pretension. I want to have a heart for people like your Son demonstrated. I want to honor you with holy character and personal integrity. I want to bless others as I live my life of faith. Please, dear Father, help me never become an expert at religious teaching while remaining ignorant of your passionate desire for holiness and of your consuming love for your children. In Jesus' name I pray. Amen.

CONTEXT: LUKE 11:45-54
Related Passages: John 3:16-21; Hebrews 3:12-13; 1 John 3:15-18

Day 218

RESPONSIBLE FOR ALL?

Luke 11:50-51

[Jesus said] "So you people who live now will be punished for the deaths of all the prophets who were killed since the beginning of the world. You will be punished for the killing of Abel. And you will be punished for the killing of Zechariah, who was killed between the altar and the Temple. Yes, I tell you that you people will be punished for them all."

KEY THOUGHT

Wow! Jesus' judgment on these folks is severe. Why is his pronouncement so harsh? How can he say such things? I believe there are three reasons. First, Jesus Christ, the Son of God (who is greater than the prophets and great souls of the past) has come to them and they will murder him to protect their religion. Second, Jesus wants them to realize how utterly flawed their approach to religion actually has become. Third, Jesus wants us to see clearly how horrible it is to try to protect our religious pre-conceptions rather than to be shaped by the truth. His words were sharp and harsh, but absolutely true and needed!

TODAY'S PRAYER

Father, I am convicted of how easily I can trade a vibrant faith in you for a flawed and self-protecting "religiosity." Please call me away from false motives, pretenses, and convictions so that I can serve you with an undivided heart. In Jesus' name I pray. Amen.

CONTEXT: LUKE 11:45-54
Related Passages: John 8:40-47; John 1:10-13; Matthew 27:24-25

Day 219

RELIGIOUS SUPERIORITY BEFORE SPIRITUAL ENCOURAGEMENT?

Luke 11:52

[Jesus said] "It will be bad for you, you experts in the law! You have taken away the key to learning about God. You yourselves would not learn, and you stopped others from learning too."

KEY THOUGHT

Unfortunately, some who are caught up in a religious movement have the genuineness of their faith usurped by a group desire to be religiously superior. Rather than encouraging, helping, and blessing those who are newer in the faith, these folks turn faith into legalism and corrupt the hopeful message of the gospel. The way they live out their religion drives away people who are seeking God and breaks the spirit of those who are new to faith. Let's make sure that we don't impose demands God doesn't require. Even more, when folks find areas where they need to grow in their obedience to God, let's be there to help and not criticize.

TODAY'S PRAYER

Father, please forgive me for the times I've not stuck close enough to new Christians. Give me eyes to see and a heart that is willing to help those who are new in the faith. Use me to be a load-lifter and load-bearer for these new followers, not a load-imposer. In the precious name of Jesus I pray. Amen.

CONTEXT: LUKE 11:45-54
Related Passages: Colossians 1:28-29; Galatians 4:19; 1 Thessalonians 2:7-8

Day 220

OBEDIENCE, RATIONALIZATION, DISINTEREST, OR FURY?

Luke 11:53-54

When Jesus went out, the teachers of the law and the Pharisees began to give him much trouble. They tried to make him answer questions about many things. They were trying to find a way to catch Jesus saying something wrong.

KEY THOUGHT

We can have four reactions to Jesus' demands in our lives. We can obey, and show by our lives that we truly believe he is Lord. We can rationalize away those demands so that we can play like we are a Jesus-follower without really being a genuine follower of the Lord. We can ignore Jesus' words and treat them as irrelevant. Or, we can respond to his convicting truths with anger and fury. What do you do with Jesus' words?

TODAY'S PRAYER

Father, thank you for sending Jesus to reveal your truth. Keep my heart open to that truth so that it will flourish and bring changes to my life as I obey the Lord Jesus, in whose name I pray. Amen.

CONTEXT: LUKE 11:45-54
Related Passages: Matthew 7:21-23; Mark 3:32-35; John 7:18

Day 221

NO REAL SECRETS!

Luke 12:1-3

Many thousands of people came together. There were so many people that they were stepping on each other. Before Jesus spoke to the people, he said to his followers, "Be careful of the yeast of the Pharisees. I mean that they are hypocrites. Everything that is hidden will be shown, and everything that is secret will be made known. What you say in the dark will be told in the light. And what you whisper in a private room will be shouted from the top of the house."

KEY THOUGHT

We must live as if we have no secrets because all of our secrets will eventually become public—now, later, or when Jesus' comes. Who we truly are in the core of our beings will be on full display when we stand before the Lord. We won't be hiding behind a public persona while trying to cover up our rotten reality or our sinful habits. Let's pray that what people see in us is a lot more like Jesus each day!

TODAY'S PRAYER

Holy and loving Father, I praise you for being the Almighty God who knows even the untold truths buried in my past, hidden in my heart. In Jesus' name I pray. Amen.

CONTEXT: LUKE 12:1-12
Related Passages: Ephesians 5:10-16; Romans 2:16; Luke 8:16-18

Day 222

SOBERING WORDS!

Luke 12:4-5

Then Jesus said to the people, "I tell you, my friends, don't be afraid of people. They can kill the body, but after that they can do nothing more to hurt you. I will show you the one to fear. You should fear God, who has the power to kill you and also to throw you into hell. Yes, he is the one you should fear."

KEY THOUGHT

Most of us much prefer to speak about God's grace, love, and mercy. Every once in awhile, however, we hit one of those "shake you to the core" passages that reminds us of God's holiness and our sinfulness. God doesn't want to punish or condemn us. Jesus is proof of that. But he is the creator and he has paid an enormous price to bring us back to himself after our rebellion. When we ignore his grace, mercy, and love we are choosing disaster and judgment. God's grace, mercy, and love is revealed and offered to us in Jesus. To reject Jesus is to reject God and his grace, mercy, and love. It is to choose judgment and condemnation. Jesus wants us to know that what we decide about him and do with his life and teachings means everything for us eternally.

TODAY'S PRAYER

Father, forgive me when I have trivialized your grace, mercy, and love that were so powerfully offered to me through Jesus. Forgive me, O God, for the times that I have not been awed by your holiness, not been touched by your sacrificial mercy, and not been wounded at the price you paid to extend me grace. Thank you with all that I am for Jesus, in whose name I offer this confession and prayer. Amen.

CONTEXT: LUKE 12:1-12
Related Passages: John 3:16-21; Luke 12:16-18; Mark 9:43-48

Day 223

BEYOND THE HARSH WORDS
TO GRACIOUSNESS!

Luke 12:6-7

[Jesus said] "When birds are sold, five small birds cost only two pennies. But God does not forget any of them. Yes, God even knows how many hairs you have on your head. Don't be afraid. You are worth much more than many birds."

KEY THOUGHT

Jesus' words in the previous sentences were strong; some would even say his words were harsh. Jesus reminds us, however, that God's desire is not to punish, harm, or bring destruction on us. His desire is to love and bless us. One clear example is to simply look at the created world and see how God has lovingly provided for all sorts of animals. Long before anyone had ever heard of PETA, God showed his love by giving each creature its space and place. Yet we are definitely more valuable than any animal or created thing. Jesus wants us to know how precious we are to God, so he teaches us this lesson in Luke 12 and then goes out and demonstrates it on the cross!

TODAY'S PRAYER

Father, thank you for knowing me, valuing me, and loving me. Most of all, dear Father, thank you for sending Jesus to show your great love for me. In Jesus' name I offer my deepest thanks and praise. Amen.

CONTEXT: LUKE 12:1-12
Related Passages: Genesis 1:26-31; Psalm 139:13-16; Romans 8:19

Day 224

CONFESSING CHRIST

Luke 12:8-9

[Jesus said] "I tell you, if you stand before others and are willing to say you believe in me, then I will say that you belong to me. I will say this in the presence of God's angels. But if you stand before others and say you do not believe in me, then I will say that you do not belong to me. I will say this in the presence of God's angels."

KEY THOUGHT

Confessing Christ is crucial! Confessing Christ can be costly in human terms. For generations, Jesus' followers have been put to death simply for saying, "Jesus Christ is Lord" rather than calling some other ruler "Lord." However, the significance of our confessing Christ is revealed most clearly by Jesus' own words here: he will claim us if we claim him!

TODAY'S PRAYER

O Lord, my Father in heaven, you are holy. I know that, just as I have acknowledged Christ as my Lord and called on his name in baptism, Jesus will acknowledge me before you and the holy angels and will call my name as your child on the day he returns. Holy God, I gladly confess that Jesus Christ, your Son, is my Savior and my Lord. It is in his precious name that I am saved and that I pray. Amen.

CONTEXT: LUKE 12:1-12
Related Passages: Romans 10:9-13; 1 Corinthians 12:3; Philippians 2:5-11

Day 225

FORGIVABLE AND UNFORGIVABLE

Luke 12:10

[Jesus said] "Whoever says something against the Son of Man can be forgiven.
But whoever speaks against the Holy Spirit will not be forgiven."

KEY THOUGHT

We can certainly be thankful that past blasphemies and past rejections
of Jesus will not be held against us. When we come to Christ, our sins are
forgiven and our guilt is removed. For this grace, we can only offer thanks and
praise to God!

TODAY'S PRAYER

Thank you, dear Father in heaven, for cleansing me of my past offenses
that insulted you and your Son. I am genuinely sorry for them and wish I
could go back and remove them. However, dear Father, since I cannot do
that, I am thankful that your grace has. In Jesus' name I pray. Amen.

CONTEXT: LUKE 12:1-12
Related Passages: Acts 2:36-41; 1 Corinthians 6:11; Psalm 103:10-12

Day 226

THE HOLY SPIRIT WILL HELP

Luke 12:11-12

[Jesus said] "When men bring you into the synagogues before the leaders and other important men, don't worry about what you will say. The Holy Spirit will teach you at that time what you should say."

KEY THOUGHT

In the previous verse, Jesus had warned against blaspheming the Holy Spirit. While it is not altogether clear what he meant in this context, in another reference to this subject Jesus is referring to those who attributed his miracles to demons rather than the Spirit of God. Nevertheless, one thing is clear: the Holy Spirit lives in and works through Jesus' followers. This is especially true when they are facing great opposition, especially political rulers. The Holy Spirit will be with them to help them know what to say. They will not be alone no matter how it may feel to them. Their words will have power because of the Spirit speaking through them. To ignore their words is to ignore the very Spirit of God speaking through them.

TODAY'S PRAYER

Father, speak through me and use me by the power of your Holy Spirit, to your glory. In Jesus' name I pray. Amen.

CONTEXT: LUKE 12:1-12
Related Passages: Acts 1:8; Acts 4:29-31; Acts 6:8-10

Day 227

GREEDY FOR FINANCIAL JUSTICE

Luke 12:13-15

One of the men in the crowd said to Jesus, "Teacher, our father just died and left some things for us. Tell my brother to share them with me."

But Jesus said to him, "Who said I should be your judge or decide how to divide your father's things between you two?" Then Jesus said to them, "Be careful and guard against all kinds of greed. People do not get life from the many things they own."

KEY THOUGHT

Most of us can really get upset when someone cheats us financially. Yet incredibly, nearly everyone of us gets cheated at something, by someone, somewhere down the line. There are plenty of folks looking to cheat honest folks. This hurts us terribly when it is a person in our physical or spiritual family. They are supposed to be people we can trust. We shouldn't be surprised when this is a problem brought to Jesus. Jesus makes it clear that he is not going to get into the middle of a family dispute about money. He is not here to insure us financial justice. Jesus is more interested in our earthly character and our eternal trajectory. Greed can manifest itself in those who are rich. However, it is an even bigger problem in those who want to be rich. The issue isn't if we're going to be cheated financially, but whether or not we handle it with character and grace.

TODAY'S PRAYER

Father, don't let greed have a foothold in my heart. I know that it is a form of idolatry, and I don't want anything to have the desires of my heart but you. In Jesus' name I pray. Amen.

CONTEXT: LUKE 12:13-21
Related Passages: 1 Timothy 6:6-10; Colossians 3:5; 1 Corinthians 6:1-6

Day 228

TRUE WEALTH

Luke 12:16-21

Then Jesus used this story: "There was a rich man who had some
land. His land grew a very good crop of food. He thought to himself,
'What will I do? I have no place to keep all my crops.'

"Then he said, 'I know what I will do. I will tear down my barns and build
bigger barns! I will put all my wheat and good things together in my new
barns. Then I can say to myself, I have many good things stored. I have
saved enough for many years. Rest, eat, drink, and enjoy life!'

"But God said to that man, 'Foolish man! Tonight you will die. So what about
the things you prepared for yourself? Who will get those things now?'

"This is how it will be for anyone who saves things only
for himself. To God that person is not rich."

KEY THOUGHT

When we are blessed financially, we can easily become arrogant and
think that we are blessed because we are smarter, better, or just work harder
than anyone else. Many followers of Jesus in the world today live in very
impoverished conditions. Those of us who are blessed with financial wealth—
and God's definition of wealth is anyone who has more than food, clothes,
and a place to sleep—have been blessed to be a blessing. This principle goes
back to God's call of Abraham (Gen. 12:1-3) and is reiterated by Paul to the
Corinthians (2 Cor. 9:8-11). Our financial blessings are simply God's way of
entrusting us with his money to do his work. We are blessed to be a blessing—
not to hoard, gloat, or become self-satisfied.

TODAY'S PRAYER

Father, thank you for all of my blessings. I ask you for the wisdom to use these blessings in
ways that reflect your will, bless others, and bring you joy. In Jesus' name I pray. Amen.

CONTEXT: LUKE 12:13-21
Related Passages: Genesis 12:1-3; 2 Corinthians 8:1-5; 2 Corinthians 9:6-10

Day 229

WHY THE BIGGER THINGS?

Luke 12:22-26

Jesus said to his followers, "So I tell you, don't worry about the things you need to live—what you will eat or what you will wear. Life is more important than food, and the body is more important than what you put on it. Look at the birds. They don't plant, harvest, or save food in houses or barns, but God feeds them. And you are worth much more than crows. None of you can add any time to your life by worrying about it. And if you can't do the little things, why worry about the big things?"

Key Thought

Life is more than food and clothing. God has reminded us of that throughout the Scriptures. Jesus reminded us of it when he faced temptation from Satan. So we shouldn't worry, because God will take care of the big stuff and the little stuff. Worrying doesn't change things, big or small, except to make those problems appear worse than they really are. So why do we let ourselves get worked up into a frenzy over "big things"? Let's cast our cares on God and then trust in his grace and providence.

Today's Prayer

Holy God, my loving Abba Father, you knew I really needed to read this passage today and think through its meaning in my life. "Don't worry!" you're telling me. Even more so, you're telling me, "Quit worrying!" I know that worrying about things can't change them. So please give me faith that you are already working on both the big and small things in my life. Help me learn to trust you to see me through any circumstance. Give me wisdom, strength, courage, generosity, and love. I pray this in Jesus' name. Amen.

Context: Luke 12:22-34
Related Passages: Philippians 4:6-7; 1 Peter 5:7; Philippians 4:19-20

Day 230

WHAT ARE YOU LIVING FOR?

Luke 12:27-32

*"Think about how the wildflowers grow. They don't work or make clothes for them-
selves. But I tell you that even Solomon, the great and rich king, was not dressed
as beautifully as one of these flowers. If God makes what grows in the field so
beautiful, what do you think he will do for you? That's just grass—one day it's
alive, and the next day someone throws it into a fire. But God cares enough to
make it beautiful. Surely he will do much more for you. Your faith is so small!*

*"So don't always think about what you will eat or what you will drink. Don't worry
about it. That's what all those people who don't know God are always thinking about.
But your Father knows that you need these things. What you should be thinking
about is God's kingdom. Then he will give you all these other things you need.*

"Don't fear, little flock. Your Father wants to share his kingdom with you."

KEY THOUGHT

What's the bottom line in these words of Jesus? Don't be afraid to live
for the Kingdom as your highest concern. God takes care of things much less
important than we are. He cares for them in ways far finer than we can provide
for ourselves. We're more important to God than those things. So let's give the
Father the joy of giving us the Kingdom by making it our highest desire. Let
him take care of the "little stuff" as we pursue the "Kingdom stuff."

TODAY'S PRAYER

*Holy Father, give me a passion for your Kingdom and your righteousness.
Make that passion burn inside me until your Kingdom becomes my highest
call. I know that my worries about other things will be driven out by the proper
passion for what you long to give me. In Jesus' name I pray. Amen.*

CONTEXT: LUKE 12:22-34
Related Passages: Matthew 6:3-10; Philippians 3:13-14; Revelation 3:15-16

Day 231

INVESTMENT FOR THE FUTURE

Luke 12:33-34

[Jesus said] "Sell the things you have and give that money to those who need it. This is the only way you can keep your riches from being lost. You will be storing treasure in heaven that lasts forever. Thieves can't steal that treasure, and moths can't destroy it. Your heart will be where your treasure is."

KEY THOUGHT

"What are your primary investment strategies?" I can still remember a financial planner asking me that question. It wasn't his first question or second, but on down the line he got around to asking it. In a way, Jesus is really challenging us to face that same question in this passage. In the cycles of our national and world economies, there are "lean" times and there are times of "plenty." No earthly investment strategy is foolproof. Only when we invest in things that are eternal can we invest in things that are truly guaranteed—things that can't be stolen, destroyed, or ruined. So what are we doing to invest in our eternal future? This question is vital, because what we value as our true treasure will be the focus of our hearts.

TODAY'S PRAYER

Father, help me build a portfolio of grace, marked by generosity to others and a commitment to things that are eternal. In Jesus' name I pray. Amen.

CONTEXT: LUKE 12:22-34
Related Passages: Luke 14:33; Galatians 6:7; 1 Timothy 6:6-7, 17-19

Day 232
BE READY!

Luke 12:35-40

[Jesus said] "Be ready! Be fully dressed and have your lights shining. Be like servants who are waiting for their master to come home from a wedding party. The master comes and knocks, and the servants immediately open the door for him. When their master sees that they are ready and waiting for him, it will be a great day for those servants. I can tell you without a doubt, the master will get himself ready to serve a meal and tell the servants to sit down. Then he will serve them. Those servants might have to wait until midnight or later for their master. But they will be glad they did when he comes in and finds them still waiting.

"Remember this: If the owner of the house knew what time a thief was coming, he would not allow the thief to enter his house. So you also must be ready, because the Son of Man will come at a time when you don't expect him!"

KEY THOUGHT

Jesus had just urged his followers to invest in things that are eternal (see the previous verses). Now he reminds them to be ready for the beginning of this eternal future. His coming is near, so be ready. His coming will be unexpected by many, so be ready. In addition, there is a great blessing for those of us who are looking for his coming and are ready for it. So are you waiting and watching and ready for Jesus' return?

TODAY'S PRAYER

Father, give me a greater sense of urgency and expectation about the coming of Christ. I want to be ready and to greet that day with celebration even though I can't know the day or hour of his coming. Give me wisdom as I seek to invest in eternal things that matter to you. Give me a sense of joyous anticipation as I await the blessing of my Savior's glorious return and ultimate victory. In Jesus' name I pray. Amen.

CONTEXT: LUKE 12:35-48
Related Passages: 1 Corinthians 15:52-55; 2 TImothy 4:6-8; 2 Thessalonians 5:1-11

Day 233

A GREATER RESPONSIBILITY

Luke 12:41-48
Peter said, "Lord, did you tell this story for us or for all people?"

The Lord said, "Who is the wise and trusted servant? The master trusts one servant to give the other servants their food at the right time. Who is the servant that the master trusts to do that work? When the master comes and finds him doing the work he gave him, it will be a day of blessing for that servant! I can tell you without a doubt, the master will choose that servant to take care of everything he owns.

"But what will happen if that servant is evil and thinks his master will not come back soon? He will begin to beat the other servants, men and women. He will eat and drink until he has had too much. Then the master will come when the servant is not ready, at a time when the servant is not expecting him. Then the master will punish that servant and send him away to be with the other people who don't obey.

"That servant knew what his master wanted him to do. But he did not make himself ready or try to do what his master wanted. So that servant will be punished very much! But what about the servant who does not know what his master wants? He also does things that deserve punishment. But he will get less punishment than the servant who knew what he should do. Whoever has been given much will be responsible for much. Much more will be expected from the one who has been given more."

KEY THOUGHT

Peter's question to Jesus addresses those of us who lead, whether in business, education, church, or family. We've been given the blessing of influence. How we lead is not just a matter of our group doing well; it is also a matter of honoring the Lord with our best efforts and with holy conduct. He has given us skill, influence, and position to be a blessing to others. If we shirk our responsibilities, if we lead unfairly or harshly, or if we "slack off" in using our gifts, we will be judged harshly. Why? We've been given much; God expects much from us!

TODAY'S PRAYER

O gracious Father, you have blessed me in many incredible ways. I want to use my gifts, abilities, and talents in ways that honor you and bless your people. May my life honor the investment that you have made in me. I pray in Jesus' name. Amen.

CONTEXT: LUKE 12:35-48
Related Passages: 1 Peter 4:10-11; 1 Peter 5:1-4; Hebrews 13:20-21

Day 234

FIRE! DIVISION! DECISION!

Luke 12:49-53

Jesus continued speaking: "I came to bring fire to the world. I wish it were already burning! There is a kind of baptism that I must suffer through. I feel very troubled until it is finished. Do you think I came to give peace to the world? No, I came to divide the world! From now on, a family of five will be divided, three against two, and two against three.

A father and son will be divided: The son will turn against his father. The father will turn against his son. A mother and her daughter will be divided: The daughter will turn against her mother. The mother will turn against her daughter. A mother-in-law and her daughter-in-law will be divided: The daughter-in-law will turn against her mother-in-law. The mother-in-law will turn against her daughter-in-law."

KEY THOUGHT

Jesus demonstrated God's love to us in many ways. He will demonstrate it incredibly when he comes to take God's children home to be with him forever. However, the cost of those blessings is high—high for him, high for God, and high for those who follow him. Jesus left heaven, came to earth, and died a horrible death to provide these blessings to us. So we must not be surprised at the powerful language Jesus uses here. His ministry calls for a radical decision. He is either God with us or he is an impostor. He is either Christ, God's Messiah and our Savior, or he is delusional. He is either Lord, King of our hearts and of all creation, or he is a liar. Making this decision will divide families and households. It will be politically incorrect because it doesn't allow for alternatives. As Jesus speaks to his early followers, he also speaks to us. If we decide for him, our decision will not make everyone happy. Not everyone will like us or approve of us. A passionate follower of Jesus will not be appreciated by all—maybe not by most!

TODAY'S PRAYER

Father, please give me the courage to fully decide to follow Jesus. Then, please grant me the wisdom to know how to deal lovingly with those who cannot accept my decision, my passion, and my discipleship. I ask this in Jesus' name. Amen.

CONTEXT: LUKE 12:49-59
Related Passages: Philippians 2:5-11; John 15:18; 1 John 3:13

Day 235

GET THINGS SETTLED

Luke 12:54-59

Then Jesus said to the people, "When you see clouds growing bigger in the west, you say, 'A rainstorm is coming.' And soon it begins to rain. When you feel the wind begin to blow from the south, you say, 'It will be a hot day.' And you are right. You hypocrites! You can understand the weather. Why don't you understand what is happening now?

"Why can't you decide for yourselves what is right? Suppose someone is suing you, and you are both going to court. Try hard to settle it on the way. If you don't settle it, you may have to go before the judge. And the judge will hand you over to the officer, who will throw you into jail. I tell you, you will not get out of there until you have paid every cent you owe."

KEY THOUGHT

Jesus has been teaching his followers about living with a sense of urgency and expectation (see the last half of Luke 12). The values of the Kingdom of God are values built around a commitment to be ready for his return. That means living with passion. That means living with many people who do not appreciate us. That means living with a sense of expectation. That means living with a sense that our decision to follow Jesus matters profoundly. With all that in mind, Jesus closes this section by urging us to get our matters settled with others. Since his coming is always near, we need to make sure our relationships are reconciled. Closing time can come at any time and we want to make sure our matters are in good shape. So let's get things right today!

TODAY'S PRAYER

Father, give me a deeper sense of urgency to get my relationships and matters in order. In Jesus' name I pray. Amen.

CONTEXT: LUKE 12:49-59
Related Passages: Ephesians 4:20-32; Matthew 6:14-15; James 5:9

Day 236

REPENT!

Luke 13:1-5

Some people there with Jesus at that time told him about what had happened to some worshipers from Galilee. Pilate had them killed. Their blood was mixed with the blood of the animals they had brought for sacrificing. Jesus answered, "Do you think this happened to those people because they were more sinful than all other people from Galilee? No, they were not. But if you don't decide now to change your lives, you will all be destroyed like those people! And what about those people who died when the tower of Siloam fell on them? Do you think they were more sinful than everyone else in Jerusalem? They were not. But I tell you if you don't decide now to change your lives, you will all be destroyed too!"

KEY THOUGHT

The word repent—to change our hearts and lives—carries with it all sorts of images depending upon one's background. Jesus is concerned that we understand one concept central to this idea: the need to turn around. He wants us to realize that living life as we think best is a disaster. We need to turn around and let him set our values, direction, and lifestyle. Left to our own best choices we are going to fail. So we need to repent—to change our hearts and lives, turn around, and follow his direction.

TODAY'S PRAYER

Father, I sometimes find myself full of pride and self-confidence, believing that I can best determine the direction of my life. Yet, dear Father, I recognize that unless I turn around and follow Jesus, my life is ultimately headed for destruction. Today I re-commit to begin each new day with a passion to live for you, guided by your Spirit, with Jesus as my Lord. Please bless me as I seek to live wholly for you. In Jesus' name I pray. Amen.

CONTEXT: LUKE 13:1-9
Related Passages: Acts 2:38-41; Acts 3:19-20; Acts 17:27-31

Day 237

ONE LAST CHANCE!

Luke 13:6-9

Jesus told this story: "A man had a fig tree. He planted it in his garden. He came looking for some fruit on it, but he found none. He had a servant who took care of his garden. So he said to his servant, 'I have been looking for fruit on this tree for three years, but I never find any. Cut it down! Why should it waste the ground?' But the servant answered, 'Master, let the tree have one more year to produce fruit. Let me dig up the dirt around it and fertilize it. Maybe the tree will have fruit on it next year. If it still does not produce, then you can cut it down.'"

KEY THOUGHT

At the end of Luke 12, Jesus reminded his followers to live with a sense of urgency about his return. Jesus began chapter 13 by calling on people to change their hearts. Now Jesus is basically reminding us that we live on borrowed time. We need to make that change in our hearts and lives now. We've been extended a season of grace to become fruitful, so it's time to be fruitful. No more playing around with religion. No more hypocrisy. No more religious talk without spiritual commitment and spiritual living. It's put up or shut up time. It's time to be fruitful.

TODAY'S PRAYER

Holy and righteous Father, I know that now is the time you want me to be fruitful. Today you want me to live for you with passion. Help me put off my religious procrastination. Bless me as I seek to lay aside my fears and inhibitions about following you. Empower me to live with holiness, urgency, and a sense of joyous expectation. I pray this in Jesus' name. Amen.

CONTEXT: LUKE 13:1-9
Related Passages: Acts 17:27-31; Acts 2:36-41; Acts 3:17-20

Day 238

PRAISE GOD!

Luke 13:10-13

Jesus taught in one of the synagogues on the Sabbath day. A woman was there who had an evil spirit inside her. It had made the woman crippled for 18 years. Her back was always bent; she could not stand up straight. When Jesus saw her, he called to her, "Woman, you have been made free from your sickness!" He laid his hands on her, and immediately she was able to stand up straight. She began praising God.

KEY THOUGHT

Coming together to worship God also involves ministering to each other. God is praised when his children feel the touch of Jesus and their brokenness is addressed with love. Worship isn't about a religious audience watching a few spiritual performers do their act, but about Jesus' body ministering to brokenness, committing to holiness, and praising God for his grace.

TODAY'S PRAYER

Father, give me eyes to see those I need to touch and bless with your grace when I go to be with your people to worship you. In Jesus' name I pray. Amen.

CONTEXT: LUKE 13:10-17
Related Passages: Colossians 3:16-17; Hebrews 10:21-25; Acts 2:46-47

GET REAL!

Luke 13:14-17

The synagogue leader was angry because Jesus healed on the Sabbath day. He said to the people, "There are six days for work. So come to be healed on one of those days. Don't come for healing on the Sabbath day."

The Lord answered, "You people are hypocrites! All of you untie your work animals and lead them to drink water every day—even on the Sabbath day. This woman that I healed is a true descendant of Abraham. But Satan has held her for 18 years. Surely it is not wrong for her to be made free from her sickness on a Sabbath day!" When Jesus said this, all those who were criticizing him felt ashamed of themselves. And all the people were happy for the wonderful things he was doing.

KEY THOUGHT

Worship of God will always mean concern for his people. In fact, worship that is not tied to living correctly with people is not worship and does not please God. While we don't like to use the word "shame" in today's politically correct world, some things are indeed shameful. One of those things is to pretend to be a God-worshipping person and then to treat his children as if they didn't matter to us or to their Father in heaven.

TODAY'S PRAYER

Father, I realize that a crucial part of worshipping you is treating people with the love, respect, kindness, and dignity with which you would treat them. Father, help me demonstrate this in my lifestyle, not just know it in my head. Use me to bless others and bring you praise. In Jesus' name I pray. Amen.

CONTEXT: LUKE 13:10-17
Related Passages: Isaiah 1:14-17; James 1:27; Luke 10:30-37

Day 240

LITTLE US, BIG KINGDOM

Luke 13:18-21

Then Jesus said, "What is God's kingdom like? What can I compare it to? God's kingdom is like the seed of the mustard plant. Someone plants this seed in their garden. The seed grows and becomes a tree, and the birds build nests on its branches."

Jesus said again, "What can I compare God's kingdom with? It is like yeast that a woman mixes into a big bowl of flour to make bread. The yeast makes all the dough rise."

KEY THOUGHT

The Kingdom isn't about logic or predictability, but about God and his sovereign power and grace! God can take something small, someone insignificant, even a person who is broken, and do phenomenal things. A huge tree comes from a small seed. A whole loaf is leavened by just a touch of yeast. God asks us to offer ourselves to him. If we do, we can be caught up into the powerful and mysterious work of God's Kingdom.

TODAY'S PRAYER

Father, Lord God Almighty, I offer you all that I am to serve you and bring glory to you. I long to be a part of the triumphant work of your Kingdom. In Jesus' name I pray. Amen.

CONTEXT: LUKE 13:18-21
Related Passages: 1 Corinthians 4:20; Matthew 6:33; 2 Corinthians 4:5-18

Day 241

A REMINDER OF URGENCY AND INTENSITY

Luke 13:22-27

Jesus was teaching in every town and village. He continued to travel toward Jerusalem. Someone said to him, "Lord, how many people will be saved? Only a few?"

Jesus said, "The door to heaven is narrow. Try hard to enter it. Many people will want to enter there, but they will not be able to go in. If a man locks the door of his house, you can stand outside and knock on the door, but he won't open it. You can say, 'Sir, open the door for us.' But he will answer, 'I don't know you. Where did you come from?' Then you will say, 'We ate and drank with you. You taught in the streets of our town.' Then he will say to you, 'I don't know you. Where did you come from? Get away from me! You are all people who do wrong!'"

KEY THOUGHT

Many in the world today have a passing fascination with Jesus, but they have no desire for Jesus to be Lord of their lives. Others see faith as something put off until a more convenient time in their lives—until they have "sown their wild oats" or "lived it up." Jesus is reminding us that only those who have truly confessed and who live with him as Lord are going to find their future glorious. God's grace (Eph. 2:8-10) is not a reason to take lightly the offer of salvation. Those who believe they are saved, but have no desire or passion to live for their Lord and work for his Kingdom are sadly mistaken (James 2:14-20). This is not salvation by works, but it is a reminder that true followers don't go on sinning simply because God is gracious (Rom. 6:1-3). Jesus gave up everything to redeem us. He asks that we recognize his sacrifice and demands that we make him Lord of our lives.

TODAY'S PRAYER

Righteous Father, I thank you for your grace. I know that Jesus paid the debt for my sin and redeemed me. I know that you raised him from the dead and that you exalted him to the highest place. I trust that Jesus is my Savior and seek to live for him as my Lord. May my life reflect my profound thanks for your grace and display the purpose, passion, and meaning you long to give me as your child. In Jesus' name I pray. Amen.

CONTEXT: LUKE 13:18-30
Related Passages: Ephesians 2:8-10; Romans 6:1-4; James 2:17-20

Day 242

TABLES TURNED

Luke 13:28-30
"You will see Abraham, Isaac, Jacob, and all the prophets in God's kingdom. But you will be left outside. There you will cry and grind your teeth with pain. People will come from the east, west, north, and south. They will sit down at the table in God's kingdom. People who have the lowest place in life now will have the highest place in God's kingdom. And people who have the highest place now will have the lowest place in God's kingdom."

KEY THOUGHT

Luke repeatedly emphasizes a very convicting theme in Jesus' ministry: the religious tables being turned at judgment. Jesus repeatedly warns religiously pretentious people of their eternal destruction. These people make a big show of their dedication. They act as if they are pious when they are not. Many of these folks look down on others out of their own self-righteousness while refusing to live with the love and the character of God. Great joy awaits God's children when his Kingdom is fully realized. But those who only appear religious will face a fearsome condemnation. Many who don't seem to be of the "right religious stripe" today actually reflect the love and character of God in their daily lives. They will enjoy the bliss of the Father's eternal blessings. Great will be their joy!

TODAY'S PRAYER

Father, I want to live as a person of spiritual integrity. I want my life to reflect your love and righteousness. Take from me any hint of hypocrisy, arrogance, and self-righteousness. Make me genuinely holy, not just by grace, but also in my daily interface with others. I want my life to bring others to you. In Jesus' name I pray. Amen.

CONTEXT: LUKE 13:18-30
Related Passages: Psalm 19:12-14; Luke 5:27-32; Matthew 20:16

Day 243

NO CONTROL OVER THE CHRIST

Luke 13:31-33

Just then some Pharisees came to Jesus and said, "Go away from here and hide. Herod wants to kill you!"

Jesus said to them, "Go tell that fox, 'Today and tomorrow I am forcing demons out of people and finishing my work of healing. Then, the next day, the work will be finished.' After that, I must go, because all prophets should die in Jerusalem."

KEY THOUGHT

God's will and Jesus' sense of mission will determine the timing, the place, and the extent of the Messiah's ministry. Herod's threats will not frighten or derail the Lord Jesus from his purpose. Like every great prophet, Jesus' destiny will be accomplished in Jerusalem. He will not be manipulated or controlled by political pressure, unfair opposition, or religious propriety. Jesus will walk his own way to accomplish God's will and fulfill his prophesied ministry.

TODAY'S PRAYER

Father, please give me the courage, boldness, integrity, and passion I need to serve you effectively with integrity, righteousness, and grace. I pray this in the name of Jesus. Amen.

CONTEXT: LUKE 13:31-35
Related Passages: 2 Timothy 2:20-21; John 7:25-31; John 4:34

Day 244

LONGING TO PROTECT THE CITY

Luke 13:34-35

"Jerusalem, Jerusalem! You kill the prophets. You stone to death the people God has sent to you. How many times I wanted to help your people. I wanted to gather them together as a hen gathers her chicks under her wings. But you did not let me. Now your home will be left completely empty. I tell you, you will not see me again until that time when you will say, 'Welcome! God bless the one who comes in the name of the Lord.'"

KEY THOUGHT

Doesn't this passage, this haunting cry of Jesus, seem very poignant even today? God longs to bless the people of Jerusalem. In fact, the Gospel of Luke and Acts of the Apostles remind us again and again of God's love for the great cities of the world—Jerusalem, Antioch, Ephesus, Athens, Corinth, Rome—and how he longs to reach them with his grace through the good news of Jesus. Yet so often the cities, like Jerusalem, are the places that reject the message of Jesus. This rejection of God's grace and ethics ends up bringing destruction on the cities. For Jerusalem, however, the rejection of Jesus is the rejection of their Messiah, their hope, and their Savior. Let's not be guilty of the same rejection. Let's understand God's desire to bring us under his wing of protection and respond by offering him our hearts, souls, minds, and strength.

TODAY'S PRAYER

Tender Shepherd, my heavenly Father, thank you for your Son and my Savior and Lord. Use me to be a blessing to my city and empower me to share your saving grace given through Jesus, in whose name I pray. Amen.

CONTEXT: LUKE 13:31-35
Related Passages: Acts 2:36-42; John 1:10-13; Luke 20:9-16

Day 245

GENUINE WORSHIP

Luke 14:1-6

On a Sabbath day, Jesus went to the home of a leading Pharisee to eat with him. The people there were all watching him very closely. A man with a bad disease was there in front of him. Jesus said to the Pharisees and experts in the law, "Is it right or wrong to heal on the Sabbath day?" But they would not answer his question. So he took the man and healed him. Then he sent the man away. Jesus said to the Pharisees and teachers of the law, "If your son or work animal falls into a well on the Sabbath day, you know you would pull him out immediately." The Pharisees and teachers of the law could say nothing against what he said.

KEY THOUGHT

We often get our priorities bent out of shape when it comes to worship. We can argue over the style of songs, appropriate dress, and even the color of the carpet. Yet God seems to be much more interested in the integrity of the heart in worship than our polished facades, rituals, and traditions. God longs to bless people—to forgive them and make them whole. We must never forget this passion of the Father that is so often demonstrated by Jesus. Let's remember that worship is as much about blessing others as it is about honoring God.

TODAY'S PRAYER

Holy God, please be with me as I prepare my heart to worship you with my brothers and sisters in Christ. Open my eyes to see how I can bless and strengthen them as I also praise and worship you. In Jesus' name I pray. Amen.

CONTEXT: LUKE 14:1-6
Related Passages: Hebrews 10:23-26; Luke 10:30-37; John 5:16-17

Day 246

EXALTED!

Luke 14:7-11

Then Jesus noticed that some of the guests were choosing the best places to sit. So he told this story: "When someone invites you to a wedding, don't sit in the most important seat. They may have invited someone more important than you. And if you are sitting in the most important seat, they will come to you and say, 'Give this man your seat!' Then you will have to move down to the last place and be embarrassed.

"So when someone invites you, go sit in the seat that is not important. Then they will come to you and say, 'Friend, move up here to this better place!' What an honor this will be for you in front of all the other guests. Everyone who makes themselves important will be made humble. But everyone who makes themselves humble will be made important."

KEY THOUGHT

Most of us detest self-promotion when we see it in someone else. However, we have a strange ability to find reasons why we "need" to promote ourselves. Jesus wants us to give up on our self-promoting ways. He calls us to be humble and then let God do the exalting. We shouldn't be surprised when the apostle Paul held Jesus up as the perfect example of humility—Jesus didn't cling to position, he emptied himself of self-promotion, he was obedient to God, and God exalted him at the proper time (Phil. 2:5-11). Pride is destructive, selfish, and poisonous to Christian service and maturity. Let's humble ourselves before God and trust him to honor us in his time.

TODAY'S PRAYER

Father, I confess to you that I feel overlooked and under-appreciated. Part of me longs for the spotlight and the accolades that come with it. Yet, dear Father, I know that it is foolish pride grabbing my heart. I know Satan longs to use that pride to incite envy, pettiness, gossip, vanity, and a host of other unholy traits in me. Humble me gently, Father, for I do trust you to do what is best for me. In Jesus' name I ask for this grace. Amen.

CONTEXT: LUKE 14:7-14
Related Passages: Isaiah 57:15; Philippians 2:5-11; 1 Peter 5:6

Day 247

MOVING BEYOND THE BARTER

Luke 14:12-14

Then Jesus said to the Pharisee who had invited him, "When you give a lunch or a dinner, don't invite only your friends, brothers, relatives, and rich neighbors. At another time they will pay you back by inviting you to eat with them. Instead, when you give a feast, invite the poor, the crippled, and the blind. Then you will have great blessings, because these people cannot pay you back. They have nothing. But God will reward you at the time when all godly people rise from death."

KEY THOUGHT

So much of life is tied up in bartering—I'll do this for you and you'll do this for me. In friendship, the expectation is not explicit. However, many relationships are built upon doing things with and for each other. This is not particularly bad. However, Jesus wants us to follow him into a more redemptive purpose in our relationships. He challenges us to bless, benefit, and befriend those who cannot repay us for our concern and kindness. This leaves the rewards for our actions to God. It allows us to be blessed simply by knowing we have helped someone and honored Jesus.

TODAY'S PRAYER

Father, open my eyes to the opportunities you provide me to bless others in Jesus' name. Forgive me when I invest all my time, effort, and interest only in those whom I already know. Use me to bless those from whom I can expect nothing. In Jesus' name I pray. Amen.

CONTEXT: LUKE 14:7-14
Related Passages: James 1:26-27; Matthew 5:43-48; Matthew 7:12

Day 248

THE PRIVILEGE OF AN INVITATION

Luke 14:15-24

One of the men sitting at the table with Jesus heard these things. The man said to him, "It will be a great blessing for anyone to eat a meal in God's kingdom!"

Jesus said to him, "A man gave a big dinner. He invited many people. When it was time to eat, he sent his servant to tell the guests, 'Come. The food is ready.' But all the guests said they could not come. Each one made an excuse. The first one said, 'I have just bought a field, so I must go look at it. Please excuse me.' Another man said, 'I have just bought five pairs of work animals; I must go and try them out. Please excuse me.' A third man said, 'I just got married; I can't come.'

"So the servant returned and told his master what happened. The master was angry. He said, 'Hurry! Go into the streets and alleys of the town. Bring me the poor, the crippled, the blind, and the lame.'

"Later, the servant said to him, 'Master, I did what you told me to do, but we still have places for more people.' The master said to the servant, 'Go out to the highways and country roads. Tell the people there to come. I want my house to be full! None of those people I invited first will get to eat any of this food.'"

KEY THOUGHT

Freedom is a great gift that many of us take for granted. The price paid to provide this blessing has been high. Often we approach our freedom with a sense of entitlement—thinking that I deserve this, this is my right. To be invited to be a recipient of God's salvation is a gift from God's mercy and grace. This is not something that we are owed. To spurn God's grace, to put off our complete response to his invitation of salvation, is to insult the One who paid such a high price to give us this opportunity. If you have been putting off your total surrender to Christ as Lord, please, listen to God's invitation and respond—today! None of us can be sure that we will be blessed with a second invitation.

TODAY'S PRAYER

Father, forgive me for procrastinating away so many opportunities to serve you with whole-hearted passion. In Jesus' name I pray. Amen.

CONTEXT: LUKE 14:15-24
Related Passages: Mark 12:28-30; Romans 12:1-2; Hebrews 13:7

Day 249

THE GREAT COST

Luke 14:25-27

Many people were traveling with Jesus. He said to them, "If you come to me but will not leave your family, you cannot be my follower. You must love me more than your father, mother, wife, children, brothers, and sisters—even more than your own life! Whoever will not carry the cross that is given to them when they follow me cannot be my follower."

KEY THOUGHT

To receive the gift of salvation is the greatest blessing any of us could receive. But such a great blessing comes at high cost. Jesus died to give us this gift. To share in the new life of salvation, he calls on us to join him in his death, burial, and resurrection. When we die with Christ in baptism, we are also putting to death the old selfish person of sin and offering ourselves to God. Jesus becomes our highest love and greatest priority. We serve him first and trust that he will bless us with what we need. Following Jesus and living for his Kingdom become our highest passions.

TODAY'S PRAYER

Almighty God, you are worthy of all worship and praise. You worked through history to fulfill your promises. Time after time you saved your rebellious children and brought them back to you. You preserved your people and used them to give us the gift of your Son. Jesus, you gave us the ultimate sacrifice. You gave your life for our sins so we could share in your Father's glory. So today, dear God, I offer myself—my heart, soul, mind, and strength—to live for you. I willingly count all my past glories as refuse in comparison to knowing your grace. I thank you, dear Father, in the name of Jesus. Amen.

CONTEXT: LUKE 14:25-35
Related Passages: Luke 9:18-26; Romans 6:1-6; Galatians 2:20

Day 250

NO EASY COMMITMENT

Luke 14:28-30

[Jesus said] "If you wanted to build a building, you would first sit down and decide how much it would cost. You must see if you have enough money to finish the job. If you don't do that, you might begin the work, but you would not be able to finish. And if you could not finish it, everyone would laugh at you. They would say, 'This man began to build, but he was not able to finish.'"

KEY THOUGHT

Dietrich Bonhoeffer said it many years ago: "When Christ calls a man, he bids him come and die." Bonhoeffer paid that cost when he died at the hands of the Nazis in WWII in a concentration camp shortly before it was liberated. Our commitment to Christ isn't a simple thing that happens between our ears. Jesus cautions us that this commitment must be heartfelt and soul deep. He warns us not to pretend to follow, but to know there is a cost that comes with following him. Jesus calls us to count the cost, and then to follow him.

TODAY'S PRAYER

Loving Father, too often I find my service to you and to the Kingdom lukewarm and passionless. Father, I not only ask for your forgiveness, but I also ask that you renew and revive me by the power of your Holy Spirit. Stir me to be the follower of Jesus you want me to be. I offer you my life, my love, and my all, in Jesus' name. Amen.

CONTEXT: LUKE 14:25-35
Related Passages: Hebrews 12:1-3; Luke 18:26-30; John 15:18

Day 251

LEAVE EVERYTHING?

Luke 14:31-33

*[Jesus said] "If a king is going to fight against another king, first he will sit down
and plan. If he has only 10,000 men, he will try to decide if he is able to defeat
the other king who has 20,000 men. If he thinks he cannot defeat the other king,
he will send some men to ask for peace while that king's army is still far away.*

*"It is the same for each of you. You must leave everything you
have to follow me. If not, you cannot be my follower."*

KEY THOUGHT

"I surrender!" That's pretty much what Jesus wants to hear from us. We
count the cost of our commitment and we see the lavishness of his grace and
realize we need to surrender—everything! Let's hold nothing back!

TODAY'S PRAYER

*Father, open my eyes to the things in my life that keep me from serving
your Son as my Lord wholeheartedly. In Jesus' name I pray. Amen.*

CONTEXT: LUKE 14:25-35
Related Passages: Luke 5:1-11; Luke 18:28-30; Luke 9:57-62

Day 252

THE SEASONING OF OUR AGE

Luke 14:34-35

[Jesus said] "Salt is a good thing. But if the salt loses its salty taste, you can't make it salty again. It is worth nothing. You can't even use it as dirt or dung. People just throw it away.

"You people who hear me, listen!"

KEY THOUGHT

We are called to be the salt of our culture and of our time. Salt is used for taste, for fertilizer, and for preservation. Jesus refers to all three uses at one time or another in his ministry. His point? If we lose our basic nature, our God-given usefulness, then we are unhelpful to the Kingdom and to God's work in the world. His message is a harsh one, but one we need to hear. Living as Kingdom people in our time is crucial—crucial to our world and to our discipleship. We are called to surrender all to Jesus to be used for his work in the world. To do anything less is to lose our "saltiness."

TODAY'S PRAYER

Father, open my eyes so that I can see any areas in my life that I have not completely surrendered to the Lordship of your Son. I want to be useful to your Kingdom and to your work in the world. I want to live a life completely committed to you so that you may be glorified, so that my life will fulfill your purposes for me, and so that my life will have an impact for good on all those around me. In Jesus' name I pray. Amen.

CONTEXT: LUKE 14:25-35
Related Passages: Matthew 5:13-16; Mark 9:50; Philippians 2:14-15

Day 253

LISTENERS REJOICE!

Luke 15:1-7

*Many tax collectors and sinners came to listen to Jesus. Then the
Pharisees and the teachers of the law began to complain, "Look,
this mana welcomes sinners and even eats with them!"*

*Then Jesus told them this story: "Suppose one of you has 100 sheep, but one of them
gets lost. What will you do? You will leave the other 99 sheep there in the field and go
out and look for the lost sheep. You will continue to search for it until you find it. And
when you find it, you will be very happy. You will carry it home, go to your friends and
neighbors and say to them, 'Be happy with me because I found my lost sheep!' In the
same way, I tell you, heaven is a happy place when one sinner decides to change. There
is more joy for that one sinner than for 99 good people who don't need to change."*

KEY THOUGHT

Sometimes the chapter divisions in the Bible get in our way. Luke 14 ends
with Jesus asking for people to listen. Notice how Luke 15 begins with the
sinners listening. They open their hearts! They did it frequently and repeatedly.
In Jesus' company, they found the hope of God. While the religiously self-
righteous look down on these "despicable" and "notorious" folks, heaven does
not! Why? God is searching for seekers. God is looking for those who know they
are lost and are looking for answers. God is longing to bring home the rebels
who know they have blown their life apart and are homesick for the love of God.
For every sinner who has longed to return, for every lost soul who has longed to
be found, for every rebel who longs to return home, for every broken heart that
longs to be healed, listen and rejoice! God is looking for us. God is planning a
party to rejoice in our repentance, our return, and our restoration.

TODAY'S PRAYER

*O God of Wonders, marvelous in power and might and generous and gracious beyond
my sinfulness, thank you! Thank you for your grace, forgiveness, and cleansing.
Thank you for the joy of your salvation. Thank you for wanting me home. Thank
you for the promise of heaven's joy. In Jesus' name I praise and thank you. Amen.*

CONTEXT: LUKE 15:1-10
Related Passages: Luke 5:32; Luke 19:5-10; Acts 17:27-28

Day 254

JOY IN FINDING!

Luke 15:8-10

[Jesus said] "Suppose a woman has ten silver coins, but she loses one of them. She will take a light and clean the house. She will look carefully for the coin until she finds it. And when she finds it, she will call her friends and neighbors and say to them, 'Be happy with me because I have found the coin that I lost!' In the same way, it's a happy time for the angels of God when one sinner decides to change."

KEY THOUGHT

To lose such a coin was terrible. The monetary value would have been immense. The possible sentimental value would have made this an enormous lost. The value of what is lost is what calls for such desperate, thorough, and passionate searching. The value of the lost coin made finding the coin a cause for great celebration—and not just for this woman and her household, but also for all of her friends. How much more valuable are the people around us than one silver coin! So how can Christians not celebrate when salvation's light reaches the dark places of a lost soul? We can't help but celebrate!

TODAY'S PRAYER

Father, please let me share in the joy of your harvest. Please use me as a person of reconciliation who helps your lost children find their way home to you. Help me to be a person of great joy and encouragement to new Christians. In Jesus' name I ask this. Amen.

CONTEXT: LUKE 15:1-10
Related Passages: Acts 13:52; Luke 10:21; Romans 14:17

Day 255

A TALE OF TWO SONS

Luke 15:11-12

Then Jesus said, "There was a man who had two sons. The younger son said to his father, 'Give me now the part of your property that I am supposed to receive someday.' So the father divided his wealth between his two sons."

KEY THOUGHT

This tale of two sons is told to illustrate God's joy over the return of a sinner. In this story, one son is rebellious and leaves home—he basically tells his dad that he is no better than dead when he asks for his inheritance before his father dies. The other son, however, never really seems to be at home with the father; he takes his share of the inheritance, the larger share, and stays at home working out of a sense of slaving duty. Neither son knows the heart of the father. Both break his heart as the story progresses. However, the father remains true to his love and seeks to bless and redeem both. My guess is that at different times in our lives, we actually play the parts of each son—self-righteous and loveless like the older son or rebellious and selfish like the younger son. How can we properly thank God for loving us when we have been both sons? How can we thank God for helping us know what it means to be his forgiven, welcomed, and holy child?

TODAY'S PRAYER

Father God, forgive me. I know that I have not always lived my life in a way that has blessed you as my Father. Thank you for your patience and your mercy. Thank you for letting me feel the sting of my sin and the consequences of my rebellion. Thank you for longing to make my life a place of joy, celebration, relationship, and reunion. In Jesus' name I offer you my thanks and praise. Amen.

CONTEXT: LUKE 15:11-32
Related Passages: Galatians 3:26-29; Romans 8:15-17; Mark 11:25

Day 256

LIFE AWAY FROM GOD

Luke 15:13-16

[Jesus said] "A few days later the younger son gathered up all that he had and left. He traveled far away to another country, and there he wasted his money living like a fool. After he spent everything he had, there was a terrible famine throughout the country. He was hungry and needed money. So he went and got a job with one of the people who lived there. The man sent him into the fields to feed pigs. He was so hungry that he wanted to eat the food the pigs were eating. But no one gave him anything. "

KEY THOUGHT

Life without God is a lonely, desolate, and disgraceful place. While you may have companions who hang around when you have something to offer them, they are usually gone and you are often alone when hard times hit. Those conditions are such a contrast with every picture we see of the joy and love in the father's house!

TODAY'S PRAYER

Righteous God, my Heavenly Father, please help me keep my mind clear about the blessings of being in your family. Help me to see the comfort, love, and joy that are mine in your family. If I stray, please humble me gently and bring me back home. My heart will only find its true joy in your presence. In Jesus' name I pray. Amen.

CONTEXT: LUKE 15:11-32
Related Passages: Colossians 1:19-23; Ephesians 2:11-13; 1 Peter 1:9

Day 257

BETTER IN MY FATHER'S HOUSE

Luke 15:17-19

[Jesus said] "The son realized that he had been very foolish. He thought, 'All my father's hired workers have plenty of food. But here I am, almost dead because I have nothing to eat. I will leave and go to my father. I will say to him: Father, I have sinned against God and have done wrong to you. I am no longer worthy to be called your son. But let me be like one of your hired workers.'"

KEY THOUGHT

We easily forget all the many ways that we have been blessed in the family of God. The rebellious young son learned this the hard way; he lost everything he had at home. Now, he had wasted his inheritance on top of everything. But as much as he had lost, he came to a life-changing realization: a slave in his father's house has it better than he did with his freedom but away from the father. Oh, that we would learn this and put it into practice!

TODAY'S PRAYER

Father, without your presence and your power, no matter where I am or what I'm doing, it will not be enough. I need your love and I need to be at home with you. I confess this in Jesus' name. Amen.

CONTEXT: LUKE 15:11-32
Related Passages: Psalm 84:10; Psalm 32:1-2; Psalm 64:10

Day 258

WHILE A LONG DISTANCE AWAY

Luke 15:20-24
[Jesus said] "So he left and went to his father.

"While the son was still a long way off, his father saw him coming and felt sorry for him. So he ran to him and hugged and kissed him. The son said, 'Father, I have sinned against God and have done wrong to you. I am no longer worthy to be called your son.'

"But the father said to his servants, 'Hurry! Bring the best clothes and put them on him. Also, put a ring on his finger and good sandals on his feet. And bring our best calf and kill it so that we can celebrate with plenty to eat. My son was dead, but now he is alive again! He was lost, but now he is found!' So they began to have a party."

KEY THOUGHT

I love the sentence, "While the son was still a long way off, his father saw him coming . . . ." The Father was longing for his son's return. He was waiting for his son's return. Our Father in heaven is filled with love and compassion for us. He sees our hearts and runs to meet us when we turn our hearts toward home—no matter how far we may have strayed. How far is your heart from the Father? Is it turned toward him? Is it open to being honest with him about your rebellion and sin? He is not looking to punish you, but to bring you home . . . to bring you back to life . . . to let the party begin.

TODAY'S PRAYER

Loving God and compassionate Father, thank you for knowing me and loving me. Look into my heart and examine my inmost thoughts. I am sorry for my sin. Thank you for making me a welcome child in your house and drawing me close to you. In Jesus' name I pray. Amen.

CONTEXT: LUKE 15:11-32
Related Passages: Psalm 51:1-4; Psalm 139:23-24; Psalm 33:20-22

Day 259

THE LOVING FATHER

Luke 15:25-30

[Jesus said] "The older son had been out in the field. When he came near the house, he heard the sound of music and dancing. So he called to one of the servant boys and asked, 'What does all this mean?' The boy said, 'Your brother has come back, and your father killed the best calf to eat. He is happy because he has his son back safe and sound.'

"The older son was angry and would not go in to the party. So his father went out and begged him to come in. But he said to his father, 'Look, for all these years I have worked like a slave for you. I have always done what you told me to do, and you never gave me even a young goat for a party with my friends. But then this son of yours comes home after wasting your money on prostitutes, and you kill the best calf for him!'

KEY THOUGHT

There is no doubt that the behavior of the older son is horrible and selfish. Notice what he says: "Look, for all these years I have worked like a slave for you." This reveals his attitude about his service to his father. He doesn't see what the younger son has discovered: it is better to be a slave in the father's house than to be without the father! The father's graciousness to this older son is amazing. He loves both sons. He has given the inheritance to both sons. So he does what a father would never have been expected to do in that day: he goes out to console his pouting and selfish son and to invite him to the banquet. Jesus' point is that our Heavenly Father doesn't want any child to be lost—not the rebellious child and not the self-righteous child. The bottom line is that the Father loves each and every one of us and wants us all to be a part of his celebration of grace no matter where we are now.

TODAY'S PRAYER

Father, thank you for your unselfish and inexhaustible love. Without your grace I would be lost. With your grace, I give thanks in anticipation of the great celebration of salvation before your throne. In Jesus' name I pray. Amen.

CONTEXT: LUKE 15:11-32
Related Passages: Ephesians 2:8-9; Matthew 25:21; Psalm 21:6

Day 260

WE MUST CELEBRATE

Luke 15:31-32

[Jesus said] "His father said to him, 'Oh, my son, you are always with me, and everything I have is yours. But this was a day to be happy and celebrate. Your brother was dead, but now he is alive. He was lost, but now he is found.'"

KEY THOUGHT

When sinners come to salvation, celebration isn't optional! The angels in heaven celebrate. The Father celebrates. God's children must celebrate. Let's celebrate!

TODAY'S PRAYER

Father, I pray for a great harvest in our day so that your people can share in the joy of heaven's celebration and the lost in our world can come to know you as their Father. In Jesus' name I pray for this grace. Amen.

CONTEXT: LUKE 15:11-32
Related Passages: Luke 15:7, 14; Luke 19:6-10; Luke 3:4-6

Day 261

ACCOUNTABLE

Luke 16:1-2

Jesus said to his followers, "Once there was a rich man. He hired a manager to take care of his business. Later, he learned that his manager was cheating him. So he called the manager in and said to him, 'I have heard bad things about you. Give me a report of what you have done with my money. You can't be my manager anymore.'"

KEY THOUGHT

In an age where feelings and intentions are often given greater value than actual behavior, Jesus' teaching on being held accountable for our actions seems harsh to many. However, Jesus wants his followers to know that his work in the lives of men and women involves the transformation of character. Character involves not only doing the right things, but also doing them for the right reasons and with the right intentions.

TODAY'S PRAYER

Father, keep my heart pure and my hands busy with your work. May my observable character and my internal desires reflect your character, faithfulness, and loving kindness. In Jesus' name I ask for this grace. Amen.

CONTEXT: LUKE 16:1-15
Related Passages: Titus 3:3-5; 2 Corinthians 3:18; 1 Peter 1:13-16

Day 262

LIVING UNDER THE DEADLINE

Luke 16:3-7

[Jesus said] "So, the manager thought to himself, 'What will I do? My master is taking my job away from me. I am not strong enough to dig ditches. I am too proud to beg. I know what I will do! I will do something to make friends, so that when I lose my job, they will welcome me into their homes.'

"So the manager called in each person who owed the master some money. He asked the first one, 'How much do you owe my master?' He answered, 'I owe him 100 jars of olive oil.' The manager said to him, 'Here is your bill. Hurry! Sit down and make the bill less. Write 50 jars.'

"Then the manager asked another one, 'How much do you owe my master?' He answered, 'I owe him 100 measures of wheat.' Then the manager said to him, 'Here is your bill; you can make it less. Write 80 measures.'"

KEY THOUGHT

How does living under a deadline impact you? If you are at all like me, your most productive days of work are always the days right before you leave on a trip. You know you have to get the important stuff done, so you don't let the less important "stuff" get in your way or distract you. The man in Jesus' story has a deadline. He is going to have to devise a strategy for how to live knowing that a deadline is approaching quickly. We, too, live under a deadline. Jesus is coming soon and we need to live each day with a sense of significance and focus. How shall we live in order to be ready for that day?

TODAY'S PRAYER

Father God, please give me a clearer sense of what time it is in the world and in my life. Help me feel the sense of urgency I need as I await the glorious coming of Jesus, in whose name I pray. Amen.

CONTEXT: LUKE 16:1-15
Related Passages: Ephesians 5:15-18; 1 Thessalonians 5:1-11; Matthew 16:27

Day 263

SPIRITUALLY SHREWD

Luke 16:8-9

[Jesus said] "Later, the master told the dishonest manager that
he had done a smart thing. Yes, worldly people are smarter in
their business with each other than spiritual people are.

"I tell you, use the worldly things you have now to make 'friends' for later. Then,
when those things are gone, you will be welcomed into a home that lasts forever."

KEY THOUGHT

Some worldly people are quite shrewd. Some can think of many ways
to use and make earthly wealth—honestly and dishonestly. Jesus, however,
wants his followers to use their worldly wealth in ways that are "spiritually
shrewd." We don't use our wealth to control others or to try to protect our
future, but to bless others. Benefiting others and using our earthly resources
to be a blessing and a friend to others are our goals. God blesses us so that we
can be a blessing. As we are faithful stewards of God's blessings, we please our
Heavenly Father and store up our treasures in heaven.

TODAY'S PRAYER

Father, make me wise in the way I use the many blessings you have lavished
upon me. Make me a conduit of your blessings. Help me find ways to
put your resources entrusted to me to work in building your Kingdom
and blessing those you would bless. In Jesus' name I pray. Amen.

CONTEXT: LUKE 16:1-15
Related Passages: Matthew 6:19-21; Mark 10:21; 2 Corinthians 9:6-11

Day 264

FAITHFULNESS MATTERS!

Luke 16:10-11

[Jesus said] "Whoever can be trusted with small things can also be trusted with big things. Whoever is dishonest in little things will be dishonest in big things too. If you cannot be trusted with worldly riches, you will not be trusted with the true riches. And if you cannot be trusted with the things that belong to someone else, you will not be given anything of your own."

KEY THOUGHT

"It's just a little thing. It won't hurt if I fudge a little, will it?" That's what we sometimes think and that's often what the world says to us. But Jesus says, "Yes, it will matter." Why? Integrity is about faithfulness to our values and to our Lord, regardless of the price. Faithfulness in small things, especially matters involving money, reveals the truth about our authenticity as Jesus' followers. What we do with a little reveals a great deal about what we will do with much.

TODAY'S PRAYER

Father, I want to be a good steward with your blessings. Keep my heart pure in matters big and small. May my words, actions, and thoughts all reflect your holy character and your freely-given grace. In Jesus' name I pray. Amen.

CONTEXT: LUKE 16:1-15
Related Passages: Matthew 25:19-21; Matthew 25:22-23; Matthew 25:24-30

Day 265

KNOW WHAT IS IMPORTANT AND WHOM TO SERVE

Luke 16:12-13

[Jesus said] "And if you cannot be trusted with the things that belong to someone else, you will not be given anything of your own.

"You cannot serve two masters at the same time. You will hate one master and love the other. Or you will be loyal to one and not care about the other. You cannot serve God and Money at the same time."

KEY THOUGHT

Money can be our master, but we must not let it. We can covet money. We can sell our virtue for money. We can be manipulated for money. We can risk our lives for money. Few things have such pull on our hearts. The apostle Paul warns that greed is a form of idolatry (Col. 3:5). In other words, money and our desire for it can become our god and our religion. Jesus makes it clear that there is room in our hearts for only one consuming love. That love will be the master of our lives. We cannot serve God if money becomes our master. We cannot worship and serve both. So which do you choose?

TODAY'S PRAYER

Father, give me a clearer sense of your purpose in blessing me. I want to serve you faithfully, using your gifts and your blessings in my life to honor you and bless others, just as you would have them blessed. In Jesus' name I pray. Amen.

CONTEXT: LUKE 16:1-15
Related Passages: 1 Timothy 6:5-10; Colossians 3:5; Luke 12:21

Day 266

WHAT THE WORLD HONORS

Luke 16:14-15

The Pharisees were listening to all these things. They criticized Jesus because they all loved money. Jesus said to them, "You make yourselves look good in front of people. But God knows what is really in your hearts. What people think is important is worth nothing to God."

KEY THOUGHT

Who switched the price tags? Our world values things very differently than God does. The Pharisees loved their money and they tried to look good in public. Many with a worldly perspective honored them for their religious dedication. After all, they were religious and blessed. God, however, knew that much of their wealth came from a covetous and greedy heart—it was a disgrace instead of a blessing. They scoffed at Jesus' words—not because Jesus' words were wrong, but because his words were right and their hearts were not. How about us? What do we dearly love? How are our hearts?

TODAY'S PRAYER

Father, I pray for a wise mind, an open heart, and a generous spirit as I use the financial blessings you have placed in my care. Guard me from greed, materialism, and covetousness. Help me see the way you want me to use my blessings for your Kingdom's work. Most of all, dear Father, please let nothing have a hold on my life other than my love for you, your Kingdom, and your righteousness. In Jesus' name I pray. Amen.

CONTEXT: LUKE 16:1-15
Related Passages: Luke 18:22-27; 1 Timothy 6:17-19; Psalm 62:10

Day 267

GOOD NEWS OF THE KINGDOM

Luke 16:16

[Jesus said] "Before John the Baptizer came, people were taught the Law of Moses and the writings of the prophets. But since the time of John, the Good News about God's kingdom is being told. And everyone is trying hard to get into it."

KEY THOUGHT

The good news of the Kingdom begins with John's preaching about the Christ. Moses and the prophets were the guides God had given for his people. But with the coming of Jesus, a new time had begun. Jesus spoke of the Kingdom; he taught Kingdom values, spoke Kingdom parables, and displayed the power of God's Kingdom. This fresh message inspired fresh hope and ignited eager hearts. Luke's Gospel is written to help us hear that good news of the Kingdom. It is a message of salvation and triumph rooted in the work of God throughout history and in Jesus. It is God's good news because it is about salvation, forgiveness, and the power of God's Spirit. It is God's Kingdom because his reign is seen in the repentance and life-change accomplished in the hearts and lives of those who confess Jesus as Lord.

TODAY'S PRAYER

Lord God Almighty, my Abba Father, thank you for your good news! Thank you for Jesus, whose life, death, resurrection, and exaltation make this good news possible. I gladly live my life with Jesus as my Lord and pray that your Kingdom may be displayed in me. In Jesus' name I offer you my thanks. Amen.

CONTEXT: LUKE 16:16-18
Related Passages: Acts 1:3; Acts 8:12; Acts 28:23-24, 30-31

Day 268

A STRONGER GRACE

Luke 16:17

[Jesus said] "But even the smallest part of a letter in the law cannot be changed. It would be easier for heaven and earth to pass away."

KEY THOUGHT

The intent of God's law was to form a holy people who reflected the character and compassion of the holy God they worshiped. Jesus' goal was not to abolish the character and call of the law, but to make it more real, permanent, and transforming in the lives of the people of God. What flawed humans couldn't do through the law, God did through his Son and the good news of the Kingdom that proclaims his work and influence in our lives. More than abolishing the purposes of the law, the good news of the Kingdom made those purposes real and more permanent. Grace does not just liberate us from law; it liberates us to live the character and compassion of God, the very things that the law sought to define and form in us.

TODAY'S PRAYER

Father, I ask that your holy character and your perfect will be displayed in what I say, how I live, and what I desire in my heart. In Jesus' name I ask for this grace. Amen.

CONTEXT: LUKE 16:16-18
Related Passages: Jeremiah 31:31-34; Romans 8:1-4; 2 Corinthians 3:6, 17-18

Day 269

DIVORCE

Luke 16:18

[Jesus said] "Any man who divorces his wife and marries another woman is guilty of adultery. And the man who marries a divorced woman is also guilty of adultery."

KEY THOUGHT

God hates divorce. It splits families. It breaks promises. It destroys people. It hurts children. It ignores the covenants people make with each other and God. It dishonors the Father's plan for marriage. God wants us to understand that his grace does not lessen his call on each of us to be faithful to our own marriage covenant. We are to be people of integrity, commitment, and faithfulness.

TODAY'S PRAYER

Father, renew our passion to have godly marriages where our covenant vows are kept and your will is lived with honor and obeyed with passion. In Jesus name I pray. Amen.

CONTEXT: LUKE 16:16-18
Related Passages: Malachi 2:13-16; Matthew 19:3-9; Hebrews 13:4

Day 270

GUT-WRENCHINGLY GRAPHIC

Luke 16:19-21

Jesus said, "There was a rich man who always dressed in the finest clothes. He was so rich that he was able to enjoy all the best things every day. There was also a very poor man named Lazarus. Lazarus' body was covered with sores. He was often put by the rich man's gate. Lazarus wanted only to eat the scraps of food left on the floor under the rich man's table. And the dogs came and licked his sores."

KEY THOUGHT

This image makes us want to vomit. However, what makes us sick is probably the thought of having dogs licking Lazarus' open sores. Yes, like other images in Scripture, this is revolting. Even more sickening to God is a man who has so much, but who is doing so little to help someone so close. Lazarus wasn't even looking for much. However, rather than anointing the sores with oil and bandaging Lazarus' wounds, the rich man spurned him and only the dogs would offer him comfort and companionship. Who is your Lazarus? God is looking for character and compassion. We are not living like his children when we abandon either of them.

TODAY'S PRAYER

Father, open my eyes to see the people you have placed in my path who need my compassion. Stir my heart with your Spirit to respond when I see them. Strip away the calloused and dead skin that surrounds my heart of compassion. Teach me the best way to show your love and grace. In Jesus' name I pray. Amen.

CONTEXT: LUKE 16:19-31
Related Passages: Luke 10:33-34; Psalm 68:4-5; Matthew 25:34-40

Day 271

WHERE FACADES DON'T MATTER

Luke 16:22-23

[Jesus said] "Later, Lazarus died. The angels took him and placed him in the arms of Abraham. The rich man also died and was buried. He was sent to the place of death and was in great pain. He saw Abraham far away with Lazarus in his arms."

KEY THOUGHT

We spend a lot of time investing in "things" that don't matter. "Things" give us an appearance of importance in our earthly journey. However, "things" don't go with us when we face God at judgment; only how we used those "things" to bless others matters. Lazarus was received with God's tender care into a place of comfort and promise. The rich man faced torment. Let's not let "things," whether they are our own or "possessed" by someone else, distract our hearts from what is important.

TODAY'S PRAYER

God, please give me the kind of heart that sees through the facades and feeble things of this world. With your Spirit, reset my heart so that it can find its focus and value in what is truly lasting and worthwhile in your sight. In Jesus' name I pray. Amen.

CONTEXT: LUKE 16:19-31
Related Passages: Luke 12:13-21; Luke 12:33-34; I Samuel 16:7

Day 272

CLOSING TIME

Luke 16:24-26

[Jesus said] "He called, 'Father Abraham, have mercy on me! Send Lazarus to me so that he can dip his finger in water and cool my tongue. I am suffering in this fire!'

"But Abraham said, 'My child, remember when you lived? You had all the good things in life. But Lazarus had nothing but problems. Now he is comforted here, and you are suffering. Also, there is a big pit between you and us. No one can cross over to help you, and no one can come here from there.'"

KEY THOUGHT

Some things are final. The rich man chose to live for the moment and neglect eternal matters. Then it was too late. Death came and stole away his chance to be a better person. There was no crossing over. There was a great chasm between. Jesus tells this story to warn us to make our lives count with eternal significance while we are alive, because when we die, there will be no more chances to invest in what matters.

TODAY'S PRAYER

Father, open my eyes and help me see things as you see them. I want to live by eternal values right now. Help me see the areas where I am procrastinating or living in denial about what needs to be done for your glory and to bless others. In Jesus' name I pray. Amen.

CONTEXT: LUKE 16:19-31
Related Passages: Proverbs 11:4; Hebrews 9:24-28; 2 Corinthians 5:10

Day 273

SOMEONE RISEN FROM THE DEAD!

Luke 16:27-31

[Jesus said] "The rich man said, 'Then please, father Abraham, send Lazarus to my father's house on earth. I have five brothers. He could warn my brothers so that they will not come to this place of pain.'

"But Abraham said, 'They have the Law of Moses and the writings of the prophets to read; let them learn from that.'

"The rich man said, 'No, father Abraham! But if someone came to them from the dead, then they would decide to change their lives.'

"But Abraham said to him, 'If your brothers won't listen to Moses and the prophets, they won't listen to someone who comes back from the dead.'"

KEY THOUGHT

God has provided many avenues for people to know his will. However, if they continually refuse his truth, or keep putting off obeying that truth, they will not repent even if miraculous things happen in their lives. Even someone rising from the dead wouldn't convince them. And, unfortunately for many, Jesus' resurrection didn't convince them. We must have seeking hearts. We must will to do God's will. We must knock on heaven's door seeking heaven's truth. If that is our passion, our heartfelt desire, then repentance is not so hard. But if we do not seek we'll certainly not repent when we are sought!

TODAY'S PRAYER

Father, keep my heart soft, pliable, and open to your will. Make me hungry to know you. Make me thirsty for your truth and righteousness. Turn my heart, O Lord, to follow after you always. In Jesus' name I pray. Amen.

CONTEXT: LUKE 16:19-31
Related Passages: Isaiah 55:6; Jeremiah 29:13; Acts 17:24-31

Day 274

DON'T HARM THE LITTLE ONES

Luke 17:1-2

Jesus said to his followers, "Things will surely happen that will make people sin. But it will be very bad for anyone who makes this happen. It will be very bad for anyone who makes one of these little children sin. It would be better for them to have a millstone tied around their neck and be drowned in the sea."

KEY THOUGHT

Jesus wants us to be aware that temptation is real, dangerous, and personal. However, it is far worse for us to be the source of someone else's temptation and sin than to have to face our own. Our sins matter in every way; they matter more, however, when we bring others down with us.

TODAY'S PRAYER

Father, thank you for strengthening me and helping me withstand the onslaught of temptation. I never want to be a stumbling block to someone else. Guide my steps, please dear Lord, so that I will not stumble or fall. Guide my influence, dear Father, so that it is used only for good and never for harm. In Jesus' name I ask this. Amen.

CONTEXT: LUKE 17:1-10
Related Passages: James 1:13-15; Romans 14:13; 1 Corinthians 8:8-9

Day 275

REDEEMING RELATIONSHIPS FROM SIN

Luke 17:3-4

[Jesus said] "So be careful! If your brother or sister in God's family does something wrong, warn them. If they are sorry for what they did, forgive them. Even if they do something wrong to you seven times in one day, but they say they are sorry each time, you should forgive them."

KEY THOUGHT

In today's polite and politically correct society, it is considered rude to step in and confront someone about his or her unethical or improper behavior. Hurting someone's feelings or impinging on his or her right of free expression is of more concern than evil acts, unethical practices, and sinful rebellion. How sad! How wrong of us as Christians! We are called to a different standard in God's Kingdom. We take sin seriously so we go after sinners, not to punish or berate them, but to help them turn from their rebellious ways and call them to Jesus. If we take sin seriously, we also must take forgiveness even more seriously. Granting forgiveness was a key reason Jesus came to earth. As Jesus' presence in the world now, it is our job to practice radical forgiveness. And facilitating forgiveness and reconciliation, whether we are the offender or the offended, is always our responsibility.

TODAY'S PRAYER

Father, help me take my sin, as well as the sin that has entrapped my Christian friends, seriously. Don't let me tone down others who want to call your people away from their sin and rebellion. Please give me a heart of compassion and words that serve, bless, and strengthen others. In Jesus' name I pray. Amen.

CONTEXT: LUKE 17:1-10
Related Passages: Luke 19:1-20; 2 Corinthians 2:5-8; James 5:16

Day 276

WE NEED MORE FAITH!

Luke 17:5
The apostles said to the Lord, "Give us more faith!"

KEY THOUGHT

How refreshing! Jesus' followers are amazingly honest. "We need more faith!" I've been there; haven't you? They want more. They want to know how to acquire more faith. So what do they do? They ask Jesus! Why don't we?

TODAY'S PRAYER

Dear Father, please increase my faith! I know faith is the doorway through which so many of your great movements of grace come. Please bless me with more faith, not for my glory, but for yours. And Lord Jesus, just like your followers of old, I ask that you increase my faith and the faith of those I am seeking to lead to you. In Jesus' name. Amen.

CONTEXT: LUKE 17:1-10
Related Passages: Hebrews 11:6; Mark 9:19-24; Hebrews 11:13-16

Day 277

EVEN A LITTLE IS VERY POWERFUL

Luke 17:6

The Lord said, "If your faith is as big as a mustard seed, you can say to this mulberry tree, 'Dig yourself up and plant yourself in the ocean!' And the tree will obey you."

KEY THOUGHT

At first glance, Jesus appears to be making an incredible promise. On a closer look, however, this is a reprimand. Even a little faith is powerful. They would have so much more impact on their world if they could muster even a little faith. Sadly, so much doesn't get done to bless others and to honor God because we have such little faith. Let's be people of faith! Lord, increase our faith!

TODAY'S PRAYER

Lord God Almighty, challenge me, stir me, move me, motivate me to live by faith and not by sight. Lord, increase my faith! In Jesus' name I ask this. Amen.

CONTEXT: LUKE 17:1-10
Related Passages: 2 Corinthians 5:1-7; 1 Timothy 4:1-4; Hebrews 10:38

Day 278

THE ATTITUDE OF A SERVANT

Luke 17:7-10

[Jesus said] "Suppose one of you has a servant who has been working in the field, plowing or caring for the sheep. When he comes in from work, what would you say to him? Would you say, 'Come in, sit down and eat'? Of course not! You would say to your servant, 'Prepare something for me to eat. Then get ready and serve me. When I finish eating and drinking, then you can eat.' The servant should not get any special thanks for doing his job. He is only doing what his master told him to do. It is the same with you. When you finish doing all that you are told to do, you should say, 'We are not worthy of any special thanks. We have only done the work we should do.'"

KEY THOUGHT

In Jesus' day, a servant did not have the rights of an owner, an heir, or a citizen. A servant had to do what pleased his or her master regardless. A servant had no right to expect approval or commendation. When a servant worked hard and completed a long list of demands, there was no expectation of praise; that servant only did what was expected. Jesus is Lord, Master, and Savior. He has called us to follow and serve him. Of course, the incredible blessing is that when we come to him as a servant, he welcomes us as family and friend.

TODAY'S PRAYER

Father, as I come and offer myself to your Son as a servant for his work and his glory, thank you for accepting me as your child and making me a sibling, a joint heir, with your precious Son and my Savior. In his name, Jesus Christ the Lord, I pray. Amen.

CONTEXT: LUKE 17:1-10
Related Passages: Galatians 3:26-4:7; Hebrews 2:14-18; John 15:15

Day 279

MERCY!

Luke 17:11-13

Jesus was traveling to Jerusalem. He went from Galilee to Samaria. He came into a small town, and ten men met him there. They did not come close to him, because they all had leprosy. But the men shouted, "Jesus! Master! Please help us!"

KEY THOUGHT

Mercy! Is that what we so often need? "Jesus! Master! Please help us!" Life is filled with many unexpected challenges. Coupled with the predictable developmental challenges that come our way, the unexpected challenges can make life seem unbearable. For those with leprosy in the days of Jesus, life was unbearable. As outcasts and beggars, they groveled out an existence while waiting to die an agonizing death. Our challenges may or may not be as severe as these ten lepers faced, but all of us do find ourselves in need of mercy. So what do we do when we find ourselves in such need? We cry out to the Lord with open, frank, and honest appraisal of his exalted position and our deep need: "Jesus! Master! Please help me!"

TODAY'S PRAYER

O Lord God, I appeal to you in the name of Jesus to help me. Have mercy on me for my weakness, hypocrisy, and sin. Lord, please do not just forgive me, but strengthen me and enable me to be a more sturdy and faithful follower. Help me in my times of confusion and need. Heal my illnesses, mend my broken heart, and still the storms of my troubled mind. Guide me as I discern the path you want me to take in the decisions I must make. Empower me with your strength, wisdom, and compassion to touch others. Lord God, and Jesus my Master in whose name I pray, please help me. Amen.

CONTEXT: LUKE 17:11-19
Related Passages: Psalm 9:13; Psalm 25:16; Psalm 57:1

Day 280

THE BLESSINGS OF OBEDIENCE

Luke 17:14
When Jesus saw the men, he said, "Go and show yourselves to the priests."
While the ten men were going to the priests, they were healed.

KEY THOUGHT

Jesus heals people in all sorts of ways. He told these ten lepers to go show themselves to the priests just as the law commanded them to do if they were healed. Jesus didn't heal them before they left, but as they were on their way to the priests. Healing happened after they stepped out in faith and obeyed. So often, many of us will not follow until the Lord does what we want. Like those with leprosy, we call Jesus "Lord" or "Master," but we want him "to do for us" rather than for us to submit to him as Lord. Let's be reminded today that if Jesus is our Lord we will obey him whether or not we see the answers to our prayers before, during, or after our obedience. Let's do what he says and trust that he will dispense his mercy and grace in a way that most blesses us for an eternity with him.

TODAY'S PRAYER

Father God, please give me the patience that comes from your Spirit's presence.
May the Spirit lead me to obey whether or not I see the answers that I seek.
I want Jesus to truly be my Lord and Master. Open my eyes so that I can see
where I need to obey him and follow his will. In Jesus' name I pray. Amen.

CONTEXT: LUKE 17:11-19
Related Passages: Matthew 7:21-23; Matthew 7:24-29; James 1:21-25

Day 281

PRAISE GOD!

Luke 17:15-16

When one of them saw that he was healed, he went back to Jesus. He praised God loudly. He bowed down at Jesus' feet and thanked him. (He was a Samaritan.)

KEY THOUGHT

How do we respond when our cries for help receive their loving answer from our Master? This story reminds us that we need to unabashedly praise and thank Jesus for his healing power, mercy, help, and grace. When was the last time you fell face down and praised Jesus? When was the last time you thanked him from the bottom of your heart and with your physical posture. One of the key words for worship means to bow ("to kiss the ground"). When was the last time you praised and thanked the Lord for all that he has done for you with a genuine heart while kneeling, bowing, or lying face down in humble gratitude?

TODAY'S PRAYER

I praise you, O God my Abba Father, for your incredible mercy and grace. Please remove my inhibitions and pride so that I can express more openly my thanks and praise through the emotions of my heart, the words that grace my lips, and the posture of my body. In Jesus' name I praise you, dear Father. Amen.

CONTEXT: LUKE 17:11-19
Related Passages: Ephesians 3:14-21; Revelation 5:8-14; Exodus 9:29

Day 282

WHERE IS THE THANKS?

Luke 17:17-19

Jesus said, "Ten men were healed; where are the other nine? This man is not even one of our people. Is he the only one who came back to give praise to God?" Then Jesus said to the man, "Stand up! You can go. You were healed because you believed."

KEY THOUGHT

"Where are the other nine?" Jesus says some sad things during his earthly ministry that tear apart our hearts: "My God, my God, why have you forsaken me?" "Peter, do you love me?" "Judas, is it with a kiss that you are betraying the Son of Man?" "Into your hands I commit my spirit." All of these statements are agonizing. Unfortunately he has to keep saying, "Where are the other nine?" or something like it quite frequently. We go to the Father using the name and authority of Jesus and ask for many things great and small. In great love and mercy, the Father, the Son, and the Spirit often bless us with precisely what we ask. Yet with so many blessings lavished on us, our prayers remain focused upon getting more rather than thanking and praising them for their generosity and grace.

TODAY'S PRAYER

Almighty God and loving Father, forgive me for my self-centered preoccupation. You have blessed me with so much and I seem to thank you for so little. I praise you for your selfless love, your abundant mercy, your costly grace, your faithfulness to your promises, and your assurance of my future with you. Thank you for your Holy Spirit who intercedes right now as I pray and who strengthens, equips, and leads me. Thank you for the breath I breathe, the food I eat, the clothes I wear, and the place I lay my head at night. For these, and thousands of other blessings from your hand, in Jesus' name I thank you. Amen.

CONTEXT: LUKE 17:11-19
Related Passages: Ephesians 5:15-21; Colossians 3:2; Psalm 95:1-6

Day 283

THE HIDDEN KINGDOM

Luke 17:20-21

Some of the Pharisees asked Jesus, "When will God's kingdom come?"

Jesus answered, "God's kingdom is coming, but not in a way that you can see it. People will not say, 'Look, God's kingdom is here!' or 'There it is!' No, God's kingdom is here with you."

KEY THOUGHT

What in the world does Jesus mean? In light of his comments in the following verses, Jesus is distinguishing between his return in glory and the Kingdom of God. He is most likely referring to the reign of God over the hearts of men and women who long to do his will and pin their hopes on his deliverance. Already that Kingdom is beginning to make its entry upon the scene with the coming of Jesus and the call of his first followers. It is not a visible territory with borders. It is not a capitol building with beautiful architecture. Instead, his Kingdom, God's Kingdom, has already begun to make its appearance as people bow their hearts to the King and offer themselves in service to his rule. The question then is not "Where is the Kingdom?" but "Is my heart yielded to King Jesus?" Has the Kingdom come to you? Have you truly yielded your heart, soul, mind, and strength to the Lord's will? Can the influence and power of God's Kingdom be seen in your life?

TODAY'S PRAYER

O Lord God Almighty, King of the ages, I praise you. I praise you for your power and glory. I praise you for your work of deliverance and salvation in the lives of men and women. I praise you for your promise of a home and a great future with you. Now I ask that your will be done in my life as I offer myself to serve and honor you as the only true and living God. In Jesus' name I praise you and offer myself to you. Amen.

CONTEXT: LUKE 17:20-25
Related Passages: Revelation 11:15; Daniel 7:14; Luke 7:28

Day 284

LONGING FOR THE SON OF MAN

Luke 17:22-24

Then Jesus said to his followers, "The time will come when you will want very much to see one of the days of the Son of Man, but you will not be able to. People will say to you, 'Look, there it is!' or 'Look, here it is!' Stay where you are; don't go away and search.

"When the Son of Man comes again, you will know it. On that day he will shine like lightning flashes across the sky."

KEY THOUGHT

Jesus warns about two things important to followers. First, they will long for the presence of the Son of Man—in other words, Jesus will be leaving them. Second, after Jesus has returned to God, people will make false claims that Jesus has returned and trouble his followers into thinking they have missed his return. Regarding the latter warning, Jesus makes a promise that when he returns, no one will miss his return. It will be as clear as lightning that shatters the darkness of the night sky. As Christians, we wait in hope for this day and we long for the appearing of the Son of Man. Until that day and while we feel this longing, let's make every moment count as we live to honor our returning Lord and King!

TODAY'S PRAYER

God, my Abba Father, I long for the day I come home to you and share in the glory of your Son and the angels that will accompany him on his return for your children. Until that day, empower me to live boldly for you. I pray this in Jesus' name. Amen.

CONTEXT: LUKE 17:20-25
Related Passages: Revelation 1:4-7; 1 Thessalonians 4:13-18; 1 Corinthians 15:52-53

Day 285

FIRST!

Luke 17:25

[Jesus said] "But first, the Son of Man must suffer many things.
The people of today will refuse to accept him."

KEY THOUGHT

Before Jesus can reign as King, he must first suffer and be rejected. Jesus' glory will follow the cross. Our deliverance comes only at the cost of Jesus' rejection. Our salvation depends upon Jesus' sacrificial suffering. We are saved, we are made a part of God's eternal Kingdom, and we are given glory at a terribly high price. Yet Jesus willingly pays that price for us and redeems us from sin and death! Jesus suffers first. Jesus is rejected first. Jesus dies first. Jesus loves first. Only then does God ask us to bow before him and confess him as Lord.

TODAY'S PRAYER

Father, thank you for going first in showing your love. Thank you for not waiting until I honored you before you sacrificed for me. I realize that my love for you, my submission to you, and my sacrifices for you come only after you have given me everything. Please accept my love, submission, and sacrifices even though they are but a poor reflection of what you have already done for me. In Jesus' name I pray this. Amen.

CONTEXT: LUKE 17:20-25
Related Passages: Romans 5:6-11; John 1:9-13; 1 John 4:9-10

Day 286

JUST LIKE IN NOAH'S DAY

Luke 17:26-27

[Jesus said] "When the Son of Man comes again, it will be the same as it was when Noah lived. People were eating, drinking, and getting married even on the day when Noah entered the boat. Then the flood came and killed them all."

KEY THOUGHT

Noah's character went totally unappreciated by his contemporaries. They ignored Noah's warnings about God's impending judgment and their need to repent. They went on doing what they had always done, even as the rain started to fall. When Jesus returns in his glory, those who have lived for him will be waiting in expectation for his return and be overjoyed. But those who have ignored the call to follow him and who have spurned his grace will be caught off guard just as much as those in Noah's day. It's sad. It's tragic. Let's try to make a difference in as many of those lives as we can!

TODAY'S PRAYER

Father, I know Jesus will come with glory. I know that his return will catch many off guard. Please use me to help those around me to be prepared and full of joy at the return of Jesus, in whose name I pray. Amen.

CONTEXT: LUKE 17:26-37
Related Passages: 1 Thessalonians 5:2-5; 2 Peter 3:10; Revelation 16:15

Day 287

NOT BUSINESS AS USUAL

Luke 17:28-30

[Jesus said] "It will be the same as during the time of Lot, when God destroyed Sodom. Those people were eating, drinking, buying, selling, planting, and building houses for themselves. They were doing these things even on the day when Lot left town. Then fire and sulfur rained down from the sky and killed them all. This is exactly how it will be when the Son of Man comes again."

KEY THOUGHT

Just as in the previous verses, Jesus warns again that people will not be paying attention when he comes. They will have settled into their ungodly lifestyles and will be totally surprised. For those not ready, it will be a time of destruction. However, it will be a time of celebration for those of us who are joyously anticipating his return. Yet even for us, the potential of Jesus' coming today should help us sharpen our focus and live with focused spiritual intensity. How would your life be lived today, tomorrow, and all the tomorrows which follow if each day you lived as if Jesus were returning that day? That's how Jesus wants us to live each day.

TODAY'S PRAYER

Holy Father, God Almighty who controls the day of the Lord's return, help me live with renewed intensity knowing that Jesus' return could happen at any time, even today. In his name I pray. Amen.

CONTEXT: LUKE 17:26-37
Related Passages: James 5:7-9; Philippians 4:4-5; 1 Peter 1:13-16

Day 288

NO CLINGING ON THIS DAY

Luke 17:31-33

[Jesus said] "On that day if a man is on his roof, he will not have time to go inside and get his things. If a man is in the field, he cannot go back home. Remember what happened to Lot's wife!

"Whoever tries to keep the life they have will lose it. But whoever gives up their life will save it."

KEY THOUGHT

Jesus' coming will be sudden and surprising. We must be ready for that coming at all times. There won't be time to prepare to go with him or to be ready for him. The things of this world will dim in comparison to the glory of his coming and the glory of our going home to God. Nothing should be allowed to interfere with this one great opportunity. Nothing!

TODAY'S PRAYER

Father, God Almighty, give me an undivided heart and undiluted passion for Jesus' return. I know it will occur unexpectedly and will happen quickly. I want to be ready. I want to be excited. I want to have no reservations. Please, dear Father, I don't want to cling to life here, but to expect your greater glory when Jesus returns. In Jesus' name I pray. Amen.

CONTEXT: LUKE 17:26-37
Related Passages: 1 Corinthians 15:51-53; 2 Timothy 4:6-8; Titus 2:11-13

Day 289

CAUGHT UP IN THE CLOUDS!

Luke 17:34-36
*[Jesus said] "That night there may be two people sleeping in one room.
One will be taken and the other will be left. There may be two women
working together. One will be taken and the other will be left."*

KEY THOUGHT

This is often called the rapture, although that term is never used in the
New Testament in this regard. I prefer to call it "caught up in the clouds."
This phrase comes from Paul's explanation of these events in 1 Thessalonians
4:13-18. When Jesus ascended into heaven, the apostles were told that Jesus
would also return in the clouds. We await this day of victory and glory that is
promised. However, for those who do not belong to the Lord, this will be a day
when they are left behind. Meanwhile, the children of God will receive their
ultimate adoption as God's children and will be ushered into his presence by
Jesus in his glory and in the glory of the angels who accompany him.

TODAY'S PRAYER

*Father, I long for and look forward to the day of Jesus' return. My only anxiety
about that day is that I want all those I know to be ready and to accompany
me into your presence. Please give me the words to say and the character of
life to show these friends, acquaintances, and loved ones how to be ready
and to anticipate this day with joy. In Jesus' name I pray. Amen.*

CONTEXT: LUKE 17:26-37
Related Passages: 1 Thessalonians 4:14-18; Acts 1:6-11; Revelation 1:5-7

Day 290

SIGNS OF THE END?

Luke 17:37
The followers asked Jesus, "Where will this be, Lord?"

*Jesus answered, "It's like looking for a dead body—you will
find it where the vultures are gathering above."*

KEY THOUGHT

There will be signs that these things (mentioned in previous verses) are about to happen. The sign of vultures in the sky alert the onlooker that something has died nearby. Well, what are these signs? Luke 17 reveals the signs Jesus has given: 1) Some will say he has already returned; 2) the Son of Man (Jesus) will have suffered terribly on the cross; 3) people will routinely be going about their daily lives. If those are Jesus' signs, then it sounds like just about any ordinary time after Jesus has been crucified. Yes, I believe that is the point. We must be ready all the time, at any time. From the day of Pentecost when the first people became Christians until today, we have been in the last days. Jesus stands close to the edge of time and when the Father says "Now!" Jesus will visibly and undeniably step back into our world and claim his followers as his own and take them home to his Father in heaven. Jesus has repeatedly warned us to always be ready. He says it again here in a slightly different way: "My coming is always near. Any day that looks like a normal day could be my time to come!"

TODAY'S PRAYER

Father, make my heart ready for the time of Jesus' return. Give me passion each day to live for you and your Kingdom as if it were my last day. Make me ready for the coming of my Lord. In Jesus' name I pray. Amen.

CONTEXT: LUKE 17:26-37
Related Passages: Acts 2:14-19; 1 Thessalonians 5:1-11; Matthew 24:36

Day 291

NEVER GIVE UP

Luke 18:1
*Then Jesus taught the followers that they should always pray and
never lose hope. He used this story to teach them: . . . .*

KEY THOUGHT

Jesus had two points he wanted to impress into the hearts of his followers.
First, he wanted them to be dedicated to prayer and have it as a constant part
of their lives. Second, he wanted them to know that they must never give up,
no matter what the circumstances. While Jesus makes his points clear, why did
he feel the need to tell a story? Stories help us remember. They connect to a
different place in our hearts and in our heads rather than just saying the main
point. Jesus used everyday stories so that the sight or experience of something
similar would bring his teaching back into the forefront of our thoughts. So
the next time you hear about a Bible teacher or preacher who tells too many
stories, remind the folks of the Master Storyteller—Jesus—and help them
repeat the story and re-tell the truth.

TODAY'S PRAYER

*Father, thank you for Jesus' ability to put your truth into everyday stories. Thank
you for the truth that they carry and the power they have in our memories.
Thank you for giving so much of your truth in Scripture in the form of stories.
Most of all, dear Father, help me to never give up as I seek your will, your
presence, and your help through prayer. In Jesus' name I pray. Amen.*

CONTEXT: LUKE 18:1-8
Related Passages: Colossians 4:2-3; 1 Thessalonians 5:16-18; Ephesians 1:15-20

Day 292

KEEP PRAYING!

Luke 18:2-7

[Jesus said] "Once there was a judge in a town. He did not care about God. He also did not care what people thought about him. In that same town there was a woman whose husband had died. She came many times to this judge and said, 'There is a man who is doing bad things to me. Give me my rights!' But the judge did not want to help the woman. After a long time, the judge thought to himself, 'I don't care about God. And I don't care about what people think. But this woman is bothering me. If I give her what she wants, then she will leave me alone. But if I don't give her what she wants, she will bother me until I am sick.'"

The Lord said, "Listen, there is meaning in what the bad judge said. God's people shout to him night and day, and he will always give them what is right. He will not be slow to answer them."

KEY THOUGHT

Jesus' point is that if an evil and unrighteous judge will eventually give in to get a complaining and persistent but powerless woman off his back, then we can surely count on God—who loves us dearly—to hear us and respond in ways that are for our good. So let's keep praying and never give up, for God will hear and respond.

TODAY'S PRAYER

Almighty and eternal Father, please hear the things that trouble me today. Hear my requests and do what is best in each situation. [Lay out the things that trouble your heart to the Lord.] Father, I am concerned about several people who are facing really challenging times. Please bless each of them with what they most need as I bring each name before you. [Share the names with the Lord.] Thank you for hearing me and working in the situations I have placed before you. In Jesus' name I pray. Amen.

CONTEXT: LUKE 18:1-8
Related Passages: Romans 5:1-5; Romans 8:26-28; Matthew 6:5-6

Day 293

NOT AN ISSUE OF JUSTICE, BUT OF FAITH

Luke 18:8

[Jesus said] "I tell you, God will help his people quickly. But when the Son of Man comes again, will he find people on earth who believe in him?"

KEY THOUGHT

One of the hardest things we face as human beings is ongoing injustice. Yet tens of thousands of believers in Jesus face injustice, hardship, brutality, and persecution each year. When believers face these hard times, it is hard to believe that they will ever receive justice. It is especially disturbing when those in power are corrupt and are the ones treating them unfairly. However, Jesus reminds us that the issue isn't injustice but faithfulness. God will settle accounts and bring justice. The real question is whether or not we'll stick in there and not give up under fire. Hang in! Pray for the Father to hear you! Don't give up, for God will not only bring justice, but he will also bring salvation and victory.

TODAY'S PRAYER

Father, through your Holy Spirit, please inspire me to faithful endurance no matter what circumstances, evil people, or Satan may bring my way. In Jesus' name I pray. Amen.

CONTEXT: LUKE 18:1-8
Related Passages: Revelation 2:8-11; Romans 8:15-18; Acts 5:41

Day 294

RELIGIOUS ARROGANCE IS THE TARGET

Luke 18:9

*There were some people who thought they were very good and looked
down on everyone else. Jesus used this story to teach them . . . .*

KEY THOUGHT

Jesus' most scathing rebukes are reserved for those who are outwardly very religious, but who are arrogant, self-righteous, and feel superior to everyone else. Once again, Jesus illustrates his point with a story so his followers will not only know the truth of his message, but so they also can visualize what this religious arrogance looks like and can remember to avoid it in their own lives. Before we examine this story of Jesus, we should look at ourselves and ask, "What is the basis of our confidence?" Is it in comparing ourselves to others? Is it in our own works of righteousness? Or is it in God's grace and mercy shown to us in Jesus?

TODAY'S PRAYER

*Father, thank you for saving me, a sinner, who cannot live up to your standards of
character, righteousness, and holiness. Thank you for making a way for your grace to
reach me and bring me into your family as your child. In Jesus' name I pray. Amen.*

CONTEXT: LUKE 18:9-14
Related Passages: 2 Timothy 1:12-17; Ephesians 2:1-10; 1 Corinthians 10:12

Day 295

TWO MEN, VAST DIFFERENCES

Luke 18:10-14

*[Jesus used this story to teach them] "One time there was a Pharisee and a
tax collector. One day they both went to the Temple to pray. The Pharisee
stood alone, away from the tax collector. When the Pharisee prayed, he said,
'O God, I thank you that I am not as bad as other people. I am not like men
who steal, cheat, or commit adultery. I thank you that I am better than this
tax collector. I fast twice a week, and I give a tenth of everything I get!'*

*"The tax collector stood alone too. But when he prayed, he would not even look
up to heaven. He felt very humble before God. He said, 'O God, have mercy on
me. I am a sinner!' I tell you, when this man finished his prayer and went home,
he was right with God. But the Pharisee, who felt that he was better than others,
was not right with God. People who make themselves important will be made
humble. But those who make themselves humble will be made important."*

KEY THOUGHT

The difference between these two men was great, but not for the reason
the Pharisee thought. No, the difference between these two men was not their
outward actions or words, but their hearts. One of these men, the sinner,
knew he needed mercy, forgiveness, and grace. The other, the outwardly
religious guy, thought he deserved to be honored by God. In fact, only one
of these men knew about grace; that was the poor and forgiven man. Jesus
reminds us that our faith isn't about religiously pretentious games, but about
our humble response to the God who has given us everything in Christ.

TODAY'S PRAYER

Father, forgive me for I am a sinner. In Jesus' name I pray. Amen.

CONTEXT: LUKE 18:9-14
Related Passages: Galatians 6:1-5; Proverbs 16:18; Proverbs 8:13

Day 296

LIKE A LITTLE CHILD

Luke 18:15-17

Some people brought their small children to Jesus so that he could lay his hands on them to bless them. But when the followers saw this, they told the people not to do this. But Jesus called the little children to him and said to his followers, "Let the little children come to me. Don't stop them, because God's kingdom belongs to people who are like these little children. The truth is, you must accept God's kingdom like a little child accepts things, or you will never enter it."

KEY THOUGHT

Jesus has been confronting the Pharisees' sense of religious entitlement and he will be confronting the legalistic sense of entitlement of a rich man who presumes that God owes him. In between these two events comes a shocking reminder of how we often miss the greatest examples of Kingdom living. Small children were a bother in the world of great theological debate and teaching. The followers of Jesus are acting as if the children are a waste of Jesus' time. In this perfect moment, Jesus reminds them—and us as well— that we must become like these children to enter the Kingdom. In fact, we must accept the Kingdom with the wide-eyed, unassuming, unpretentious joy of a child who has no sense of entitlement. And if we can't live with this child-like sense of wonder, this recognition of the absolute grace of receiving a gift from God, then we will never enter the Kingdom.

TODAY'S PRAYER

O Abba Father, forgive me for any sense of entitlement and for any arrogance to think I could ever deserve or merit your love. Thank you for bringing me into your family and may I never lose my child-like sense of wonder at your grace. In Jesus' name I pray. Amen.

CONTEXT: LUKE 18:9-30
Related Passages: John 3:3-7; Titus 3:3-7; Ephesians 2:1-10

Day 297

THE MOST IMPORTANT QUESTION.

Luke 18:18-19

A religious leader asked Jesus, "Good Teacher, what must I do to get eternal life?"

Jesus said to him, "Why do you call me good? Only God is good."

KEY THOUGHT

Can you think of a more important question than the one this leader asks? I can think of several that are equally important, but they all ultimately come down to the same basic issue: am I confident that I am going to live forever with God? Are we confident in life with Christ, forever? God wants us to be! Now whether the religious leader's motives were perfectly pure is not really relevant to our asking the same question. We can ask it from a pure and undefiled heart, seeking to honor and glorify God. When we do, we can know where we stand and with whom we stand. Jesus is challenging the religious leader to wake up and understand the truth that stands right in front of him. If he is calling Jesus "good," then he must come to understand that Jesus is God and not play religious games, but come to truly believe.

TODAY'S PRAYER

Holy and righteous Father, open my heart and my mind so I can better understand your incarnation in Jesus of Nazareth. Thank you for showing your love for us in such clearly demonstrable ways by entering our world in a physical way to bring us home to you and give us eternal life. In Jesus' name I pray. Amen.

CONTEXT: LUKE 18:18-30
Related Passages: 1 John 5:13-15; John 5:24-29; Acts 2:37-42

Day 298

I'VE OBEYED ALL THESE?

Luke 18:20-21

[Jesus said] "And you know his commands: 'You must not commit adultery, you must not murder anyone, you must not steal, you must not tell lies about others, you must respect your father and mother ....'"

But the leader said, "I have obeyed all these commands since I was a boy."

KEY THOUGHT

While many of us can say we have never been guilty of murder, adultery, or possibly even stealing, very few of us can honestly say that we have never spoken false words in conversation and have always done what is honorable toward our parents. Even in the best of lives, there is some hedging of the truth or exaggeration that slips into conversation. Even in the best of children there are weak moments and difficult spans of time where we have done less than we could and should to honor our parents. Jesus helps the young man confront the real issue in his life by answering his question even though the basis of the question was probably false. This man, however, claims to be a law keeper deluxe! He has obeyed them all since he was young. But I'm not sure he was being fully honest with himself. I know I couldn't say what he said and I have never met a person who could say it and be completely honest. How about you? Can you justify yourself on the basis of keeping law? Are you trying to be righteous simply by being better and obeying more completely than others? In the discussion that follows, Jesus penetrates to the heart of the issue.

TODAY'S PRAYER

Father, eternal God, thank you for your forgiving grace. Forgive me of my moments of self-righteous arrogance. Humble me gently till I can see that my righteousness is based on Jesus' perfect gift and not my perfect obedience. Then, dear Father, I ask by the power of your Holy Spirit that you conform me more perfectly to the person you want me to be. In Jesus' name I ask this. Amen.

CONTEXT: LUKE 18:18-30
Related Passages: Romans 8:1-4; 2 Corinthians 3:17-18; Romans 3:23-26

Day 299

JUST ONE THING!

Luke 18:22-23

When Jesus heard this, he said to the leader, "But there is still one thing you need to do. Sell everything you have and give the money to those who are poor. You will have riches in heaven. Then come and follow me." But when the man heard Jesus tell him to give away his money, he was sad. He didn't want to do this, because he was very rich.

KEY THOUGHT

"There is still one thing you need to do." For the rich young man, the one thing Jesus called him to surrender was huge. Our one thing can be huge, too! Clearly, this story impacts us at two levels. It calls us to be generous people, showing we have the heart of God. However, it also asks us to look at our life circumstances and determine what the one thing most difficult for us to give up for Jesus would be. Then it calls us to give it up. So the message for you and me, dear friend, is this: that we be generous and not let anything interfere with our wholehearted devotion to the Lord Jesus.

TODAY'S PRAYER

Dear Father in heaven, please never, ever, let anything crowd into my heart and become a rival to your Son. In Jesus' name I pray. Amen.

CONTEXT: LUKE 18:18-30
Related Passages: Luke 10:25-27; Romans 12:1-2; Luke 14:33

Day 300

THE DANGER OF RICHES

Luke 18:24-25
When Jesus saw that the man was sad, he said, "It will be very hard for rich people to enter God's kingdom. It is easier for a camel to go through the eye of a needle than for a rich person to enter God's kingdom."

KEY THOUGHT

While material riches can be a great blessing and can be used to bless many in need and to do great things for the Kingdom, they can also be traps for us. The Gospel of Luke lets us hear Jesus teach repeatedly about the danger of riches. Jesus' point here is that riches can be an incredible danger to the heart of believers. This young man is the living example of this danger. As the apostle Paul warned, greed and a desire for riches are idolatry and they will destroy us. Let's yield every area of our lives, including our use of wealth, to the Lordship of Jesus.

TODAY'S PRAYER

Father, thank you for your many rich blessings. Help me use these blessings to your glory. I do not want anything to interfere with my total devotion to you. In Jesus' name I pray. Amen.

CONTEXT: LUKE 18:18-30
Related Passages: Luke 13:13-21; 1 Timothy 6:6-10; Colossians 3:5

POSSIBLE!

Luke 18:26-27

When the people heard this, they said, "Then who can be saved?"

Jesus answered, "God can do things that are not possible for people to do!"

KEY THOUGHT

Many things are hard for us. Others seem impossible. Jesus wants us to realize that when we live for the Kingdom—if we trust in God's power to ork within us—then we can do far more than we would ever imagine possible. The real issue is putting God first and not letting anything take his place of preeminence in our hearts. The bottom line is plain: "God can do things that are not possible for people to do!"

TODAY'S PRAYER

O Lord God Almighty, I believe you parted the sea for Moses, stilled the storm through Jesus, and healed the lame man through Peter and John. I know you can also do amazing things in my life as I live for you and your Kingdom. In Jesus' name I confess your glory. Amen.

CONTEXT: LUKE 18:18-30
Related Passages: Ephesians 3:20-21; Philippians 2:13; Luke 1:28-37

Day 302

YOU CAN'T

Luke 18:28-30

Peter said, "Look, we left everything we had and followed you."

Jesus said, "I can promise that everyone who has left their home, wife, brothers, parents, or children for God's kingdom will get much more than they left. They will get many times more in this life. And in the world that is coming they will get the reward of eternal life."

KEY THOUGHT

No matter what we may give up for the sake of the Kingdom and to honor the Lord, it will be nothing compared to what God has promised us. Bottom line: we cannot out-give God! When our motives are to honor him, to bless his people, and to empower the work of the Kingdom, then we can be assured that God will not forget.

TODAY'S PRAYER

Father, thank you so much for your generous grace. I also want to thank you in advance for your generous reward and abundant blessings that lie ahead. I ask, dear Lord, that you help me not let my passion and desire to honor you be diluted by life's challenges. In Jesus' name I pray these things. Amen.

CONTEXT: LUKE 18:18-30
Related Passages: Romans 8:17-19; 1 Corinthians 2:16-17; Matthew 6:5-6

Day 303

FAILED TO GRASP IT

Luke 18:31-34

Then Jesus talked to the twelve apostles alone. He said to them, "Listen, we are going to Jerusalem. Everything that God told the prophets to write about the Son of Man will happen. He will be handed over to the foreigners, who will laugh at him, insult him, and spit on him. They will beat him with whips and then kill him. But on the third day after his death, he will rise to life again." The apostles tried to understand this, but they could not; the meaning was hidden from them.

KEY THOUGHT

Jesus' words cannot help them understand. Jesus' best efforts will only give them words to remember and to put things into perspective, at a later time after he has been crucified and raised from the dead. Jesus' destiny in Jerusalem was simply incomprehensible to them. They had seen the good he had done. They had experienced his life-changing presence firsthand. They believed him to be the Messiah. How could God's Messiah be crucified? How could he be executed for the deeds of kindness he had performed and the words of truth he had spoken? Jesus is going to Jerusalem knowing full well that he will be persecuted, rejected, and tortured. Yet he goes anyway, to honor God and to pay the price for our sin.

TODAY'S PRAYER

Lord Jesus, I thank you for going to the cross knowing that it was coming and yet enduring it for the sake of my salvation. To you, O Lord and Christ, belong all glory, honor, blessing, and praise. Amen.

CONTEXT: LUKE 18:31-43
Related Passages: Philippians 2:5-11; Hebrews 12:2; John 12:23-28

SHOUT LOUDER!

Luke 18:35-39

Jesus came near the city of Jericho. There was a blind man sitting beside the road. He was begging people for money. When he heard the people coming down the road, he asked, "What is happening?"

They told him, "Jesus, the one from Nazareth, is coming here."

The blind man was excited and said, "Jesus, Son of David, please help me!"

The people who were in front, leading the group, criticized the blind man. They told him to be quiet. But he shouted more and more, "Son of David, please help me!"

KEY THOUGHT

Often we let the noise and commotion of our crowded lives distract us from Jesus' presence in our lives. Deep down, we know that we need time in his presence—time that comes from prayer and reading the Gospels (Matthew, Mark, Luke, and John). So let's intentionally cry out each day, "Jesus, Son of David, have mercy on me!" Let's invite Jesus into our busy lives. When we let all our distractions and responsibilities crowd Jesus out of our lives, let's shout louder! If the blind man in Jesus' day wouldn't be silenced until he came into the presence of Jesus, then we shouldn't settle for anything less today.

TODAY'S PRAYER

Father, forgive me for letting the noise and busyness of my life crowd Jesus out. Make my heart yearn to learn more of Jesus each day. In Jesus' name I ask for this grace. Amen.

CONTEXT: LUKE 18:31-43
Related Passages: Revelation 3:20; Luke 19:1-10; Luke 7:36-38

Day 305

JESUS WANTS TO HEAR ABOUT YOUR BURDENS

Luke 18:40-41

Jesus stopped there and said, "Bring that man to me!" When he came close, Jesus asked him, "What do you want me to do for you?"

He said, "Lord, I want to see again."

KEY THOUGHT

You see them on the street. "How you doing?" they ask. "Fine." Your reply is automatic and instinctive. But you are not fine. You just know that they don't really want to hear about your burdens. They are just being nice and giving you a perfunctory greeting. If you are blessed, you may actually have a few folks close to you who are interested in the heaviness in your heart, but the vast majority don't want to hear about it. In fact, many folks don't have a single person who really wants to share the burdens of their heart. Jesus, however, will take the time to listen and has the heart to hear. Offer him the burdens of your heart!

TODAY'S PRAYER

Thank you, Father, for your desire to hear the burdens of my heart by showing your love through Jesus. In his name I offer my thanks. Amen.

CONTEXT: LUKE 18:31-43
Related Passages: Mark 1:40-42; Philippians 4:6-7; Luke 7:1-10

Day 306

BRINGING PRAISE TO GOD

Luke 18:42-43

Jesus said to him, "You can see now. You are healed because you believed."

Then the man was able to see. He followed Jesus, thanking God.
Everyone who saw this praised God for what happened.

KEY THOUGHT

The crowds knew that Jesus' acts of compassion were not done to draw attention to himself, but to bring praise to God. Just as Jesus lived to glorify God, we too are put here to bring God glory. If our best achievements and the events in our everyday lives bring the Father praise, then we have succeeded in life.

TODAY'S PRAYER

Father, may all good things that I do and the way that I live each day
bring you honor and praise. In Jesus' name I pray. Amen.

CONTEXT: LUKE 18:31-43
Related Passages: Luke 7:12-16; Ephesians 1:12-14; Revelation 15:4

Day 307

SEEKING THE LOST

Luke 19:1-5

Jesus was going through the city of Jericho. In Jericho there was a man named Zacchaeus. He was a wealthy, very important tax collector. He wanted to see who Jesus was. There were many others who wanted to see Jesus too. Zacchaeus was too short to see above the people. So he ran to a place where he knew Jesus would come. Then he climbed a sycamore tree so he could see him.

When Jesus came to where Zacchaeus was, he looked up and saw him in the tree. Jesus said, "Zacchaeus, hurry! Come down! I must stay at your house today."

KEY THOUGHT

When Zacchaeus demonstrated his desire to see Jesus, Jesus looked up and saw him. Jesus then told Zacchaeus that he needed to stay with him. God wants us to know that when people are actively seeking the Lord, he seeks after them until he finds them. Not only does he willingly listen to those whose hearts are burdened (Luke 18:1-14), he also reaches out for those who are seeking him.

TODAY'S PRAYER

Father, I know you longed for me to be your child even before I had begun to seek you. Thank you for finding me and bringing me into your family through the gift of your Son. In Jesus' name I praise and thank you for your grace that has brought my salvation. Amen.

CONTEXT: LUKE 19:1-10
Related Passages: Acts 17:27-28; Luke 11:9-13; Hebrews 11:6

Day 308

THE JOY OF SINNERS IN JESUS

Luke 19:6-7

Zacchaeus hurried and came down. He was happy to have Jesus in his house. Everyone saw this. They began to complain, "Look at the kind of man Jesus is staying with. Zacchaeus is a sinner!"

KEY THOUGHT

I'm not sure how those of us who are Christians today would react to the actions of Jesus with sinners if he was still physically among us. I do know, however, that many who regard themselves as sinners are still excited to know they are actually welcomed by Jesus into his grace. Those of us who have been in Christ a long time need to be re-awakened to the hunger that many people have for the Lord. Let's help them find him by looking for those seeking to find him. Then, let's welcome them as Jesus did.

TODAY'S PRAYER

Father, open my eyes to see those around me who are seeking after your Son. Please give me the wisdom to know when to speak, what to say, and how to act so that I can be helpful in their search to come to know Jesus, in whose name I pray. Amen.

CONTEXT: LUKE 19:1-10
Related Passages: 1 Peter 3:13-16; Luke 15:1-7; James 5:19-20

Day 309

REPENTANCE MEANS CHANGE!

Luke 19:8-9

Zacchaeus said to the Lord, "I want to do good. I will give half of my money to the poor. If I have cheated anyone, I will pay them back four times more."

Jesus said, "Today is the day for this family to be saved from sin. Yes, even this tax collector is one of God's chosen people."

KEY THOUGHT

Zacchaeus is a living example of repentance in this passage. Repentance is a change of heart that leads to a change of life. Zacchaeus was so touched by the Lord's loving presence that his heart was changed and he committed to changing his lifestyle. That kind of change is the mark of salvation and the guarantee of a new person.

TODAY'S PRAYER

Father, I praise you for the joy and hope my salvation has brought to me. Please empower me with your Spirit to produce the fruit of repentance, a life that blesses others and brings glory to you. In the name of Jesus Christ, my Lord, I pray. Amen.

CONTEXT: LUKE 19:1-10
Related Passages: Acts 2:37-42; Acts 3:17-21; Acts 17:30

Day 310

JESUS CAME TO SAVE THE LOST!

Luke 19:10
"The Son of Man came to find lost people and save them."

KEY THOUGHT

Jesus didn't come to please the religious crowd. Jesus didn't come to pander to the social crowd. Jesus didn't come to hang out with the wild bunch. Instead, Jesus entered the world to save sinners. When we look back over the Gospel of Luke, we see Jesus reach out to men and women, young and old, powerful and forgotten, demon possessed, and the politically connected. He came to save sinners of all shapes, sizes, and stripes. He came to save you and me.

TODAY'S PRAYER

Holy and righteous God, thank you for your great desire to bring salvation to all people—even me. Open my heart and move me to reach out to others who need to know your grace. Even more, dear Father, stir me to seek the lost as passionately as your Son did, and still does. In Jesus' name I pray. Amen.

CONTEXT: LUKE 19:1-10
Related Passages: Luke 5:32; Mark 1:35-39; John 10:10

Day 311

UNHEALTHY RUSH

Luke 19:11-14

As the crowd listened to what he was saying, Jesus went on to tell a story. He was now near Jerusalem and knew that the people thought it was almost time for God's kingdom to come. So he said, "A very important man was preparing to go to a country far away to be made a king. Then he planned to return home and rule his people. So he called ten of his servants together. He gave a bag of money to each servant. He said, 'Do business with this money until I come back.' But the people in the kingdom hated the man. They sent a group to follow him to the other country. There they said, 'We don't want this man to be our king.'"

KEY THOUGHT

Jesus is trying to slow down the rush running through the crowd. The rumor has gotten started that the Kingdom of God is going to begin immediately on his arrival in Jerusalem. He chooses to use a story to dispel this myth. However, we should notice how the followers of Jesus want to rush his work rather than letting him fulfill matters based upon his Father's timing and will. Our impatience with the Lord's timing can lead us into making poor decisions.

TODAY'S PRAYER

Father, give me the wisdom to know your will in my life and the patient endurance to wait on your timing. Forgive me for my foolish impatience. Through your Spirit, please develop my self-control, patience, and peace. I pray this in Jesus' name. Amen.

CONTEXT: LUKE 19:11-27
Related Passages: Galatians 5:22-23; Colossians 1:11-12; 2 Peter 3:9-10

Day 312

WELL DONE!

Luke 19:15-19

"But the man was made king. When he came home, he said, 'Call those servants who have my money. I want to know how much more money they earned with it.' The first servant came and said, 'Sir, I earned ten bags of money with the one bag you gave me.' The king said to him, 'That's great! You are a good servant. I see that I can trust you with small things. So now I will let you rule over ten of my cities.'

"The second servant said, 'Sir, with your one bag of money I earned five bags.' The king said to this servant, 'You can rule over five cities.'"

KEY THOUGHT

Such sweet words are these to hear! Another translation puts it, "Well done, my good servant!" (TNIV) God longs to give us his blessing and praise. He showed us this at his Son's baptism, "You are my beloved Son, and I am fully pleased with you." God does not forget our works done to honor him and he always notices the effort made in our stewardship. So know that even if no one else notices your efforts to honor God, you can be assured that he notices them and is blessed.

TODAY'S PRAYER

Father, may all I do bring you joy, honor, and praise. Thank you for reassuring me that my efforts to honor you are not in vain. In Jesus' name I pray. Amen.

CONTEXT: LUKE 19:11-27
Related Passages: Luke 3:21-22; Hebrews 6:10; Matthew 6:1-4

Day 313

THE GREATEST RISK

Luke 19:20-27

"Then another servant came in and said to the king, 'Sir, here is your bag of money. I wrapped it in a piece of cloth and hid it. I was afraid of you because you are a hard man. You even take money that you didn't earn and gather food that you didn't grow.'

"Then the king said to him, 'What a bad servant you are! I will use your own words to condemn you. You said that I am a hard man. You said that I even take money that I didn't earn and gather food that I didn't grow. If that is true, you should have put my money in the bank. Then, when I came back, my money would have earned some interest.' Then the king said to the men who were watching, 'Take the bag of money away from this servant and give it to the servant who earned ten bags of money.'

"The men said to the king, 'But sir, that servant already has ten bags of money.'

"The king said, 'People who use what they have will get more. But those who do not use what they have will have everything taken away from them. Now where are my enemies? Where are the people who did not want me to be king? Bring my enemies here and kill them. I will watch them die.'"

KEY THOUGHT

If the first two servants who received the king's bags of money made good use of them, the third did just the opposite. His view of the king was very negative and he was afraid to take risks in using the money entrusted to him. His fears made him take the greatest risk of all: doing nothing. Fear immobilizes us. Jesus doesn't want us to be afraid to risk for the Kingdom; in fact, he wants us to know that the greatest risk of all is to look fearfully at God and to think we are playing it safe by just hiding all that he has entrusted to us to use for his glory.

TODAY'S PRAYER

Father, keep my heart from being afraid to make great efforts to do great things. While I know that there is always a chance of an embarrassing failure, I also realize that an even greater embarrassment would be to do nothing with all that you have entrusted to me. Give me wisdom and confidence in putting to use your truth and blessings in my life. In Jesus' name I pray for courage to use your gifts for your glory. Amen.

CONTEXT: LUKE 19:11-27
Related Passages: Ephesians 3:20-21; 2 Corinthians 9:10-11; 1 John 4:18

Day 314

THE LORD NEEDS IT!

Luke 19:28-35

After Jesus said these things, he continued traveling toward Jerusalem. He came near Bethphage and Bethany, towns near the hill called the Mount of Olives. He sent out two of his followers. He said, "Go into the town you can see there. When you enter the town, you will find a young donkey tied there that no one has ever ridden. Untie it, and bring it here to me. If anyone asks you why you are taking the donkey, you should say, 'The Master needs it.'"

The two followers went into town. They found the donkey exactly like Jesus told them. They untied it, but its owners came out. They said to the followers, "Why are you untying our donkey?"

The followers answered, "The Master needs it." So the followers brought the donkey to Jesus. They put their coats on its back. Then they put Jesus on the donkey.

KEY THOUGHT

What an attitude! If the Lord needs it, I'll offer it. If the Lord wants it, I'll do it. No questions asked. No explanation needed. No hesitation found. We've seen a rich young man turn back from following because the Lord asked him something he wouldn't do. This is not the case here. "The Lord needs it!" Such a simple explanation was met with an equally simple response—no words, just compliance. Little did the owners know that their act of submission and obedience to Jesus would bring about such a glorious event—the Triumphal Entry described in the following verses. So the question for each of us today is this: "What does the Lord need from me?" May our responses be the same as the unnamed owners of the donkey.

TODAY'S PRAYER

God of glory and grace, my heavenly Father, please work on my heart. Do what is necessary to keep it soft and responsive to your will. May I always be open to whatever your Son needs of me. May I respond without hesitation. Most of all, may you be glorified and your Kingdom be served in my willingness to obey. In Jesus' name. Amen.

CONTEXT: LUKE 19:28-40
Related Passages: Luke 18:18-23; Luke 9:21-27; Luke 14:33

Day 315

THE STONES WOULD CHEER!

Luke 19:36-40
*He rode along the road toward Jerusalem. The followers
spread their coats on the road before him.*

*Jesus was coming close to Jerusalem. He was already near the bottom of the Mount of
Olives. The whole group of followers was happy. They were very excited and praised God.
They thanked God for all the powerful things they had seen. They said, "'Welcome! God
bless the king who comes in the name of the Lord.' Peace in heaven and glory to God!"*

Some of the Pharisees said to Jesus, "Teacher, tell your followers not to say these things."

*But Jesus answered, "I tell you, if my followers didn't
say them, these stones would shout them."*

KEY THOUGHT

Isn't it sad that people still get upset when they think that people are too
exuberant over the presence of Jesus in worship? Creation shouts Jesus' praise
and the angels of heaven shout out to honor his glory. Let's not let anyone or
anything shame us into silence about our glorious Savior.

TODAY'S PRAYER

*Father, your Son is marvelous, glorious, gracious, and precious to me. I want the
world to know that he is not only my Savior, but also the Savior of all people.
Give me wisdom to know how best to communicate this truth in each situation
in which I find myself. However, dear Father, may my spoken admiration
for your Son and my life's witness to his grace never be withheld because I'm
afraid of what others may think of me. In Jesus' name I pray. Amen.*

CONTEXT: LUKE 19:28-40
Related Passages: Luke 9:24-27; 2 Timothy 1:6-8; Philippians 2:9-11

Day 316

REJECTED!

Luke 19:41-44

Jesus came near Jerusalem. Looking at the city, he began to cry for it and said, "I wish you knew today what would bring you peace. But it is hidden from you now. A time is coming when your enemies will build a wall around you and hold you in on all sides. They will destroy you and all your people. Not one stone of your buildings will stay on top of another. All this will happen because you did not know the time when God came to save you."

KEY THOUGHT

We easily assume that if an opportunity is presented to us, then we will have many other chances to respond. But experience eventually teaches us what God had tried to get us to see much earlier: opportunities are offered and then pass by us never to be offered quite the same way again. Jerusalem stood on the brink of history. Accepting Jesus as the way to peace offered great opportunity. Rejecting Jesus led to the destruction that would follow. Unfortunately this same rejection plays itself out repeatedly on a much smaller scale in the lives of many people. They reject the way of the Lord in their youth, or in a time of rebellion, and think that he will be there for them to follow whenever and however they may choose. While they may eventually come to the Lord, they will waste much time, and they will also forfeit much peace as the consequences of rebellion and procrastination bring heartache after heartache. In addition, some can have their hearts so hardened that they never try to return to the Lord. Let's live with urgency with those we love and ask God to help us reach them for Jesus so their lives and their eternities will not be squandered on what is not peace!

TODAY'S PRAYER

Father, give me wisdom and "urgent patience" to know how best to share Jesus with those I love who do not know him as their Lord. I do not want to rush them in ways that close their hearts to him. At the same time, dear Father, I don't want to be lackadaisical in my approach. Help me be a peace-bringer as I seek to share the Lord. In Jesus' name I ask it. Amen.

CONTEXT: LUKE 19:41-48
Related Passages: Matthew 5:9; John 14:27-29; Philippians 4:4-7

Day 317

THEY HUNG ON EVERY WORD

Luke 19:45-48

Jesus went into the Temple area. He began to throw out the people who were selling things there. He said, "The Scriptures say, 'My Temple will be a house of prayer.' But you have changed it into a 'hiding place for thieves.'"

Jesus taught the people in the Temple area every day. The leading priests, the teachers of the law, and some of the leaders of the people wanted to kill him. But they did not know how they could do it, because everyone was listening to him. The people were very interested in what Jesus said.

KEY THOUGHT

Those in power wanted to shut Jesus up; they were so adamant about it, they plotted to kill him. However, the everyday folks heard the voice of God in Jesus' words and hung on everything he said. Our journey through the Gospel of Luke this year has been based upon our need to hear the voice of Jesus and to know his ministry first hand. Some people will read a bestselling Christian author before they will read their Bible. They will read books about Jesus rather than reading the Gospels that the Holy Spirit provided us to know the story of Jesus. I want to issue you a challenge: join me in using these next sixty day to read through each of the Gospels (Matthew, Mark, Luke, and John) at least once. Hang on to Jesus' every word. Ask the Holy Spirit to help you know Jesus more completely so that you can become like Jesus more fully.

TODAY'S PRAYER

O righteous and holy Father, God of all creation, please reveal your Son to me and in me as I seek to know him better in the closing weeks of this year. In Jesus' name I pray. Amen.

CONTEXT: LUKE 19:41-48
Related Passages: 2 Corinthians 3:17-18; John 1:36-41; John 5:32-40

Day 318

BY WHOSE AUTHORITY?

Luke 20:1-8

One day Jesus was in the Temple area teaching the people. He was telling them the Good News. The leading priests, teachers of the law, and older Jewish leaders came to talk to Jesus. They said, "Tell us what authority you have to do these things. Who gave you this authority?"

Jesus answered, "I will ask you a question too. Tell me: When John baptized people, did his authority come from God or was it only from other people?"

The priests, the teachers of the law, and the Jewish leaders all talked about this. They said to each other, "If we answer, 'John's baptism was from God,' then he will say, 'Then why did you not believe John?' But if we say that John's baptism was from someone else, the people will stone us to death. They all believe that John was a prophet." So they answered, "We don't know the answer."

So Jesus said to them, "Then I will not tell you who gave me the authority to do these things."

KEY THOUGHT

Jesus has now entered the battlefield. Yes, he is in the Temple of God. However, his opponents are now going to bombard him with questions in hopes of getting him to commit some heinous religious offense that they can use to make him seem scandalous. Jesus' agenda, on the other hand, is to share the good news. Outwitting his opponents at their own game, he sends them away with a question they didn't want to answer. He is there to minister. He won't get caught up in their games with the end so near. Let's remember that we must not let religious games take the place of God's mission and ministry through us. Jesus serves and teaches with compassion even while under attack. We can, too!

TODAY'S PRAYER

Father, forgive me for getting so upset sometimes with religious questions. I know there are important issues of truth. Please help me see these. On the other hand, Father, I don't want to get caught up in the religious arguments and miss the opportunity to minister to others. Please remove any contentious spirit from me and help me to focus on the things that are matters of your concern. In Jesus' name I pray for this wisdom. Amen.

CONTEXT: LUKE 20:1-8
Related Passages: 1 Timothy 6:20; Titus 2:15; Romans 15:17-20

Day 319

THE OWNER'S STORY

Luke 20:9-13

Then Jesus told the people this story: "A man planted a vineyard. He leased the land to some farmers. Then he went away for a long time. Later, it was time for the grapes to be picked. So the man sent a servant to those farmers so that they would give him his share of the grapes. But they beat the servant and sent him away with nothing. So the man sent another servant. They beat this servant too and showed no respect for him. They sent the servant away with nothing. So the man sent a third servant to the farmers. They hurt this servant badly and threw him out.

"The owner of the vineyard said, 'What will I do now? I will send my son. I love my son very much. Maybe the farmers will respect my son.'"

KEY THOUGHT

This parable is very autobiographical for Jesus. He is clearly referring to what God has done. Religious leaders ruled over God's people. They did it their own way. They resisted God's desires and true representatives to the point of abusing and killing them. So God would send someone who is more than just an owner's representative; he would send his cherished Son. Jesus is that cherished Son! What unfolds in the events that follow happened to God's beloved Son. God loves enough to send his cherished Son to save us—even if it means rejection and abuse from those who are supposed to serve him.

TODAY'S PRAYER

Father, thank you for your indescribable gift of Jesus, in whose name I pray. Amen.

CONTEXT: LUKE 20:9-19
Related Passages: John 3:16-17; Romans 5:6-11; 1 John 4:9-10

Day 320

GOD FORBID!

Luke 20:14-16

[Jesus continued teaching] "When the farmers saw the son, they said to each other, 'This is the owner's son. This vineyard will be his. If we kill him, it will be ours.' So the farmers threw the son out of the vineyard and killed him.

"What will the owner of the vineyard do? He will come and kill those farmers. Then he will lease the land to some other farmers."

When the people heard this story, they said, "This should never happen!"

KEY THOUGHT

"This should never happen!" the people cried out when they heard Jesus' story. But God didn't stop the horrible events of the trial, rejection, and crucifixion from happening. In fact, these events show his love for us and demonstrate Jesus' obedience to God. Jesus' crucifixion is horrible . . . unconscionable . . . and despicable. In normal human circumstances they would have been deplorable. Jesus, however, is much more than the son of the farm owner described in his parable; he is the Son of God and heir to all that belongs to God. Yet he will be treated with utmost contempt. It is so sad—yet it is also our salvation!

TODAY'S PRAYER

Father, thank you for your mercy and grace. I am sorry that it cost so much to share it with me and that Jesus had to endure so much for me. Make me worthy of this great cost by the sanctifying power of your Holy Spirit. I pray this in Jesus' name. Amen.

CONTEXT: LUKE 20:9-19
Related Passages: Acts 2:22-24; 1 Corinthians 1:20-25; 2 Corinthians 5:21

Day 321

JUST GOT MAD!

Luke 20:17-19

But Jesus looked into their eyes and said, "Then what does this verse mean: 'The stone that the builders refused to accept became the cornerstone'? Everyone who falls on that stone will be broken. If that stone falls on you, it will crush you!"

When the teachers of the law and the leading priests heard this story, they knew it was about them. So they wanted to arrest Jesus right then, but they were afraid of what the people would do.

KEY THOUGHT

There are three ways to respond when Jesus speaks the truth about our sin. First, we can ignore it and pretend it doesn't apply to us. Second, we can do what the religious leaders did here—we can become enraged at the truth and try to get rid of the truth-teller. Third, we can be convicted in our hearts and change our lives. While the events in which we face these three choices are not as significant as what is happening with Jesus in Jerusalem, they do happen for us. Let's not be like Jesus' opponents here, and seek to be rid of the truth-teller. Instead, let's welcome the truth and the truth-teller by changing our hearts and welcoming him into our lives.

TODAY'S PRAYER

Father, when I hear the truth, please convict my heart and help me change my life. I don't want to ignore or rationalize my sin. I don't want to let Satan harden my heart to the truth. Help me be convicted of my sin and commit to live your truth no matter the cost to me. In Jesus' name I ask for this grace. Amen.

CONTEXT: LUKE 20:9-19
Related Passages: Acts 2:37-39; Acts 3:17-20; Acts 17:30

Day 322
AMAZING!

Luke 20:20-26

So the Jewish leaders waited for the right time to get Jesus. They sent some men to him, who pretended to be sincere. They wanted to find something wrong with what Jesus said. (If they found something wrong, then they could hand him over to the governor, who had the authority to arrest him.) So the men said to Jesus, "Teacher, we know that what you say and teach is true. It doesn't matter who is listening—you teach the same to all people. You always teach the truth about God's way. Tell us, is it right for us to pay taxes to Caesar or not?"

But Jesus knew that these men were trying to trick him. He said to them, "Show me a silver coin. Whose name and picture are on it?"

They said, "Caesar's."

He said to them, "Then give to Caesar what belongs to Caesar, and give to God what belongs to God."

The men were amazed at his wise answer. They could say nothing. They were not able to trick Jesus there in front of the people. He said nothing they could use against him.

KEY THOUGHT

Isn't it interesting that Jesus' public ministry is ending very similarly to the way it began—with people being amazed at his teaching. The smartest and the best minds tried to trap Jesus in social and religious conflict. But Jesus' answers are not only wise; they are also true. Let's seek our answers in him and let him silence the doubts and answer the questions of our hearts.

TODAY'S PRAYER

Holy God, please help me find my answers in Jesus as I seek your truth. In Jesus' name I ask for your grace. Amen.

CONTEXT: LUKE 20:20-40
Related Passages: Luke 4:22, 32, 36; John 6:60-69; Matthew 28:18-20

Day 323

OUR QUESTIONS BETRAY OUR HEARTS

Luke 20:27-33

Some Sadducees came to Jesus. (Sadducees believe that people will not rise from death.) They asked him, "Teacher, Moses wrote that if a married man dies and had no children, his brother must marry his widow. Then they will have children for the dead brother. One time there were seven brothers. The first brother married a woman but died. He had no children. Then the second brother married the woman, and he died. And the third brother married the woman, and he died. The same thing happened with all the other brothers. They all died and had no children. The woman was the last to die. But all seven brothers married her. So when people rise from death, whose wife will this woman be?"

KEY THOUGHT

Ever notice how the questions we ask often betray what is really in our hearts? The Sadducees didn't believe in a resurrection. So their question was a trap, not an earnest seeking of truth. Their hearts were hardened and their goal was destroying Jesus. Jesus longs to hear our honest questions and help us find the truth. Sometimes, however, we need to listen to our own questions and ask the Lord what they reveal about our hearts.

TODAY'S PRAYER

Father, give me a clean heart and pure motives as I seek your truth. May the words of my mouth and the mediations of my heart be pleasing in your sight, O Lord, my Rock and Savior. In Jesus' name I ask it. Amen.

CONTEXT: LUKE 20:20-40
Related Passages: Luke 11:9-13; Psalm 51:10; Psalm 19:12-14

Day 324

NO MARRIAGE?

Luke 20:34-40

Jesus said to the Sadducees, "On earth, people marry each other. Some people will be worthy to be raised from death and live again after this life. In that life they will not marry. In that life people are like angels and cannot die. They are children of God, because they have been raised from death. Moses clearly showed that people are raised from death. When Moses wrote about the burning bush, he said that the Lord is 'the God of Abraham, the God of Isaac, and the God of Jacob.' So they were not still dead, because he is the God only of living people. Yes, to God they are all still living."

Some of the teachers of the law said, "Teacher, your answer was very good." No one was brave enough to ask him another question.

KEY THOUGHT

No marriage in heaven? Some folks worry about this. Jesus' point, however, is that every relationship is raised to a new level and that we find a heightened and holy existence that far transcends anything we can experience or even imagine here, so marriage in heaven will not be an issue for us. Just remember, good things await us in the presence of God with whom we will spend forever . . . and those good things are better than anything we can ask or imagine!

TODAY'S PRAYER

Father, thank you for a bright and shining future with you that is far better than anything I can imagine, much less understand. I await your future with joyous expectation. In Jesus' name. Amen.

CONTEXT: LUKE 20:20-40

Related Passages: 1 Thessalonians 4:15-18; Philippians 3:20-21; Revelation 7:14-17

Day 325

DAVID'S SON

Luke 20:41-44

Then Jesus said, "Why do people say that the Christ is the Son of David? In the book of Psalms, David himself says, 'The Lord God said to my Lord: Sit by me at my right side, and I will put your enemies under your power.' David calls the Christ 'Lord.' So how can the Christ also be David's son?"

KEY THOUGHT

As Jesus' opponents repeatedly tried to "trip him up" with their religious questioning, Jesus turns the tables on them and asks them a question. As a descendant of King David, Jesus could claim to be David's son. But, as Jesus points out using their own method of interpretation, David also calls the Messiah his Lord! How can this be so? Of course Jesus is not only taking part in religious banter, he is also trying to jolt them out of their steadfast desire to get rid of him. He is also trying to open their eyes to see who it is that chooses to walk among them—Jesus, the Messiah, the Son of David, and the Son of God.

TODAY'S PRAYER

Father, I do believe that Jesus is my Lord, the Messiah and Christ, my Savior, and my King. Forgive me for not living out that faith with more passion and more character. Empower me with your Spirit to become more like him each day. In Jesus' name I pray. Amen.

CONTEXT: LUKE 20:41-47; 21:1-4
Related Passages: Acts 2:22-24, 31-33; Acts 10:36; Romans 14:9

Day 326

GREATER PUNISHMENT

Luke 20:45-47

While all the people were listening to Jesus, he said to his followers, "Be careful of the teachers of the law. They like to walk around wearing clothes that look important. And they love for people to show respect to them in the marketplaces. They love to have the most important seats in the synagogues and the places of honor at banquets. But they cheat widows and take their homes. Then they try to make themselves look good by saying long prayers. God will punish them very much."

KEY THOUGHT

Three great sins are pronounced upon the religious leaders of Jesus' day: first, they are pretentious, loving to be recognized as important religious people; second, they cheat the helpless in society whom they are supposed to protect; and third, they are hypocrites who try to cover their hypocrisy by appearing to be pious. Those of us who are invested in living our faith passionately need to know that God is pleased with our passion. However, our Heavenly Father does not want us to make a big show of our religious zeal, especially when we find ways to justify living in contradiction to his revealed will for us in Scripture.

TODAY'S PRAYER

Father, may I never again be guilty of the Pharisees' sins! Forgive me, dear God, for those times when I've wanted to appear religious, but lived my life in hypocrisy and sin. Through your blessed and powerful Holy Spirit conform me more to your Son each day. In Jesus' name I ask this. Amen.

CONTEXT: LUKE 20:41-21:4
Related Passages: Proverbs 6:16-19; James 1:27; Amos 5:21-24

Day 327

MORE THAN THE SHOW CAN DISPLAY

Luke 21:1-4

Jesus looked up and saw some rich people putting their gifts to God into the Temple collection box. Then he saw a poor widow put two small copper coins into the box. He said, "This poor widow gave only two small coins. But the truth is, she gave more than all those rich people. They have plenty, and they gave only what they did not need. This woman is very poor, but she gave all she had to live on."

KEY THOUGHT

If we are not careful, we can easily jump to judgment based on external demonstrations of piety. We can easily reach the point where we honor those with money because their gifts are large even though their sacrifices may be small in terms of actual personal sacrifice. God, however, knows our hearts when we give. He knows what we hold back and why. He also knows how much we sacrifice and the attitude prompting that sacrifice. All around us are people who are living for the Lord, but who will seldom receive human recognition. Jesus, however, notices. He knows people's hearts as they give. Not one kindness we do in the name of Jesus and for the glory of the Lord's Kingdom will be forgotten. Not one sacrifice for the Savior will go unnoticed. He knows the truth behind our gifts and is blessed when these gifts come from generous, joyous, and sacrificial hearts.

TODAY'S PRAYER

Father God, you own everything in the heavens and on the earth; please break me from the sinful habits of greed, worldliness, and covetousness e. What your Son has done for me is much greater than any of my fleeting and temporary accomplishments. I pray this in Jesus' name. Amen.

CONTEXT: LUKE 20:41-21:4
Related Passages: James 2:1-5; 2 Corinthians 8:1-5; 2 Corinthians 9:6-8

Day 328

IT WON'T BE LEFT STANDING!

Luke 21:5-7

*Some of the followers were talking about the Temple. They said,
"This is a beautiful Temple, built with the best stones. Look at
the many good gifts that have been offered to God."*

*But Jesus said, "The time will come when all that you see here will
be destroyed. Every stone of these buildings will be thrown down
to the ground. Not one stone will be left on another."*

*Some followers asked Jesus, "Teacher, when will these things happen?
What will show us that it is time for these things to happen?"*

KEY THOUGHT

Jesus has three powerful messages about standing firm in the troubles of
life. The first message has to do with the Temple, while the other two can be
found in the following verses. Jesus' point is that no matter how beautiful the
Temple in Jerusalem may be, it will be destroyed and left in a rubble heap—
earthly temples made by hands will not and cannot last. Our finest and most
holy buildings won't last forever. Jesus wants us to know that we must invest
ourselves in what is lasting and be ready for him when he returns in his glory.

TODAY'S PRAYER

*Holy God, give me the wisdom and the courage to invest myself in your
Kingdom and things that last. Help me see those areas of my life where
my heart is too attached to things that are not lasting and change my
heart and my actions to honor Jesus, in whose name I pray. Amen.*

CONTEXT: LUKE 21:5-19
Related Passages: 2 Peter 3:8-13; 1 Thessalonians 4:13-17; Matthew 6:19-21

Day 329

DON'T BE MISLEAD

Luke 21:8-11

*Jesus said, "Be careful! Don't be fooled. Many people will come using my
name. They will say, 'I am the Christ' and 'The right time has come!' But
don't follow them. When you hear about wars and riots, don't be afraid.
These things must happen first. Then the end will come later."*

*Then Jesus said to them, "Nations will fight against other nations. Kingdoms will fight
against other kingdoms. There will be great earthquakes, sicknesses, and other bad
things in many places. In some places there will be no food for the people to eat. Terrible
things will happen, and amazing things will come from heaven to warn people."*

KEY THOUGHT

Misunderstanding about Jesus' return has been a problem for ages. Many
have been misled by signs they think they see in our world. Jesus, however,
warns that many things will happen before his return—wars, rebellions,
earthquakes, famines, epidemics, and heavenly signs. The key thing in each
of these events is not to panic. God is in control and he will have Jesus come at
the proper time and will bless his people. We just need to be prepared.

TODAY'S PRAYER

*Father, with so many disturbing things going on in our world today, please still the
struggles in my heart and allow me to remain calm and faithful during troubling
times. I know that I belong to you and I also know that when Jesus returns I will go
to be with you—no matter when that time may come. In Jesus' name I pray. Amen.*

CONTEXT: LUKE 21:5-19
Related Passages: 1 Thessalonians 5:1-10; 2 Peter 3:10; Revelation 16:15

Day 330

STAND FIRM!

Luke 21:12-19

[Jesus said] "But before all these things happen, people will arrest you and do bad things to you. They will judge you in their synagogues and put you in jail. You will be forced to stand before kings and governors. They will do all these things to you because you follow me. But this will give you an opportunity to tell about me. Decide now not to worry about what you will say. I will give you the wisdom to say things that none of your enemies can answer. Even your parents, brothers, relatives, and friends will turn against you. They will have some of you killed. Everyone will hate you because you follow me. But none of these things can really harm you. You will save yourselves by continuing strong in your faith through all these things."

KEY THOUGHT

If Jesus' first point in previous verses was that the Temple would be destroyed and that we need to invest in what is permanent, his second point is equally important: remain firm and we will be saved!

TODAY'S PRAYER

Holy and loving Father, please give me the strength I need to stand firm in my faith no matter what outward circumstances may surround me. In Jesus' name I ask for this strength. Amen.

CONTEXT: LUKE 21:5-19
Related Passages: 1 Corinthians 16:13; Colossians 1:21-23; Hebrews 3:14

Day 331

ESCAPE JERUSALEM, EXPECT HIS COMING

Luke 21:20-28

[Jesus said] "You will see armies all around Jerusalem. Then you will know that the time for its destruction has come. The people in Judea at that time should run away to the mountains. The people in Jerusalem must leave quickly. If you are near the city, don't go in! The prophets wrote many things about the time when God will punish his people. The time I am talking about is when all these things must happen. During that time, it will be hard for women who are pregnant or have small babies, because very bad times will come to this land. God will be angry with these people. Some of the people will be killed by soldiers. Others will be made prisoners and taken to all the different countries. The holy city of Jerusalem will be under the control of foreigners until their time is completed.

"Amazing things will happen to the sun, moon, and stars. And people all over the earth will be upset and confused by the noise of the sea and its crashing waves. They will be afraid and worried about what will happen to the world. Everything in the sky will be changed. Then people will see the Son of Man coming in a cloud with power and great glory. When these things begin to happen, stand up tall and don't be afraid. Know that it is almost time for God to free you!"

KEY THOUGHT

Jesus warned that the destruction of Jerusalem would come. The inhabitants needed to be ready to escape that disaster. Many of the Christians in Jerusalem followed Jesus' word and did escape to safety when the time came. So they needed not fear, but only look forward to that day with hope and confidence. As for us, there will come a time when Jesus will return in glory with salvation. We, too, need to look forward to that day with confidence and hope, knowing that even in our worst moments, the Lord is near and his return is never far away.

TODAY'S PRAYER

Gracious God and Almighty Lord, I look forward to the day of Jesus' return in glory. Use me to help others prepare for that day and to be ready to greet it with confidence. Until then, make my hope in your Son's return burn brightly in my heart until the sky shines brightly with his glory. In Jesus' name I anticipate this day to come soon! Amen.

CONTEXT: LUKE 21:20-38
Related Passages: 2 Timothy 4:6-8; Philippians 3:20-21; Romans 8:18-23

Day 332

HIS LASTING WORD

Luke 21:29-33

Then Jesus told this story: "Look at all the trees. The fig tree is a good example. When it turns green, you know that summer is near. In the same way, when you see all these things happening, you will know that God's kingdom is coming very soon.

"I assure you that all these things will happen while some of the people of this time are still living. The whole world, earth and sky, will be destroyed, but my words will last forever."

KEY THOUGHT

While the Temple will become rubble, Jerusalem will be destroyed, and the heavens and the earth will pass away, one thing will last forever: Jesus' word! His promises are faithful and secure. His words are true and lasting. So let's give thanks for his word and for his sharing it with us.

TODAY'S PRAYER

O Father, thank you for the message of Jesus and for every word he spoke and every promise he made. Help me as I seek to learn them, to incorporate them into my daily life, and to build my future upon their truths and promises. In Jesus' name I ask this. Amen.

CONTEXT: LUKE 21:20-38
Related Passages: 1 Peter 1:21-23; Isaiah 40:8; John 6:68-69

STAY ALERT!

Luke 21:34-36

[Jesus warned] "Be careful not to spend your time having parties and getting drunk or worrying about this life. If you do that, you won't be able to think straight, and the end might come when you are not ready. It will come as a surprise to everyone on earth. So be ready all the time. Pray that you will be able to get through all these things that will happen and stand safe before the Son of Man."

KEY THOUGHT

Jesus repeatedly warned his followers during the latter part of his ministry to stay alert and be ready for his return. But what does being ready mean? Does it mean knowing the exact time of his return—the day or the hour? No, we can't know that. So what does it mean? It means to live with faithful vigilance, expectation, and hope for Jesus' return. He stands near and can return at any time. Let's live to be ready for that day!

TODAY'S PRAYER

Holy and righteous Father, the Eternal God and Creator of the universe, work in me your righteous will to make me ready for your Son's glorious return. In Jesus' name I pray. Amen.

CONTEXT: LUKE 21:20-38
Related Passages: 1 Thessalonians 5:1-6; Mark 13:33; Ephesians 6:18

Day 334

PREDICTABLE PATTERN, EAGER LISTENERS

Luke 21:37-38

During the day Jesus taught the people in the Temple area. At night he went out of the city and stayed all night on the Mount of Olives. Every morning all the people got up early to go listen to Jesus at the Temple.

KEY THOUGHT

Jesus found eager listeners. His habit during this last week in Jerusalem was predictable. If folks wanted to find him, they could. The Mount of Olives was his place of rest and prayer. The Temple was his location during the day. The people could find him, and they did. They drew near to listen to him. Little did they know they were hearing his last words. But, they were his last words before his fretful hours with his followers and his trip to the cross. So let's draw near and listen carefully to hear what was on Jesus' heart. Let us give thanks that God has chosen to reveal himself to us in such a human way.

TODAY'S PRAYER

Father, how can I thank you for letting me overhear the last words of Jesus as he speaks to the crowds in the Temple, goes to the Mount of Olives, and ultimately goes to the cross? Help me not only to hear his words, but also to be touched and changed by them. In Jesus' name I pray. Amen.

CONTEXT: LUKE 21:20-38
Related Passages: Luke 14:34-15:1; Luke 5:1; Luke 9:28-36

Day 335

THE DEVIL'S HENCHMEN

Luke 22:1-6

It was almost time for the Jewish Festival of Unleavened Bread, called the Passover. The leading priests and teachers of the law wanted to kill Jesus. But they were trying to find a quiet way to do it, because they were afraid of what the people would do.

One of Jesus' twelve apostles was named Judas Iscariot. Satan entered him, and he went and talked with the leading priests and some of the soldiers who guarded the Temple. He talked to them about a way to hand Jesus over to them. The priests were very happy about this. They promised to give Judas money for doing this. He agreed. Then he waited for the best time to hand him over to them. He wanted to do it when no one was around to see it.

KEY THOUGHT

I cannot help feeling unbelievably sad when I read this passage. Men who are called by God to intercede for his people and to expertly interpret the Scriptures for his people are plotting the worst of all things—the murder of the Son of God. Judas, one of Jesus' twelve apostles, comes up with a plot to betray the Lord to the religious leaders. The Temple guard is in on the murderous scheming. Satan, of course, is behind it all. I wish that we could say these things don't happen today. Unfortunately, when God's leaders get caught up in self-interest and religious politics, Satan steps in and leads them astray and horrible things happen. Pray that God will protect his leaders from the devious ways of the evil one who seeks to rip apart godly leaders and destroy the work of the Kingdom.

TODAY'S PRAYER

Father, please intervene directly in the lives of our church leaders and cast out the influence of Satan, all self-seeking and party spirit, and every hint of life-destroying political scheming. In Jesus' name I ask for this to your glory and the growth of your Kingdom. Amen.

CONTEXT: LUKE 22:1-13
Related Passages: John 12:42-43; John 7:16-18; Mark 13:11-13

Day 336

JUST AS JESUS SAID

Luke 22:7-13

*The Day of Unleavened Bread came. This was the day when the
Jews always killed the lambs for the Passover. Jesus said to Peter and
John, "Go and prepare the Passover meal for us to eat."*

*They said to him, "Where do you want us to prepare the meal?" He said to them, "When
you go into the city, you will see a man carrying a jar of water. Follow him. He will
go into a house. Tell the owner of the house, 'The Teacher asks that you please show
us the room where he and his followers can eat the Passover meal.' Then the owner
will show you a large room upstairs that is ready for us. Prepare the meal there."*

*So Peter and John left. Everything happened the way Jesus
said. So they prepared the Passover meal.*

KEY THOUGHT

While we may have as many questions about this passage as there are
answers, one thing is certain: when Jesus asks, his followers obey and they find
things to be just as Jesus said. So how are you doing in focusing on the Lord
and his words? Why not rev up your commitment to read through each of the
Gospels at least once in the next month or so? Ask the Father to help you not
only to hear his truth revealed by Jesus, but to also obey it!

TODAY'S PRAYER

*Father, thank you that Jesus' words are sure and certain. Be with me
as I seek to know your Son better, obey his words more completely, and
reflect his character more completely. I pray in Jesus' name. Amen.*

CONTEXT: LUKE 22:1-13
Related Passages: John 2:1-5; Matthew 7:21-27; Luke 8:21

Day 337

THE THREE DIMENSIONAL SUPPER

Luke 22:14-20

The time came for them to eat the Passover meal. Jesus and the apostles were together at the table. Jesus said to them, "I wanted very much to eat this Passover meal with you before I die. I will never eat another Passover meal until it is given its full meaning in God's kingdom."

Then Jesus took a cup of wine. He gave thanks to God for it and said, "Take this cup and give it to everyone here. I will never drink wine again until God's kingdom comes."

Then he took some bread and thanked God for it. He broke off some pieces, gave them to the apostles and said, "This bread is my body that I am giving for you. Eat this to remember me." In the same way, after supper, Jesus took the cup of wine and said, "This wine represents the new agreement from God to his people. It will begin when my blood is poured out for you."

KEY THOUGHT

Jesus speaks in anticipation of sharing two special meals with his followers. The first is the Passover meal where he utters these words. This is the beginning of his Passion. What lies ahead of him is a horrible ordeal involving great suffering, humiliating rejection, and the anguish of abandonment by his friends. This meal is Jesus' last with them and he wants to use it to prepare them for all that lies ahead. The second meal is the one Jesus anticipates sharing with his followers beyond his death, at the fulfillment in the Kingdom. Jesus gives us, his followers, a three-fold understanding of the Supper. We recognize our Savior's agony in offering his body and blood to save us. We celebrate his victory over death by eating the Supper on the day of his resurrection—Sunday, the first day of the week. We anticipate the glory of our Lord's return and our sharing in a victory supper with our Savior.

TODAY'S PRAYER

O holy and righteous Father, thank you! I praise you for your love in sending your Son to suffer and die so that I could be delivered from my sin. I praise you for the great supper that lies ahead when I get to share in the victory of Jesus' return. I praise you in Jesus' name. Amen.

CONTEXT: LUKE 22:14-30
Related Passages: 1 Corinthians 11:23-26; Acts 20:7; Acts 2:46-47

Day 338

IS IT ME?

Luke 22:21-23

Jesus said, "But here on this table is the hand of the one who will hand me over to my enemies. The Son of Man will do what God has planned. But it will be very bad for the one who hands over the Son of Man to be killed."

Then the apostles asked each other, "Which one of us would do that?"

KEY THOUGHT

"Surely I wouldn't do that?" That's the basic question that Jesus' followers are asking him. It is also the question that we need to be asking when taking the Lord's Supper. The Supper is a great time for us to take seriously our need for self-examination. Let's be honest about our possible failure in the face of temptation, trial, and persecution. However, rather than anticipating failure or getting stuck in our past failures, let's re-commit to serve the Lord faithfully as we share in the Lord's Supper.

TODAY'S PRAYER

Father, I know that I can be weak and vulnerable to temptation and sin. Without your power working in me through your Holy Spirit, I know I cannot withstand the onslaught of the devil's attacks. Please help me trust fully that your forgiveness frees me to take of the Supper in spite of my failings. Strengthen and empower me to live a pure life and honor your Son whose sacrifice has cleansed me and made me whole. In his name I pray. Amen.

CONTEXT: LUKE 22:14-30
Related Passages: 2 Corinthians 13:3-6; 1 Corinthians 11:27-32; John 13:21-30

Day 339

THE GREATNESS OF OUR LORD

Luke 22:24-27

Later, the apostles began to argue about which one of them was the most important. But Jesus said to them, "The kings of the world rule over their people, and those who have authority over others want to be called 'the great providers for the people.' But you must not be like that. The one with the most authority among you should act as if he is the least important. The one who leads should be like one who serves. Who is more important: the one serving or the one sitting at the table being served? Everyone thinks it's the one being served, right? But I have been with you as the one who serves."

KEY THOUGHT

You can usually tell who the important people are by those who wait upon them and by those to whom they can give orders. Not in Jesus' Kingdom! Jesus reminds his followers (including us today) that as the Master and Lord he could order folks around, but instead he serves them. That is the definition of greatness in Jesus' Kingdom. So let's honestly ask ourselves how well we stack up on the greatness scale of the Master.

TODAY'S PRAYER

Righteous and merciful Father, I confess to you that I sometimes use the wrong criteria when evaluating a person's importance. This causes me to desire status, rank, and recognition rather than quietly serving others. Please forgive me. Mold my heart by your Holy Spirit to serve others just as your Son has served and blessed me. In Jesus' name I pray. Amen.

CONTEXT: LUKE 22:14-30
Related Passages: 1 Peter 5:1-4; John 13:12-17; Luke 9:48

Day 340
TRUE!

Luke 22:28-30

[Jesus said] "You men have stayed with me through many struggles. So I give you authority to rule with me in the kingdom the Father has given me. You will eat and drink at my table in that kingdom. You will sit on thrones and judge the twelve tribes of Israel."

KEY THOUGHT

While most, if not all, of Jesus' followers will forsake him and run away during his arrest, trial, and crucifixion, they have been true to him through his ministry to this point. He lets them know that they have places of honor in the coming Kingdom. While they may not know all that will happen in that Kingdom, they do know that they will be in the presence of the Lord, will eat at his table, will reign on thrones, and will judge his people. While their earthly struggles are great and their rewards in this life seem paltry, Jesus assures them that they will reign with him in glory.

TODAY'S PRAYER

Father, give me the faith to wait for the dawning of your day of victory. Help me to not give up when I'm discouraged. Keep me passionate as I seek to serve you with all of my heart, soul, mind, and strength. I know that all that I offer to you will be small in the face of all that awaits me in your presence. In Jesus' name I praise and thank you. Amen.

CONTEXT: LUKE 22:14-30
Related Passages: Romans 8:15-21; 1 Corinthians 6:3; Luke 18:28-30

Day 341

REDEFINING FAILURE

Luke 22:31-32

"Satan has asked to test you men like a farmer tests his wheat. O Simon, Simon, I have prayed that you will not lose your faith! Help your brothers be stronger when you come back to me."

KEY THOUGHT

Most of us would define Peter's denials of the Lord as failure Peter was denying he had any connection with the Lord even though a short time before his denials he had been adamant that he would never turn away from the Lord. We can learn two very important lessons. First, our failures don't have to be the defining characteristic of our walk with Jesus. Peter was weak, stumbled, and fell. Yet because of his deep repentance, the Lord's help, and the power of the Holy Spirit, the Lord later mightily used him. Second, we must never relegate anyone, not even ourselves, to the junk heap for letting the Lord down at one time or another. He is gracious and compassionate and will forgive our sin when we genuinely turn our hearts back to him. Then the Lord will use our failures to better equip us to serve others.

TODAY'S PRAYER

Father, please forgive me for the times I've given up on one of your other children or on myself because of failures in faith. Help me to be more gracious to others and to myself, and help me to be more committed to helping others serve through their brokenness and stumbling. In Jesus' name I ask for this grace. Amen.

CONTEXT: LUKE 22:31-38
Related Passages: Matthew 18:21-22; James 5:19-20; Romans 14:1-4

Day 342

OVERSTATING OUR COURAGE

Luke 22:33-34

But Peter said to Jesus, "Lord, I am ready to go to jail with you. I will even die with you!"

But Jesus said, "Peter, before the rooster crows tomorrow morning, you will say you don't know me. You will say this three times."

KEY THOUGHT

One of our weaknesses as mere mortals is to overstate our courage. We often fail to realize the power of fear—why else would the Bible contain so many commands not to be afraid? Peter's intentions are genuine, but the power of discouragement, despair, disillusionment, and fear is greater. What commitments have you made to the Lord that you did not keep? Even though Peter would deny his Lord three times, the Lord worked in Peter's life so that he would not be destroyed. He can do the same for you in your times of failure and loss. However, we should take Peter's warning as our own. When we feel strong, we are often the most vulnerable. Our strength must come from the Lord and not our feelings of invincible faith.

TODAY'S PRAYER

O Lord God, thank you for loving Peter even though you knew he would let you down. Thank you for restoring and using him after his sinfulness and failure. My desire, O God, is never to trust in my own strength, but in your power at work in me. When I begin to get too full of myself and too confident in my own power, please humble me gently so that in crucial moments I will not fail you! In Jesus' name I ask this. Amen.

CONTEXT: LUKE 22:31-38
Related Passages: John 21:15-19; 2 Corinthians 12:8-9; Proverbs 16:18

IT IS TIME!

Luke 22:35-38

Then Jesus said to the apostles, "Remember when I sent you out without money, a bag, or sandals? Did you need anything?"

The apostles said, "No."

Jesus said to them, "But now if you have money or a bag, carry that with you. If you don't have a sword, sell your coat and buy one. The Scriptures say, 'He was considered a criminal.'

This Scripture must happen. It was written about me, and it is happening now."

The followers said, "Look, Lord, here are two swords."

Jesus said to them, "That's enough."

KEY THOUGHT

Jesus knows it is now time for him to face the path of suffering and rejection. His followers don't have a clue about what is going to happen to him even though he has repeatedly warned them. In other words, Jesus knows he must face his suffering and rejection alone and abandoned. For us today, this story can be a great comfort for two reasons. First, Jesus understands what it means to be abandoned by friends and left to face suffering and rejection all alone. When we face that kind of challenge, we can trust that he understands our pain and know that he will never abandon us. Second, even though his closest followers blow it, the Lord remakes and reclaims them, making them useful to the Kingdom. We know that our own lapses do not disqualify us from being useful to him. If we are genuinely repentant, he will remake and reclaim us, too!

TODAY'S PRAYER

Heavenly Father, I hate that Jesus had to die for my sins and face his horrors all alone, without his friends to support him. Yet this helps me know that in times when I feel so alone, I know Jesus cares, understands, and stands with me. In Jesus' name I thank you. Amen.

CONTEXT: LUKE 22:31-38
Related Passages: Romans 8:31-39; Mark 14:45-50; Hebrews 13:5b-6

Day 344

THE USUAL PLACE

Luke 22:39-46

Jesus left the city and went to the Mount of Olives. His followers went with him. (He went there often.) He said to his followers, "Pray for strength against temptation."

Then Jesus went about 50 steps away from them. He knelt down and prayed, "Father, if you are willing, please don't make me drink from this cup. But do what you want, not what I want." Then an angel from heaven came to help him. Jesus was full of pain; he struggled hard in prayer. Sweat dripped from his face like drops of blood falling to the ground. When he finished praying, he went to his followers. He found them asleep, worn out from their grieving. Jesus said to them, "Why are you sleeping? Get up and pray for strength against temptation."

KEY THOUGHT

Jesus warns his followers again about the temptation that is about to engulf them. He does it in "the usual place"—his place of prayer. Everything about this event is surrealistic, bizarre, and horrifying, except this place of prayer. Jesus had walked with God his entire ministry. Prayer had been his connecting link with his Father. It was the place where he re-centered his sense of ministry, where he gained strength, where he rejoiced, and where he spoke honestly of his own struggles. Do you have a time carved out in your day where you surrender your will to the Father? Do you have "the usual place" where you offer your heart to God? It can be at your computer as you take time each day to draw close to the Father and offer him your heart. It can be in the quiet of the morning, or the evening, or even at noon. The important thing is that you have "the usual place" where you meet God and say, "Father, I want your will, not mine." When you do, you can be sure he hears you, sends his angels to attend you, and works in your life to ultimately bring you into his glory.

TODAY'S PRAYER

Father, thank you for meeting me in "the usual place." I submit my will and my life to you, trusting in your gracious promises to me and your glorious future for me. Please give me the courage to follow where you lead me. In Jesus' name I pray. Amen.

CONTEXT: LUKE 22:39-53
Related Passages: Hebrews 5:7; Hebrews 1:14; Philippians 2:5-11

BETRAYAL

Luke 22:47-48

While Jesus was speaking, a crowd came up. It was led by Judas, one of the twelve apostles. He came over to Jesus to kiss him.

But Jesus said to him, "Judas, are you using the kiss of friendship to hand over the Son of Man to his enemies?"

KEY THOUGHT

The phrase that hurts me most for Jesus in this verse is "one of the twelve apostles." Jesus is betrayed by one of his own. Not only that, he was betrayed by an act of loving greeting. Everything about this event is hurtful. How can someone with whom you've shared your most intimate moments and deepest truths give you up to those who hate you? Unfortunately, it happens all too frequently. However, when we go through such trials, we can be assured that Jesus knows our pain and lovingly draws alongside to comfort us. He has been there. He has suffered excruciating pain all set up by the betrayal of one of his closest friends. So in our hurt, let us draw near to him and know that he is there to help us make it through our hours of deepest darkness and despair.

TODAY'S PRAYER

Father, thank you for being up close and personal. Thank you for not being far off and detached. Thank you for experiencing our earthly pain as one of us. I now draw near to receive your grace and your help in my time of need. In the name of Jesus, my faithful friend, Lord, and Savior I pray. Amen.

CONTEXT: LUKE 22:39-53
Related Passages: Psalm 55:16-23; Proverbs 27:6; Hebrews 4:14-16

Day 346

WHEN THE POWER OF DARKNESS REIGNS

Luke 22:49-53

The followers of Jesus were standing there too. They saw what was happening and said to Jesus, "Lord, should we use our swords?" And one of them did use his sword. He cut off the right ear of the servant of the high priest.

Jesus said, "Stop!" Then he touched the servant's ear and healed him.

Jesus spoke to the group that came to arrest him. They were the leading priests, the older Jewish leaders, and the Jewish soldiers. He said to them, "Why did you come out here with swords and clubs? Do you think I am a criminal? I was with you every day in the Temple area. Why didn't you try to arrest me there? But this is your time—the time when darkness rules."

KEY THOUGHT

We forget, I fear, that we don't live in this world alone. We face a foe seeking to harm us. He is seeking to disable, discredit, and destroy us. He will have his moments of victory, leading us to stumble and fall. There will be times on this earth when the power of darkness does reign. However, because Jesus won the ultimate victory in this battle beginning in the garden and leading to the cross, our victory in the war against Satan, sin, and death is assured. Darkness had its moment, but it could not snuff out the light of God. The light and love of God reign because of the victory of Jesus.

TODAY'S PRAYER

Father, please never let me forget that in your Son I have the ultimate victory—especially in those moments when darkness rules and I feel alone. In Jesus' name I pray. Amen.

CONTEXT: LUKE 22:39-53
Related Passages: Colossians 3:1-4; Romans 8:35-37; Acts 26:16-18

Day 347

THE BROKENNESS OF SIN AND SHAME

Luke 22:54-62

They arrested Jesus and took him away to the house of the high priest. Peter followed Jesus but stayed back at a distance. The soldiers started a fire in the middle of the yard and sat together. Peter sat with them. A servant girl saw him sitting there. She could see because of the light from the fire. She looked closely at Peter's face. Then she said, "This man was also with Jesus."

But Peter said this was not true. He said, "Lady, I don't know him." A short time later, someone else saw Peter and said, "You are also one of them."

But Peter said, "Man, I am not!"

About an hour later, another man said, "It's true. I'm sure this man was with him, because he is from Galilee."

But Peter said, "Man, I don't know what you are talking about!"

Immediately, while he was still speaking, a rooster crowed. Then the Lord turned and looked into Peter's eyes. And Peter remembered what the Lord had said, "Before the rooster crows in the morning, you will say three times that you don't know me." Then Peter went outside and cried bitterly.

KEY THOUGHT

Peter suffered the brokenness of sin and shame. The Lord had warned him, yet he failed. Despite his rash promises, Peter denied the Lord—three times. The crowing rooster ushered Peter into the bitter, undeniable reality of his sin. I've had a moment or two like that. Maybe you have, too. It's that moment when we realize that we've dishonored the Lord and let him down . . . again. Peter is our great reminder: failures don't have to determine our future with the Lord. God can take our failures and make something good of them.

TODAY'S PRAYER

Abba Father, forgive me for my weakness and sin. Forgive me for trying to battle Satan's power with my own strength. I trust in your powerful and transforming forgiveness. Take my failures, restore me, and use me to bless others. In Jesus' name I pray. Amen.

CONTEXT: LUKE 22:54-71
Related Passages: 2 Corinthians 1:3-4; 1 John 1:8-2:2; John 21:15-17

Day 348

YOU ARE RIGHT ... BUT WRONG

Luke 22:63-71

The men guarding Jesus made fun of him and beat him. They covered his eyes so that he could not see them. Then they hit him and said, "Be a prophet and tell us who hit you!" And they shouted all kinds of insults at him.

The next morning, the older leaders of the people, the leading priests, and the teachers of the law came together. They led Jesus away to their high council. They said, "If you are the Christ, then tell us that you are."

Jesus said to them, "If I tell you I am the Christ, you will not believe me. And if I ask you, you will not answer. But beginning now, the Son of Man will sit at the right side of God All-Powerful."

They all said, "Then are you the Son of God?" Jesus said to them, "You are right in saying that I am."

They said, "Why do we need witnesses now? We all heard what he said!"

KEY THOUGHT

The irony of this event is that Jesus' enemies are right in their accusation—he is the Messiah, the Son of God. They are also wrong—they won't believe in Jesus as Messiah and Son of God, but instead are intent on killing him. They are the vivid reminder that we can say the right things and yet refuse to believe them. We can say the right things, but say them in ridicule and be guilty of sin. The battle we face is an issue of our hearts. Are we seeking God's will or are we protecting our religious interests? Let's continually seek to have our hearts open for God's truth and God's will.

TODAY'S PRAYER

Father, as I seek truth, help me seek you and your will first. I know that I cannot authentically live in obedience to your truth without seeking to honor you. Purify my heart and create a right spirit in me. In Jesus' name I ask this. Amen.

CONTEXT: LUKE 22:54-71
Related Passages: Psalm 51:10; John 7:16-17; John 5:39-40

Day 349

NOT GUILTY

Luke 23:1-4

Then the whole group stood up and led Jesus away to Pilate. They began to accuse Jesus and said to Pilate, "We caught this man trying to change the thinking of our people. He says we should not pay taxes to Caesar. He calls himself the Christ, a king." Pilate asked Jesus, "Are you the king of the Jews?" Jesus answered, "Yes, what you say is true."

Pilate said to the leading priests and the people, "I find nothing wrong with this man."

KEY THOUGHT

The charges that the enemies of Jesus present are all lies. Pilate sees through these lies and goes to the crucial question: Is Jesus King of the Jews? Jesus acknowledges that he is. Pilate pronounces him not guilty. Finding nothing wrong with Jesus and even recognizing him as an important teacher or a righteous leader is not enough. Do we believe that Jesus is the Son of God, our Savior and Lord? Are we willing to base our lives on his death, burial, and resurrection by confessing him and sharing with him in his saving work through baptism? Do we believe that he can transform us totally by pouring his Holy Spirit into our hearts and working his will in our lives? Jesus must be far more than a good guy and a great teacher. He must be our Lord! If he is not, then we will simply put him into the most convenient place in our lives rather than letting him transform us.

TODAY'S PRAYER

Holy and righteous Father, please do your work in my life. I believe that Jesus, your Son, is the Messiah, my Savior and my Lord. I fully trust that he lived on earth as a human like me and that he gave up his life on the cross, that he was buried, and that you raised him from the dead. Please conform me to his character through the Holy Spirit who is at work in me. I ask for this grace in Jesus' name. Amen.

CONTEXT: LUKE 23:1-12
Related Passages: Romans 10:9-13; Romans 6:3-8; Titus 3:3-7

Day 350

TREACHERY BEHIND THE SCENES

Luke 23:5-12

*But they kept on saying, "His teaching is causing trouble all
over Judea. He began in Galilee, and now he is here!"*

*Pilate heard this and asked if Jesus was from Galilee. He learned that Jesus was under
Herod's authority. Herod was in Jerusalem at that time, so Pilate sent Jesus to him.*

*When Herod saw Jesus, he was very happy. He had heard all about him and had
wanted to meet him for a long time. Herod wanted to see a miracle, so he was hoping
that Jesus would do one. He asked him many questions, but Jesus said nothing. The
leading priests and teachers of the law were standing there shouting things against
Jesus. Then Herod and his soldiers laughed at him. They made fun of him by dressing
him in clothes like kings wear. Then Herod sent him back to Pilate. In the past
Pilate and Herod had always been enemies. But on that day they became friends.*

KEY THOUGHT

The trials of Jesus were a mockery. None of them was about justice. The
Sanhedrin was not supposed to meet secretly at night. Pilate pronounced
Jesus innocent, yet kept the legal proceedings going for political expediency.
Herod had no desire to do the right thing; he was determined to do the
politically correct thing. This was nothing more than treachery. Jesus was
not treated fairly. He did not receive justice. What was done to him was what
God decried throughout the Old Testament through the prophets—there
was no justice in the courts and those with money and power misused their
influence. Sinners and traitors convicted Jesus. He was the innocent lamb led
to slaughter. He was the perfect sacrifice for all who are sinners.

TODAY'S PRAYER

*Father, it breaks my heart to see your Son treated with such treachery. While it
angers me, it also helps me bear up under those times when I am treated unfairly.
I know that Jesus is with me in those times and that he fully understands my
emotions. Thank you for walking in this unfair and often cruel world as one of
us so that I can share eternity with you. In Jesus' name I thank you. Amen.*

CONTEXT: LUKE 23:1-12
Related Passages: Isaiah 53:7-9; Isaiah 59:14; Amos 5:10-15

NOTHING!

Luke 23:13-16

Pilate called all the people together with the leading priests and the Jewish leaders. He said to them, "You brought this man to me. You said he was trying to change the people. But I judged him before you all and have not found him guilty of the things you say he has done. Herod didn't find him guilty either. He sent him back to us. Look, he has done nothing bad enough for the death penalty. So, after I punish him a little, I will let him go free."

KEY THOUGHT

"Nothing this man has done calls for the death penalty." That pretty much settles it. Jesus didn't deserve to die. He was falsely arrested, falsely accused, falsely tried, and falsely executed. He doesn't die for crimes he committed, but for our sins so that we can be set free and made children of God.

TODAY'S PRAYER

Father in heaven, thank you for your grace. Precious Lord and Savior, thank you for your willing sacrifice for my sins. Holy Spirit, thank you for your transforming work in my life. May my life never be an affront to the grace given me, the sacrifice made for me, and the Spirit that lives in me. In Jesus' name I pray. Amen.

CONTEXT: LUKE 23:13-25
Related Passages: 2 Corinthians 5:21; Romans 5:6-11; 1 Peter 3:18

Day 352

THEIR VOICES PREVAILED

Luke 23:17-25

But they all shouted, "Kill him! Let Barabbas go free!" (Barabbas was a man who was in jail for starting a riot in the city and for murder.)

Pilate wanted to let Jesus go free. So again Pilate told them that he would let him go. But they shouted again, "Kill him! Kill him on a cross!"

A third time Pilate said to the people, "Why? What wrong has he done? He is not guilty. I can find no reason to kill him. So I will let him go free after I punish him a little."

But the people continued to shout. They demanded that Jesus be killed on a cross. Their shouting got so loud that Pilate decided to give them what they wanted. They wanted Barabbas to go free—the one who was in jail for starting a riot and for murder. Pilate let Barabbas go free. And he handed Jesus over to be killed. This is what the people wanted.

KEY THOUGHT

Pilate didn't have the courage to buck the crowd's will. Instead, he read the poll numbers rather than doing the right thing. So Pilate "handed Jesus over to be killed," giving "what the people wanted." They had requested that a murderer be released and Jesus be crucified. As insane as this seems, this is what often happens when the crowd determines the agenda. All throughout Jesus' ministry, the crowd has sought to possess him and make him into what they wanted him to be. Jesus wouldn't let them. Now the crowd calls for his death. The crowd gets its wish with Pilate. Will the crowd get its wish with us and with our lives? Or will we choose Jesus and the way of the Lord? Let's remember that the way of Christ is quite often unacceptable to the crowd. If we ever doubt this truth, all we have to do is to be reminded of the cross and of our Savior.

TODAY'S PRAYER

Father in heaven, help me never base my life on the will of the crowd, but to have the courage to follow the way of the Lord. In Jesus' name I pray. Amen.

CONTEXT: LUKE 23:13-25
Related Passages: John 2:23-25; John 6:14-16, 25-27; Luke 6:26

Day 353

DAUGHTERS OF JERUSALEM

Luke 23:26-31

The soldiers led Jesus away. At that same time there was a man from Cyrene named Simon coming into the city from the fields. The soldiers forced him to carry Jesus' cross and walk behind him.

A large crowd followed Jesus. Some of the women were sad and crying. They felt sorry for him. But Jesus turned and said to the women, "Women of Jerusalem, don't cry for me. Cry for yourselves and for your children too. The time is coming when people will say, 'The women who cannot have babies are the ones God has blessed. It's really a blessing that they have no children to care for.' Then the people will say to the mountains, 'Fall on us!' They will say to the hills, 'Cover us!' If this can happen to someone who is good, what will happen to those who are guilty?"

KEY THOUGHT

One of the key groups in Jesus' passion and resurrection is "the women." While Jesus' male followers abandon him, "the women" are with him on the way to Golgotha, at the foot of the cross, and at the tomb on resurrection Sunday. They are also there in the days awaiting the coming of the Spirit in the early chapters of Acts of the Apostles. "The women" are faithful examples of true followers of Jesus through his whole ordeal. These women are the great reminder that often the most faithful and loyal of Jesus' followers are not those who are best known to us. However, they are treasured and honored by God. All around us are heroic, faithful, and exemplary followers who love the Lord, yet we often focus on those who fail. Let these women be a reminder that our heritage is not just built on the faith of the well known, but also on the faith of the loyal, courageous, and lesser-known heroes of faith, many of whom are women.

TODAY'S PRAYER

Father in heaven, the Almighty God, thank you for the women of faith who have been examples through the ages. Thank you for their courage, loyalty, and strength. Thank you for their willingness to play important roles in your story of grace . Thank you, O God, for the women of faith who have played such a vital and powerful role in my life. In Jesus' name I thank you. Amen.

CONTEXT: LUKE 23:26-43
Related Passages: Luke 8:1-3; Luke 23:55-56; Luke 24:1-12

Day 354

THE GAMBLE

Luke 23:32-34

There were also two criminals led out with Jesus to be killed. They were led to a place called "The Skull." There the soldiers nailed Jesus to the cross. They also nailed the criminals to crosses beside Jesus—one on the right and the other on the left.

Jesus said, "Father, forgive them. They don't know what they are doing."

The soldiers threw dice to divide Jesus' clothes between them.

KEY THOUGHT

The obvious gamble in this story occurs with the soldiers trying to win a game of chance to get the clothes of the crucified Jesus. In another sense, however, three other implicit "gambles" take place here. First, the "gamble" made by the crowd, epitomized by crucifying Jesus between two criminals; their gamble is that Jesus is not the Son of God, but a criminal worthy of crucifixion. Second, the "gamble" made by Jesus and epitomized by his words of forgiveness toward those who hate him and kill him—the gamble that his sacrificial and forgiving death would somehow touch our hearts and win us to himself. Third, what we do with this story is our "gamble." Do we believe that Jesus is God's Son, our Savior, God's Messiah, and our Lord? If we do, then we will base the rest of our lives on this conviction. But having heard this story, having been brought to the cross of Jesus, we are forced to make a choice. So what's your choice?

TODAY'S PRAYER

Father, I believe that your love and grace have been powerfully demonstrated by Jesus' death on the cross. I gladly entrust my life to this love and grace, believing that Jesus is your Son, the Messiah of Israel's hopes, my Savior, and the Lord of all. I do not consider the investment of my life in this story to be a gamble, but the basis of my confident hope for a bright future with you. In Jesus' name I offer my thanks and praise for this indescribable gift. Amen.

CONTEXT: LUKE 23:26-43
Related Passages: Joshua 24:14-21; Acts 2:36-40; Acts 4:10-12

Day 355

RIGHT TITLES, WRONG HEARTS

Luke 23:35-39

The people stood there watching everything. The Jewish leaders laughed at Jesus. They said, "If he is God's Chosen One, the Christ, then let him save himself. He saved others, didn't he?"

Even the soldiers laughed at Jesus and made fun of him. They came and offered him some sour wine. They said, "If you are the king of the Jews, save yourself!" (At the top of the cross these words were written: "THIS IS THE KING OF THE JEWS.")

One of the criminals hanging there began to shout insults at Jesus: "Aren't you the Christ? Then save yourself, and save us too!"

KEY THOUGHT

Isn't it amazing how the mocking crowd, the scoffing leaders, the cruel soldiers, and the sarcastic criminal on the cross nearby all call Jesus the right thing? They call him, "God's Chosen One," "the Christ," "king of the Jews," and "the Christ." Yet none of these groups put their faith in Jesus! Even the devil can confess the truth about Christ (James 2:19), but it takes a seeking heart to believe, follow, and be saved. The truth about Jesus is there if our hearts are seeking. Jesus is the one who saves. Jesus is God's Chosen One. Jesus is the Messiah. Jesus is King of the Jews. The real question is not his identity, but whether or not he is your Lord and mine!

TODAY'S PRAYER

Father in heaven, I believe that Jesus Christ is Lord. I trust that he died for my sins. I believe that he could have come down from the cross and saved himself, but instead chose to suffer death for my sins and then to be raised to life for my salvation. In Jesus, I put my trust and make my confession. Amen.

CONTEXT: LUKE 23:26-43
Related Passages: Philippians 2:5-11; Romans 4:23-25; Philippians 1:18-22

Day 356

REMEMBER ME!

Luke 23:40-43

But the other criminal stopped him. He said, "You should fear God. All of us will die soon. You and I are guilty. We deserve to die because we did wrong. But this man has done nothing wrong." Then he said, "Jesus, remember me when you begin ruling as king!"

Then Jesus said to him, "I promise you, today you will be with me in paradise."

KEY THOUGHT

Jesus had told his followers, "Remember me!" as they shared in the Lord's Supper. So for thousands of years, Christians all around the world take the bread and fruit of the vine during the Lord's Supper to remember Jesus' life, death, and resurrection. Ironically, even while the thief is dying on a cross near Jesus, he confesses Jesus' innocence and then asks that Jesus "Remember me." So in the horror of his own crucifixion, Jesus offers this dying man a special moment of grace. Jesus reassures the dying criminal that he will share paradise with Jesus. Jesus will remember him! Jesus will also remember our confessions of faith, deeds of kindness done in his name, and our faithfulness to the Father. "Remember me!" we cry out to the Lord; thankfully, we already know his answer.

TODAY'S PRAYER

Father, never ever let me outlive my faith in Jesus and my hope that is stirred every time I remember what he has done for me. In Jesus' name I request this grace. Amen.

CONTEXT: LUKE 23:26-43
Related Passages: Luke 12:8; 2 Timothy 2:8-13; Hebrews 6:10

Day 357

RICH WITH GRACE

Luke 23:44-46

It was about noon, but it turned dark throughout the land until three o'clock in the afternoon, because the sun stopped shining. The curtain in the Temple was torn into two pieces. Jesus shouted, "Father, I put my life in your hands!" After Jesus said this, he died.

KEY THOUGHT

These few words are filled with great richness. Jesus' death occurs in deep darkness. This darkness has its way for a brief spell before its stranglehold on us is broken forever by Jesus' resurrection. The veil is torn in the Temple; Jesus opens up the way for us to enter the Holy of Holies with confidence and find grace at the Mercy Seat of God (Heb. 10:19-22). In his final breath, Jesus entrusts everything to his Father in faith; in our worst moments, we can know that no matter how forsaken we may feel, God will bring us to himself in glory. Jesus takes his last breath and dies; each of us must one day give up our last breath, but because of Jesus' death and subsequent resurrection, we can die with confidence. Which message do you need most today? Choose one and look to Jesus and trust in his grace.

TODAY'S PRAYER

Father, what can I say in response to the gift of your Son? All praise to you, the God Almighty, the Father of mercy, and the Sovereign God of grace. Jesus, thank you for your example and the price you paid to provide it for me. Now I finish this prayer with the request that you, O Holy Spirit, fill and empower me to have the same trust in my struggles as the Lord displayed as he faced his trials. In the name of Jesus, my Lord and Savior, I pray. Amen.

CONTEXT: LUKE 23:44-56
Related Passages: Hebrews 10:19-25; Hebrews 2:14-18; Hebrews 4:14-16

Day 358

REACTIONS TO THE CROSS

Luke 23:47-49
The army officer there saw what happened. He praised God,
saying, "I know this man was a good man!"

Many people had come out of the city to see all this. When they saw it,
they felt very sorry and left. The people who were close friends of Jesus were
there. Also, there were some women who had followed Jesus from Galilee.
They all stood far away from the cross and watched these things.

KEY THOUGHT

What happens in your heart when you think of Jesus on the cross? The seasoned Roman officer handling the execution praised God, saying that Jesus was a good man. The crowd went home with deep sorrow. Jesus' friends watched from a distance in sadness and loss. Which one best describes your reaction? Why? Don't you find it amazing that probably the least preferable reaction, the least exemplary, was the reaction of Jesus' friends? Let's not just be observers of the cross! We can be deeply sorrowed by ours sins that took Jesus to the cross, but in our sorrow, let's make sure we don't let grief consume us. Instead, let's praise God for the grace and salvation he provided for us through the cross. Then, rather than going into hiding like the fearful friends of Jesus, let's go share Jesus' grace with others.

TODAY'S PRAYER

Holy and Almighty God, it breaks my heart that Jesus had to die as a sacrifice
for sin, especially my sin. However, I praise you for your plan of grace,
for providing mercy at the expense of your own heartbreak, and for your
overwhelming love for people like me. In Jesus' name I thank you. Amen.

CONTEXT: LUKE 23:44-56
Related Passages: Romans 4:24-25; Romans 5:6-11; 1 Corinthians 1:20-25

Day 359

HONOR GOD!

Luke 23:50-56

A man named Joseph was there from the Jewish town of Arimathea. He was a good man, who lived the way God wanted. He was waiting for God's kingdom to come. Joseph was a member of the Jewish council. But he did not agree when the other Jewish leaders decided to kill Jesus. He went to Pilate and asked for the body of Jesus. He took the body down from the cross and wrapped it in cloth. Then he put it in a tomb that was dug in a wall of rock. This tomb had never been used before. It was late on Preparation day. When the sun went down, the Sabbath day would begin.

The women who had come from Galilee with Jesus followed Joseph. They saw the tomb. Inside they saw where he put Jesus' body. Then they left to prepare some sweet-smelling spices to put on the body.

On the Sabbath day they rested, as commanded in the Law of Moses.

KEY THOUGHT

What do you do when all seems lost and life makes no sense? Joseph and the women are our example to follow in the worst moments of horror in our lives. They do the decent, kind, and generous thing—they honor Jesus in his death with a decent and honorable burial even though it involved personal cost and great danger. They honor the will of God as they know it from Scripture even though all seemed lost—they honor the Sabbath as required by the Law. We will all face times of desperation and trial. Let's remember the examples of Joseph and the women. Often our obedient actions, infused with the Holy Spirit's help, are what we most need to get us through our time of horror and to prepare us for the joy that is on the horizon.

TODAY'S PRAYER

Holy and tender Father, please give me the courage to hold fast to my faith in the difficult times. Give me the faith to live with honor and decency even though no one else seems to value these qualities. In addition, dear Father, help me have the discipline and the will to honor you in simple obedience, especially when times are hard. In Jesus' name I pray. Amen.

CONTEXT: LUKE 23:44-56
Related Passages: Matthew 12:46-50; Luke 8:1-3; 1 Samuel 15:22

Day 360

THEN THEY REMEMBERED!

Luke 24:1-8

Very early Sunday morning, the women came to the tomb where Jesus' body was laid. They brought the sweet-smelling spices they had prepared. They saw that the heavy stone that covered the entrance had been rolled away. They went in, but they did not find the body of the Lord Jesus. They did not understand this. While they were wondering about it, two men in shining clothes stood beside them. The women were very afraid. They bowed down with their faces to the ground. The men said to them, "Why are you looking for a living person here? This is a place for dead people. Jesus is not here. He has risen from death. Do you remember what he said in Galilee? He said the Son of Man must be handed over to the control of sinful men, be killed on a cross, and rise from death on the third day." Then the women remembered what Jesus had said.

KEY THOUGHT

Don't you just love "the women" and their example of faithfulness? Their faithful commitment enables them to discover God's incredible miracle with Jesus—they are the first to learn of his resurrection! However, the most powerful insight in this passage to me is the simple sentence at the end: "Then they remembered that he had said this." Jesus' resurrection changes everything. One of the important areas of change was in the memory of his most faithful followers. After the resurrection, things Jesus had said in his ministry come flooding back into their minds with understanding, excitement, and conviction. Promises that seemed obscure suddenly become clear. Prophetic words that seemed undiscoverable are uncovered and seen in their full glory. Their insight is to be our insight as well. All of Jesus' ministry, his healing and his teaching, can now be more fully understood on this side of the resurrection.

TODAY'S PRAYER

Father, as I study your Son's life on earth, please never let me forget that he died for my sins and was raised back to life with power. Help me know that his promises are true, his teaching is proven, and his service is worth my emulation because it is demonstrated to be the way of life. In Jesus' name I ask this. Amen.

CONTEXT: LUKE 24:1-12
Related Passages: Romans 1:2-4; 2 Corinthians 1:18-20; John 2:18-22

Day 361

NONSENSE?

Luke 24:9-12

The women left the tomb and went to the eleven apostles and the other followers.
They told them everything that happened at the tomb. These women were Mary
Magdalene, Joanna, Mary, the mother of James, and some others. They told the
apostles everything that happened. But the apostles did not believe what they
said. It sounded like nonsense. But Peter got up and ran to the tomb to see. He
looked in, but he saw only the cloth that Jesus' body had been wrapped in. It was
just lying there. Peter went away to be alone, wondering what had happened.

KEY THOUGHT

These women have been more faithful than any of Jesus' male followers.
They have stood by their Lord in his journey to the cross and the tomb. When
these faithful women tell the rest of Jesus' followers what has happened, their
testimony is dismissed as mere nonsense. Yet these women were the earliest
witnesses of the resurrected Jesus; they stood by him through his ministry, his
death, all the way to his resurrection. These trailblazing heroes of our faith in
the resurrected Savior include "Mary Magdalene, Joanna, Mary the mother of
James, and several others." I don't know about you, but there are a number of
women who have pioneered the way for my faith to find the resurrected Jesus,
as well.

TODAY'S PRAYER

Father, thank you so much for the influence of faithful women who have blazed the trail
that has led me to believe in your risen Son. Bless them in ways that help them know
the eternal difference they have made in my life. In Jesus' name I thank you. Amen.

CONTEXT: LUKE 24:1-12
Related Passages: Luke 10:38-42; Acts 1:9-14; Luke 17:1-4

Day 362

WE HAD HOPED!

Luke 24:13-27

That same day two of Jesus' followers were going to a town named Emmaus. It is about seven miles from Jerusalem. They were talking about everything that had happened. While they were talking, discussing these things, Jesus himself came near and walked with them. (But the two men were not allowed to recognize Jesus.) He asked them, "What's this I hear you discussing with each other as you walk?"

The two men stopped, their faces looking very sad. The one named Cleopas said, "You must be the only person in Jerusalem who doesn't know what has just happened there."

Jesus said, "What are you talking about?"

They said, "It's about Jesus, the one from Nazareth. To God and to all the people he was a great prophet. He said and did many powerful things. But our leaders and the leading priests handed him over to be judged and killed. They nailed him to a cross. We were hoping that he would be the one to free Israel. But then all this happened.

"And now something else: It has been three days since he was killed, but today some of our women told us an amazing thing. Early this morning they went to the tomb where the body of Jesus was laid. But they did not find his body there. They came and told us they had seen some angels in a vision. The angels told them Jesus was alive! So some of our group went to the tomb too. It was just as the women said. They saw the tomb, but they did not see Jesus."

Then Jesus said to the two men, "You are foolish and slow to realize what is true. You should believe everything the prophets said. The prophets said the Christ must suffer these things before he begins his time of glory." Then he began to explain everything that had been written about himself in the Scriptures. He started with the books of Moses and then he talked about what the prophets had said about him.

KEY THOUGHT

Jesus' resurrection restores hope, fulfills Scripture, and ensures that we can trust him, even in the face of great disappointment.

TODAY'S PRAYER

Holy God, there are places of disappointment in my heart. Please open my heart as Jesus draws near to help overcome my confusion and unbelief. In Jesus' name I pray. Amen.

CONTEXT: LUKE 24:13-35
Related Passages: James 4:8; 2 Corinthians 2:10-16; Hebrews 13:5-6

Day 363

RECOGNIZED IN THE BREAKING
OF THE BREAD

Luke 24:28-35

They came near the town of Emmaus, and Jesus acted as if he did not plan to stop there. But they wanted him to stay. They begged him, "Stay with us. It's almost night. There's hardly any daylight left." So he went in to stay with them.

Joining them at the supper table, Jesus took some bread and gave thanks. Then he broke some off and gave it to them. Just then the men were allowed to recognize him. But when they saw who he was, he disappeared. They said to each other, "When he talked to us on the road, it felt like a fire burning in us. How exciting it was when he explained to us the true meaning of the Scriptures!"

So the two men got up then and went back to Jerusalem. There they found the followers of Jesus meeting together. The eleven apostles and the people with them said, "The Lord really has risen from death! He appeared to Simon."

Then the two men told what had happened on the road. They talked about how they recognized Jesus when he shared the bread with them.

KEY THOUGHT

Every meal is sacred when Christians share it together. When we share the Lord's Supper, we are most certainly to recognize the presence of the Lord with us. This meal is a reminder that even the most common times of table fellowship are sacred and precious moments of Jesus' presence. When we eat together, let's never let a single meal pass without our conscious realization and recognition of the Lord being with us.

TODAY'S PRAYER

Holy Father, thank you for making meals sacred moments with your Son. Forgive me for trivializing mealtime with my family in Christ. I get so busy and rushed that I often miss the opportunity to welcome the Savior into our fellowship. I confess this in Jesus' name. Amen.

CONTEXT: LUKE 24:35-43
Related Passages: Acts 2:41-47; Revelation 3:20; 1 Corinthians 10:16-17

NO GHOST!

Luke 24:36-43

While the two men were saying these things to the other followers, Jesus himself came and stood among them. He said to them, "Peace be with you."

This surprised the followers. They were afraid. They thought they were seeing a ghost. But Jesus said, "Why are you troubled? Why do you doubt what you see? Look at my hands and my feet. It's really me. Touch me. You can see that I have a living body; a ghost does not have a body like this."

After Jesus told them this, he showed them his hands and his feet. The followers were amazed and very, very happy to see that Jesus was alive. They still could not believe what they saw. He said to them, "Do you have any food here?" They gave him a piece of cooked fish. While the followers watched, he took the fish and ate it.

KEY THOUGHT

"If it seems too good to be true, then it probably is!" We are taught this principle to keep from getting duped and scammed. Jesus' followers had trouble believing in his resurrection because it seemed too good to be true. So Jesus goes to great lengths to help them understand that he is not a ghost or a figment of their imaginations. He had them touch him and see his scars. He ate fish in their presence. Jesus' resurrection is too good to be true—but it is true and because it is, everything good is suddenly possible for Jesus' followers!

TODAY'S PRAYER

Father, give me the eyes to see and the ears to hear the great news you have given me in Jesus' resurrection. I know it is too good to be true, but I believe that it is true. I want to live out my life based on this faith. Strengthen this conviction through your Holy Spirit. In Jesus' name I pray. Amen.

CONTEXT: LUKE 24:36-53
Related Passages: Ephesians 1:19-21; 1 Thessalonians 4:13-14; Colossians 3:1-4

Day 365

FILLED WITH JOY AND PRAISE

Luke 24:44-53

Jesus said to them, "Remember when I was with you before? I said that everything written about me must happen—everything written in the Law of Moses, the books of the prophets, and the Psalms."

Then Jesus helped the followers understand these Scriptures about him. Jesus said to them, "It is written that the Christ would be killed and rise from death on the third day. You saw these things happen—you are witnesses. You must go and tell people that they must change and turn to God, which will bring them his forgiveness. You must start from Jerusalem and tell this message in my name to the people of all nations. Remember that I will send you the one my Father promised. Stay in the city until you are given that power from heaven."

KEY THOUGHT

What is our purpose now that we fully believe that Jesus is risen from the dead? What should be our response to this year of walking with Jesus through the Gospel of Luke? Very simply put, we should be filled with joy that leads us to praise God. Jesus has come and lived among us as one of us. He loved us so much that he would rather die for us than live without us. God's power enabled him to triumph over sin, death, and the devil. We now enjoy God's great victory in Jesus. Our future is fused with his future. We must be a people of joy! We must praise our God of powerful grace and mighty mercy! And because we've received "power from heaven"—the Holy Spirit—we begin where we are sharing this message to the nations!

TODAY'S PRAYER

Holy and Almighty God, I praise you for the victory you have given me through your Son's life, death, and resurrection. You are worthy of all glory, honor, praise, and adoration. You have sacrificed so much to bring me to your presence as your cleansed and holy child. My heart overflows with joy knowing that my home is with you. Bless me now as I commit to be your person—a person of joy and praise, sharing the message of Jesus, in whose name I pray. Amen.

CONTEXT: LUKE 24:36-53
Related Passages: Philippians 4:4-5; Romans 5:1-5; Ephesians 1:12-14